GOD IN PATRISTIC
THOUGHT

SPCK Large Paperbacks

GOD IN PATRISTIC THOUGHT

BY

G. L. PRESTIGE D.D.

LONDON

S · P · C · K

First published in 1936
by William Heinemann Ltd
Second edition, S.P.C.K., 1952
S.P.C.K. Paperback 1964
Reprinted 1969, 1975
S.P.C.K., Holy Trinity Church, Marylebone Road, London NW1 4DU

Printed in Great Britain by
Hollen Street Press Ltd., Slough, Berks.

ISBN 0 281 00510 9

CONTENTS

CONTENTS

CONTENTS

CONTENTS

INTRODUCTION
[1936]

(i)

IN GENERAL, it is a sensible rule that the less an author says in prefacing his work, the better. Nevertheless I am not leaving my book to introduce itself, but am writing an Introduction, and that, in part, a controversial one. This course has at any rate the advantage that controversy can be kept out of the text proper; professed scholars may turn at once to the first chapter and judge for themselves what I have to say. I am told, however, that it would be convenient to less mature students if they were given some indication of my line of argument before being plunged into the detailed evidence; and, more especially, that it would be unfair and confusing to them, if their attention were not explicitly directed to certain points at which my conclusions traverse assertions commonly stated in the text-books tŏ which theological students have recourse. There seems to be substance in this representation. Accordingly, I venture to prefix to the work itself some preliminary observations on its character and contents.

Its scope is largely determined by its origin. At the end of 1921 I was invited by the late Professor C. H. Turner to undertake research work for the projected Lexicon of Patristic Greek, which, it is hoped, will be published by the Oxford University Press. It fell to me to investigate, among other subjects, nearly all the words of main importance for the doctrines of the Trinity and the Incarnation. Since a considerable mass of material was accumulated, far more than could be printed in the actual Lexicon or published as articles in learned periodicals, the Committee of the Lexicon gave me free consent to make such use as I thought fit of the information which I had amassed. For this generous permission, and for the courteous friendship of Dr. Stone, the editor of the Lexicon, with whom it was both a pleasure and an education to work, I cannot be too grateful. The basis, therefore, of the present book is the extended research made for the Lexicon into the meanings, both technical and popular, theological and secular, of those words which acquired special importance for Greek patristic thought. Before attempting to estimate the value of what the Fathers taught, I have tried to ascertain as exactly as possible the meaning of what they said, interpreting their language not so much by speculative reconstruction of their supposed intellectual systems, as by examination of the facts of linguistic usage. Something of the kind has been attempted before, but, so far as I am aware, on nothing like so wide a scale. My particular advantages have consisted in the increase of modern critical editions and of thorough indexing, and in having the resources of the Lexicon at my disposal.

I have not confined attention solely to the Greek Fathers. Their teaching has been illustrated, from time to time, by reference to Latin writers; and certain broad differences have been pointed out between the Greek doctrine of the Trinity and the Latin. But, in the main, it is the Greek Fathers who form the subject of this study. There is ample justification for making this limitation. The Greek Fathers are more philosophical, alike in treatment and in aim, than their

INTRODUCTION

(ii)

I must make clear my fundamental outlook. I do not believe that the importation of Hellenic rationalism, to expound and explain the facts of Christian history, was illegitimate. Finite minds can never adequately theorise the infinite. But human reason is a valid instrument for unfolding the implications of human experience. There is nothing particularly Hellenic, still less pagan, about rational method, except that the Greeks had the providential privilege of its discovery and development. In itself, it is part of the equipment with which human nature has been endowed by God who made mankind. From this point of view, Harnack's famous attack on Christian rationalism, as a process of secularisation, seems an appeal to illiberal prejudice. There are always dangers in thinking. Thought that outranges its premisses and explains away its data is bound to be misleading. Theology, like any other science, can provide instances of such results. But there are even worse dangers in refusing to think at all. There is greater room for misunderstanding when the data are uncriticised than when they are badly criticised. My own conviction is that the Christian doctrine of the Trinity is a legitimate rational construction founded on the facts of Christian experience.

The statement that the doctrinal process was less one of rational development than one of intellectual choice between a number of conflicting ideas current in the Hellenistic world, seems to me greatly exaggerated. Ideas were certainly adopted from pagan sources in the different efforts made to give a Christian explanation. But I do not think that any one such idea was ever imported without undergoing substantial modification to suit its new environment. The idea was cut to fit the Christian faith, not the faith trimmed to square with the imported conception. Conceptions of pagan philosophy were radically altered in their Christian context, and not seldom utterly discarded after trial. During their period of testing, there was often risk of a wrong bias being given to theological development. Some thinkers were weighed down unduly by the pressure of a new idea, especially when they found, as often happened, that the Bible seemed to afford it textual support. In this way heresies arose. But thinkers in the central plane of the theological process, though sometimes overweighted, never kicked the beam. There was always some element of counterbalance in their thought, not perhaps prominent, but none the less fundamental. They must be judged according to the whole effect conveyed by their teaching. Origen, the common father of Arianism and of Cappadocian orthodoxy, is the obvious example. And in judging them we must not expect to find their minds entirely free from contradictions. It is not the men who first see the value of a new idea that always recognise exactly where or how it contradicts some other element in their own thought. One of the most striking features of modern theological enquiry is its tendency to absolve teachers whose disciples, more irresponsible or less balanced than themselves, formed schools of heresy. Not every heresiarch was himself a heretic. If we read more into a man's teaching than he is prepared to acknowledge in it, we cease to be impartial; inconsistent he may be, but inconsistency is too common to be criminal. I do not then deny the influence of externally imported ideas, but I think, all the same, that the doctrine of the Trinity was reached by true rational development, and not by syncretism between Christianity and paganism.

The reaction against dogmatic construction has proceeded to extreme lengths. It is thought that to exercise reason about divine things promotes arid intellectualism. It certainly did not in Athanasius or Augustine. It possibly did in Leontius of Byzantium. The question is further raised, whether the effort to define the deity of Christ does not obscure and destroy all proper interest in His historical earthly life; whether the attempt to formulate a meta-physical doctrine of the being of God does not lead to regions so remote and an atmosphere so refined that the practical, ethical, religious values of Christianity are starved and stifled. The question can only be answered by appeal to actual results. Is it the case that those Christians who have cared most for the assertion of Christ's absolute deity have failed conspicuously as a class in devotion to His human qualities? Or that those who have been brought most fully under the influence of doctrinal orthodoxy have most neglected practical Christian morality? No doubt divergent answers might be given in different quarters. But for myself, I can only say that unless redemption and sanctification can be presented as acts of God Himself, that is, unless Christ and the Holy Spirit can be preached as truly divine, religion and morality seem to have no absolute value. Thoughtful people want to be reasonably well assured that the revelation of Christ and the holiness of the Spirit are really one with ultimate transcendent reality, if they are asked to count the world well lost for them. And I also think that, on a broad view of history, human society as a whole is disposed to demand the same assurance. Christian morality does not appear to survive for many generations after the loss of Christian dogmatic faith.

Nevertheless, the other side has sometimes been maintained with great emphasis during the last half-century. A typical instance is provided by Dr. James Mackinnon in his recently published book, *From Christ to Constantine*. From many of his judgments on the teaching of particular Fathers I should strongly dissent. But that is not the crucial point. His whole attitude is opposed to Christian rationalism. He adopts Harnack's phrase about the 'Hellenisation' of Christianity. Origen, he complains, created a "strange medley of high thought and traditional beliefs and fancies," which would probably have astonished the prophets and apostles by the Platonic influence which it displays. The suggestion is that Platonism could not help to explain, but could only contaminate the Gospel. Paul of Samosata "was repelled by the growing tendency within the Church to Hellenise the historic Jesus" by identifying Him with the Logos and presenting Him as the Second Person of the Trinity; Paul's own conception, recognised by Dr. Mackinnon as being virtually Unitarian, "is certainly nearer the historic reality." Here Dr. Mackinnon seems to confuse the historic Jesus with the theories propounded, whether by Paul or his opponents, to account for His significance. He asks, in connection with Athanasius, whether it is absolutely necessary that in order to redeem humanity Christ must be God Himself. Arianism, at any rate in its early stages, was "a plea for liberty of theological discussion," as against the intellectual intolerance of the Athanasian party. Apparently one doctrine is as good as another; or even better, if it does not link Christ to transcendental reality.

Greek theology in general is described as an accommodation between Christianity and culture, as a means of "adapting Christianity to its wider culture environment," in order to increase its effectiveness as a missionary religion in the Græco-Roman world. "The use of an abstruse philosophical terminology might well repel, as an unscriptural and artificial method of diagnosing the concrete Christ, and at the same time burdening the faith of His followers with alien concepts under the influence of Greek and Jewish-Hellenist speculation." Dr. Mackinnon admits that this speculative influence is already strongly marked in various parts of the New Testament itself. Its primitive origin thus renders much more difficult and paradoxical the task of repudiating the validity of its principles. And he does not adequately take into account the fact that it permeated the very atmosphere mentally absorbed by Christians of the second and third centuries, even more completely than simplified biology and third-hand physics pervade the popular intellectual atmosphere of the twentieth century. Indeed, the ancient environment was the more admirable, for it possessed, what the intellectual atmosphere of the modern populace does not possess, a really critical and philosophical basis. If people thought at all, they could only think in that kind of medium. No other rational method existed then, or exists now, but what has been derived ultimately from the great Greek philosophical schools. But Dr. Mackinnon does not want Christianity explained by reference to absolute categories. He desires "a more historic and less metaphysical train of thought."

His point of view is not to be dismissed off-hand; it demands careful consideration. But it is not possible to discuss it further here. I can only submit that I find it difficult to reconcile with the belief that the world is a rational universe and that God is intelligent Mind. And I must express the conviction that, if Dr. Mackinnon's outlook were adopted generally, the most disastrous results would follow for evangelical Christianity. The whole of the book which follows is designed to support the opposite point of view, by trying to show that the theological development which Dr. Mackinnon deprecates was, so far as relates to the Trinity, a natural and necessary outcome of Christian thought about Christian rudiments.

(iii)

I can now turn from more general questions to describe the particular contents of the work that follows. The first three chapters have no direct concern with the doctrine of the Trinity. They make an attempt to paint in something of the theistic background. Without any claim to be exhaustive, they call attention to some highly important features of Hellenistic Christian thought about God. I have not given any assessment of the Hebrew theism which Christianity inherited. It lies outside my scope, and must for present purposes be taken for granted. My readers will, however, detect repeated signs that it formed the basis of patristic theism. In fact, these chapters really show how Hebrew theism looked to sympathetic Hellenistic minds.

Chapter I opens with some derivations of the title 'God,'

which, though fanciful, depict Him as the supreme disposer of the universe and the first cause of life and progress. Moral qualities are suggested by the rather later emphasis on universal oversight and combustion of evil. This shows how little desire there was to disregard Hebrew notions: God humbles Himself to behold the things that are in heaven and earth (*ps.* cxiii. 6); He is consuming fire (*Deut.* iv. 24). Illustrations are then given of the manner in which the infinite being of God is commonly described in the Fathers. The terms used are often, though not wholly, negative in form, but they convey a sense which is definite and positive. They aim at expressing His complete independence of all created existence, either materially or morally, and His sole responsibility for all the things that are. It is noticeable that, great as was the use made of Stoic conceptions to illustrate Christian theistic belief, the crucial point in which Christianity contradicted Stoic thought is strongly emphasised. The danger of misconception due to Hebrew anthropomorphism is at the same time expressly excluded. The doctrines of divine unity and self-consistency are clearly taught, the first to guard against polytheism (hence the insistence that the being of God is not susceptible of compound relationships), the second to preserve His absolute perfection.

A concrete expression of the divine 'form' (i.e. content) was furnished in the familiarly Hebrew, as well as thoroughly Greek, conception of 'spirit.' Spirit is regarded, to use an inevitable metaphor, as the stuff or matter of which God consists. It is a synonym for 'the divine nature.' Failure to appreciate this patristic commonplace is the cause of considerable misunderstanding of familiar texts, from the

New Testament onwards. It is quite absurd to treat every mention of 'spirit' as a reference to the particularised conception of the Holy Spirit. And another idea, this time exclusively Hebrew, of great frequency and importance, is that of God's holiness. This term implies not only the "awful purity" which fills the minds of the Hebrew prophets, but also the mysteriously supernatural power of which they were no less fully conscious.

Chapter II deals in more precise detail with divine transcendence. As one writer says, God is not only the maker of all but also the best of all. This subject brought into prominence some of the difficulties involved in the relations between a transcendent deity and the created world, and again Stoicism, in its pantheistic tendencies, was explicitly rejected, in favour of a conception drawn from pre-Christian Biblical sources. God, it was asserted, pervades the creation but is not confined to it. He is not represented as too far aloof, or too holy, to permit Himself to be contaminated by association with the physical world, as Epicureans and Gnostics tried to affirm. A place is kept both for divine creation and for divine immanence. But His transcendence is vigorously maintained. Since transcendence, though a characteristically Hebrew idea, is nowhere philosophically expounded in the Bible, a term had to be adopted to express its definition. This was found in the word agenetos, 'uncreated.' The idea of creation was therein contrasted with that of self-grounded existence. To call God uncreated was tantamount to calling Him infinite perfection, independent reality, and the source of all finite being: He alone is absolute; all else is dependent and contingent. As the vast significance of this term is commonly overlooked, some space is devoted to its illustration, and to unravelling the tangle caused by Gnostic confusion between metaphysical and biological concepts of transmitting existence.

Chapter III passes from the nature of God to the manner of His self-manifestation. No man can see God; He is to be discerned through His activities. Where the face of the Lord is, there is peace and exultation. In so far as He is pleased to declare Himself to human hearts, so far is He knowable. The knowledge of God therefore depends on recognition of His 'economy' or dispensations; the word economy covers both general and special providence, divine government, divine revelation, and divine grace, the whole culminating in the incarnation. Since the universe was regarded as being fundamentally a spiritual system, no difficulty was experienced in following Hebrew precedent and acknowledging the existence of inferior spiritual 'powers,' possessed of particular activities. And since the principle and ground of all being was found in God, the word 'god,' again in accordance with Biblical precedent, was sometimes employed in a relative sense of those beings which shared to some degree in delegated spiritual functions. On this principle it was possible to recognise a spiritual, though perverted, influence in heathen deities, and to speak, in an analogical sense, of the deification of Christian men.

With chapter IV we reach the problem of the Trinity. The overwhelming sense of divine redemption in Christ led Christians to ascribe absolute deity to their Redeemer. This happened—and the fact must not be overlooked—before and not after the rise to prominence of the Logos doctrine. Logos theories were an attempt to explain an already accepted belief in the deity of the Son, not the cause of such a belief gaining acceptance. This means that the doctrine of the Trinity sprang from the inherent necessity to account for the religious data of Christianity, not from the importation of pagan metaphysical presuppositions.

The deity of the Holy Spirit was far less widely and less explicitly asserted, for the first three centuries of Christendom, than that of the Son. There were reasons for the delay. But this is not to say that His deity went unrecognised. It would be truer to say that it was commonly assumed and taken for granted, without occasion arising for its implications to be thought out. This view is supported by the fact that the early Adoptionists, who regarded Christ as a mere man, seem to have shown no hesitation in giving personal recognition to the Spirit. It was not until Paul of Samosata, in the third century, that Adoptionists were led by a logical inference to reduce the Spirit to the level on which they placed the Son. Divine attributes were commonly ascribed to the Spirit, and His action was specially identified with the process of Biblical inspiration and the phenomena of Christian prophecy. Whenever a line· is drawn between God and creatures, it is regularly drawn so as to include the Holy Spirit on the side of God. Long before the word 'triad' came into use, at the end of the second century, both in East and West, a triad had been recognised in fact. At one time, as the Biblical Word was identified with the Son, an attempt was made to identify the Biblical Wisdom with the Holy Spirit. It is simply untrue that the problem of the third Person in the Trinity was ignored.

Dr. Kirk has recently given enlarged currency, in his contribution to *Essays on the Trinity and the Incarnation*, to the idea that a powerful strain of 'Binitarianism,' or belief

in only two divine Persons, was from the first entwined with
Trinitarian belief. The fact that he finds both strains
expressed in St. Paul and the Fourth Gospel greatly mini-
mises the significance of his contention, for, if from the
middle of the first century the same people were both
Binitarians and Trinitarians, their Binitarianism cannot
have amounted to much in actual fact. It only means that
there were times and occasions on which they were content
to concentrate attention on two Persons, without ceasing
to believe in three. His tendency to accept as genuine the
purely modern confusion between the Son and the Spirit
is largely due to his failure to recognise the common
patristic sense of 'spirit' as equivalent to 'divine being.'
Christ is constantly described as a 'spirit' by the Fathers, in
virtue of His divine nature; but this usage has nothing to do
with an identification between Him and 'the Holy Spirit.'
And it must be plainly stated that some of the quotations
by which it is sought to illustrate denial of divinity to the
Holy Spirit derive their only force from mistranslation.

Thus Athenagoras is said to define Christians as "men
who hold the Father to be God and the Son God and the
Spirit Holy"(*op. cit.* p.217). What Athenagoras actually
says (*suppl.* 10.3) is this: "It is astonishing to hear the name
of atheists applied to people who present a God the Father
and a divine Son and a Holy Spirit, and teach the power
of these in unity and their distinction in order." He calls
attention to the unity and power of all three Persons, and
cites the fact of belief in the Holy Spirit together with the
other two as evidence that Christians were not atheists. If
they did not hold the Spirit to be God, His citation impairs
the very argument which Athenagoras is advancing. An

even more flagrant error is made in an alleged quotation
from Eusebius, that "the Holy Spirit cannot be called God,
being one of the things made by the Son" (*loc. cit.*). Eusebius
says nothing of the kind. The following is the whole
passage (*eccl. theol.* 3.6.3). "The 'one God-and-Father' of
our Lord Jesus Christ can alone be called such; the Son is
God-only-begotten who is in the bosom of the Father;
the Paraclete-Spirit is neither God nor Son (since He receives
His origin from the Father not in such fashion as the Son
does, but is one of the beings that derive through the
Son: 'all have come into being through Him, and apart
from Him has nothing come into being'). These broadly are
the 'mysteries' declared by the holy and Catholic Church
through the divine titles; but Marcellus has confused them
all." When Eusebius denies that the Spirit is "either
God or Son," a thorough acquaintance with patristic
usage, or even careful attention to the context itself, shows
that 'God' means 'God the Father.' The Spirit is not
to be identified either with the Father or with the Son.
Eusebius is simply maintaining, as against the theory
of Marcellus, the distinction and reality of the three
Persons. Marcellus, he continues, is part Sabellian (that
is, confuses the three Persons into one), and part Samosatene
(that is, denies ultimately the personality of the second and
third of them). Eusebius, on the contrary, distinguishes
three Persons, and recognises the title (φωνή) of each as
"divine." Seeing that Binitarianism depends on such
mishandling of the sources, one must regretfully conclude
that Dr. Kirk has mistaken the shadow of oversea Imaginative Theology for the historical substance of patristic
thought.

INTRODUCTION

It needs to be emphasised that the word 'Trinity,' which in quotations, at least from the earlier period, I have normally represented by the less question-begging term 'triad,' originally had no association with the conception of divine unity. It was adopted to express the conviction that the godhead, in one true sense, was not a unity. The word expressing the principle of divine unity is 'monarchy.' Though modern writers have used the name Monarchian to denote a complex of heretical opinions, there is really nothing heretical whatever in its ancient application. 'Monarchy' is employed by the most respectable Fathers in the sense of what we call 'monotheism.'

Chapter V describes an interesting and rather neglected effort, made by Tertullian and Hippolytus, to produce a theological statement which should reconcile monotheism with the acceptance of a divine triad. So far as concerns the doctrine of the Trinity, Tertullian should be recognised as belonging more to Greek theology than to Latin, as frankly as Hippolytus is so accepted. The movement for minimising the 'juristic' character ascribed to his thought, and emphasising its philosophical quality, needs to be still further strengthened. If this effort to enunciate an 'organic monotheism' had succeeded, the term 'economy,' which Tertullian employed for the purpose, would have become the technical description of the Trinity instead of the Incarnation. Its ensuing adoption for the Incarnation possibly helped to throw the suggestions of Tertullian and Hippolytus into complete oblivion.

Chapter VI opens with a brief consideration of alternative theories of the divine being. Sabellianism abolished the distinctions between the three Persons, making them

INTRODUCTION

nothing more than temporary or successive modes of manifestation to the subjective apprehension of creatures, with no real ground in the nature of God. The Gnostics pointed the way towards an emanationary solution, by which each Person after the first was progressively further removed from pure deity; this train of thought issued historically in subordinationism. The Adoptionists, treating Christ as a mere man, though uniquely inspired, groped towards the unitarianism more consistently thought out by Paul of Samosata. Paul's is a rather baffling figure, which reappears in Chapter X, in connection with a notorious difficulty of interpretation. Prof. Loofs has lately endeavoured to improve Paul's theological reputation, and is followed with entire confidence by Canon F. W. Green, who asserts, in *Essays on the Trinity and the Incarnation*, that Paul was certainly not a unitarian. Without entering into a long controversial discussion, I can only say that I think this confidence entirely misplaced.

Subordinationism came to exercise a profound influence on theology, far surpassing that of unitarianism or Sabellianism. It entered largely in connection with the doctrine of the Logos, which was developed in opposition to Gnosticism; thus Gnosticism was met and defeated with the aid of weapons in principle not unlike its own. Logos in patristic use is associated with the ideas of revelation, of rationality, and of the divine command or will. Its roots are therefore by no means either purely Hellenistic or purely metaphysical. But it had signified an immanent rational principle in the Stoic system, and this fact fastened attention largely on the cosmic aspect of the Son, when He was identified with the Logos. For an experimental period the conception was tested, but later repudiated, of the second Person of the Trinity as first an immanent Thought within the paternal Mind, then as 'uttered' in the act of creation. It was discarded, because it limited the distinct being of the Son by making it dependent on creation, and thus contravened the principle that God, in revealing Himself to mankind, so far as they are capable of apprehending Him, has made a revelation consistent with what He really is.

Chapter VII contains an extended survey of subordinationism. Origen was strongly imbued with this tendency. His greatest problem lay in trying to preserve his belief in the genuine deity of the Son and the Holy Spirit while maintaining the principle that all their divine attributes were derived from the being of the Father. Only with acute difficulty did he avoid the identification of derivation with such degree of inferiority as would abolish the claim to deity. No formula had as yet been found which would adequately express derivation as distinct from creation. But when Canon Green (*op. cit.* p.250 note 3) accuses Origen of asserting that the Logos is "of another substance" than the Father, he is mistaken. What Origen means (*de orat.* 15.1) is that the Son is "a distinct being" (ἕτερος κατ' οὐσίαν), as the context shows. Origen was followed by Eusebius, a great historian, but a rather confused theologian.

Apart from this embarrassment, which was partly of Biblical origin, the situation was further confused by the tentative introduction of the Platonistic expression 'second god.' Eusebius in particular allowed himself to be hampered by its adoption. Origen had already paved the way by distinguishing between 'the God' and 'God' (a difference corresponding roughly to that between 'God' and 'god'), permitting only the latter expression to be applied to the Son. Arius and his party gathered up all the threads of subordinationism, pressing to its logical conclusion every metaphor which tended to represent the Son as definitely inferior to the Father, or to make the pre-cosmic Logos an impersonal function of God.

Chapter VIII investigates the meaning of the Greek word 'person' (prosopon). It never means a mask in theology, though modern writers constantly repeat that the Sabellians used it in that sense. In reality, the Sabellians appear to have held only one prosopon in the godhead, and the word uniformly means 'individual.' Persona is simply Tertullian's Latin translation of prosopon; it was re-translated into Greek by Hippolytus, and continued in orthodox use to the end of the Greek patristic period. Hypostasis bears an essentially different significance. As applied to the Persons of God, it expresses objectivity, or, in the concrete, an object. This meaning emerges clearly from a variety of other senses, employed in different connections. Its use in reference to the divine Persons implies that they are not mere names or functions or attributes, but substantive objects. The statement that hypostasis ever received "a sense midway between 'person' and 'attribute,' inclining to the former," is pure delusion, though it is derived ultimately from Harnack (*Hist. Dogm.* iv. p.85). The Greeks were never misty-minded, and knew exactly what they meant by their terminology.

Chapter IX continues the theological illustration of hypostasis, showing that, though it was not till the middle of the fourth century that its application to the three Persons was finally freed from all misconception, the idea which it conveyed was substantially accepted. It seems to have gained a temporary currency in the East as a literal translation of the Latin substantia, but only as a Latinism. When that stumbling block had been cleared away by Athanasius, the formula of three hypostaseis and one ousia (substance) was generally accepted. Ousia also means 'object,' but with a difference. While hypostasis lays the stress on concrete independence, ousia lays it on intrinsic constitution. Hypostasis means 'a reality *ad alios*,' ousia 'a reality *in se*'; the one word denotes God as manifest, the other connotes God as being. Athanasius taught that in God one and the same identical 'substance' or object, without any division, substitution, or differentiation of content, is permanently presented in three distinct objective forms. It is one in content and consciousness, but three to contact and apprehension. Humanly speaking, this is a paradox. But it has the justification that any human thought about the infinite must of necessity be paradoxical. It does not pretend to be the formula by which God veritably lives, but it does provide a concept by which He can be presented to human understanding, according to its capacity to receive a measure of genuine enlightenment.

Chapter X introduces the 'homoousion,' the term by which the Nicene creed sought to exclude Arianism. The history of the word is discussed, and it is sought to show that its true meaning is 'of the same stuff.' In the creed it implies that the Son is as truly God as is God the Father. It has no direct or essential bearing on the problem of divine unity, though the followers of Athanasius seem to have read into it their own views on that subject. This was an accidental and temporary consequence of the circumstances of the time. A review is made of the disputed interpretation to be set on the term in connection with Paul of Samosata. Harnack, Ottley, Dr. C. E. Raven (*Apollinarianism* p.64), Canon Green (*op. cit.* p.260, following Prof. Loofs), all more or less confidently conclude that Paul used the word homoousios in a sense, not quite that of Athanasius, but one that implied the essential unity of the Son with the Father. I give my reasons for thinking that this conclusion is wrong. (Canon Green's quotation of "enousios Wisdom" from Athanasius *de syn.* 41 fin. [not 42 as cited, *op. cit.* p.261 note 2], means not 'immanent in the substance of God,' but the same as enhypostatos, i.e. 'concrete,' 'a substantive being,' or, as the Benedictine Latin translation renders, 'Sapientiam substantia praeditam.') The official doctrine agreed on at Nicæa left the problem of divine unity unsolved, though Athanasius had his own solution, which afterwards came to be accepted in substance.

In Chapter XI this solution is further examined. It took shape in the doctrine of Identity of Substance, the immense importance of which has been very inadequately recognised in the text-books, though it forms the whole basis of the orthodox theory of divine unity. Athanasius, in works little known in England, perhaps because not [till 1951] translated into English, expressly included the Holy Spirit in his statement of this Identity. But conservative opinion was alarmed after the Council of Nicæa by the speculations of Marcellus, and for a time was thrown into a protective alliance with the extreme subordinationist views of the Arian school, putting forth the formula homœousios ('of like substance') as less open to Sabellian interpretation. This meant that the problem of divine unity was shelved. Meantime the Macedonian wing of Arians, accepting the Son as a demi-god, banished the Holy Spirit altogether from the godhead. This was too much for the conservatives, who were gradually led, through the teaching of Athanasius, and under the guidance of Basil of Cæsarea and his associates, to full acceptance of the Identity of Substance. It was Athanasius rather than the Council of Nicæa that saved Christian monotheism. At the conclusion of the chapter some illustrations are given of the recognition by Latin writers of the difference between Eastern and Western doctrines of the Trinity, ranging from Augustine to Thomas Aquinas.

Chapter XII deals with some details in the Cappadocian Settlement, defining the individuality of the divine Persons. The sole distinctions of the several Persons are said to be Fatherhood, Sonship, and Sanctification. The one divine being exists in the three 'modes' of ingeneracy, generation, and procession. These are 'modes of existence,' in which the three distinctions mentioned are objectively expressed. It is most misleading to refer to them as 'essences.' That was the mistake made by Aetius and Eunomius, but warmly repudiated by orthodox thinkers. The only remaining relics of subordinationism are to be found in the doctrine of the 'monarchy,' that the divine being has its sole source in the Father, and in the doctrine of the double procession of the Holy Spirit, from the Father through the Son. But when Harnack claims (*Hist. Dogm.* iv. p. 87) that the Cappadocians rested their view of the divine unity on the principle of the monarchy and not on the homoousion, he is going far beyond the facts. They really based it, as shown in Chapter XI., on the Substantial Identity, which was precisely what Athanasius understood by the homoousion. The 'organic' character of the godhead, to which Tertullian had long before called attention, was thus recognised, and contributed to a new appreciation of the divine unity. It was clearly enunciated that in the whole godhead there is only one function of will and one principle of action. The three 'Persons' are not to be regarded as three independent consciousnesses.

Chapter XIII sketches the rise of an abstract tendency of thought, which came to a head in Leontius of Byzantium and Leontius of Jerusalem, whose love of schematic formalism led them to force the doctrine of the Trinity into verbal assimilation with that of the incarnation. They also had a passion for reproducing in theology the whole system of Aristotelian logic. In the result they replaced constructive metaphysics with logical formalism, and by making 'substance' abstract undermined the doctrine of Identity of Substance. This achievement deeply affected subsequent theology. The situation was only retrieved by an unknown thinker at the end of the seventh century, whose work was to a large extent incorporated in his own influential treatise by John of Damascus.

Chapter XIV deals with the doctrine of the co-inherence of the divine Persons, by which the situation thus restored was permanently safeguarded. The prevalence of abstract thought had promoted an outbreak of tritheism, and co-inherence was the orthodox reply, formulated by the same anonymous thinker. In substance, this doctrine goes back to theologians of the fourth century. Canon Green (*op. cit.* p. 293) credits Hilary with the invention of the term circumincessio, by which the Latins came to express the co-inherence, and also seems to state (*ib.* p.292) that the corresponding Greek term perichoresis was employed by the Cappadocians. I cannot find evidence for the first assertion, and am sure that the second is due to a misconception. The painstaking and generally accurate Dorner is wrong in supposing that perichoresis had been applied to the Persons of the Trinity long before John of Damascus. In fact it was by origin a Christological term, and was only just transferred to the Trinitarian field in time for John of Damascus to adopt it. But it afforded an extraordinarily timely and fruitful formula for the idea that the being of the whole three Persons was contained in that of each, and so re-affirmed from a fresh angle the crucial doctrine of Substantial Identity.

I do not like to end this long-drawn review of my own book without expressing regret at having been under the necessity of criticising somewhat vigorously conclusions advanced by two close personal friends. It is harder to criticise friends than strangers. But I hope they may agree that it offers greater consolation, because the insidious temptation to indulge in *odium theologicum* is transcended by the consciousness of *concordia amicabilis*. And I want to make public expression of thanks to two other friends for their most generous help—to Miss M. King, who took down a large portion of the book from my dictation, and to Dr. F. L. Cross, who made the Index of patristic references.

G.L.P.

NOTE TO SECOND EDITION

IN ISSUING a second edition the opportunity has been taken
to modify some of the judgements expressed in the first, and
to correct a number of false ascriptions of authorship relating
to documents of which the authenticity can no longer be
maintained. My warm thanks are due to another friend,
Fr. Henri de Riedmatten, O.P., for generous advice in
making these corrections, and in particular for the illuminating suggestion recorded on page 209 with reference to the
Council of Antioch.

G. L. P.

November 1, 1950

CHAPTER I

ELEMENTS OF THEISM

AN obvious starting point for an enquiry into ancient theistic thought is with the word θεός or 'God.' Some interesting light is thrown on the mind of many of the early Fathers by their discussion of the various derivations propounded for it. The derivations suggested are all fanciful and unhistorical, but this very fact helps to indicate the nature of some of the ideas with which the word was commonly associated in the minds of thinking men. Following Herodotus (*hist.* 2.52), some Fathers, including Theophilus, Clement of Alexandria, and Dionysius of Alexandria, connect the word with τίθημι (dispose). "God is so called because He 'disposed' all things" (Theoph. *ad Aut.* 1.4). "He has been called God on the ground of institution (θέσις) and regulation—as Disposer" (Clem. *strom.* 1.29, 182.2). A second derivation, which comes from Plato (*Crat.* 397c) and is quoted by the three Fathers mentioned, and by Eusebius, connects the title with θέω (run), an idea that recalls trains of thought which persisted into the Middle Ages. According to this notion God is the *primum mobile*, the source of motion, activity, and progress of every kind. " 'God' because He 'goes'; to go (θέω) means to run and move and activate and nourish and foresee and govern and give life to everything" (Theoph. *loc. cit.*). This idea was taken from contemplation of the stars and is not wholly free from association with the theories of astrology, as is suggested by Clement (*protrept.* 2, 26.1), when he says that the stars were called gods "because they go." On the other hand, the Latin Father Tertullian, who unlike most Latins read Greek in the original, says (*ad nat.* 2.4) that it is more reasonable to suppose that the name was borrowed from the title of the true God than from any running or motion.

A third line of thought comes into prominence a little later. Eusebius seems to be the first to bring forward the suggestion (*prep. ev.* 5.3, 182D) that the gods originally acquired their name from the fact that they occasioned the visibility of the world of sight, another reference to astronomy if not to astrology. The Greek verbs on which this fanciful derivation was based are θεωρέω or θεάομαι. Pseudo-Basil states (*ep.* 8.11) that God is so called "from having disposed all things or from beholding all things." Gregory of Nyssa has a striking passage on this subject (*c. Eun.* 2, 584, Migne 1108 A). "The conceptions which arise in us about the divine nature we translate into express names, so that no title is adopted for the divine nature apart from some particular idea." He states that the word 'God' has received acceptance on account of His activity in overseeing, "for believing that the deity is present to all and beholds all and pervades all, we express this thought by that name. . . . He is named God from His beholding." Finally an even more fanciful derivation is propounded by Gregory of Nazianzus, who mentions (*or.* 30.18) that the experts in such subjects had suggested an etymology which connected θεός with αἴθειν (to blaze), because the deity is in perpetual motion and consumes evil habits. This conceit is repeated together with other derivations by

2

John of Damascus (*fid. orth.* 1.9), one of the most diligent compilers known to ecclesiastical record.

Some leading ideas about the nature of God may be illustrated in a few quotations from early writers. Tatian writes (*ad Gr.* 4.1, 2), "Our God does not have his constitution in time. He alone is without beginning; He Himself constitutes the source (ἀρχή) of the universe. God is spirit. He does not extend through matter, but is the author of material spirits and of the figures (σχήματα) in matter. He is invisible and intangible." Athenagoras (*suppl.* 10.1) expresses allegiance to "one God, the uncreated, eternal, invisible, impassible, incomprehensible, uncontainable, comprehended only by mind and reason, clothed in light and beauty and spirit and power indescribable, by whom the totality has come to be." The precise meaning of certain of these terms will be more fully explained later. But, in brief, this statement implies that God is transcendent and everlasting; free alike from limitations of time or space and from subjection to sense or affections; and possessed of supreme supernatural power and glory. Theophilus speaks similarly (*ad. Aut.* 1.3) of the abstract qualities of the deity. "The form of God is ineffable . . . in glory He is uncontainable, in greatness incomprehensible, in height inconceivable, in might incomparable, in wisdom without peer, in goodness inimitable, in well-doing indescribable. . . He is without beginning because He is uncreated, and He is unchangeable because He is immortal." And again (*ib.* 2.3), "it belongs to God, the highest and almighty and the truly God, not only to be everywhere, but also to overlook all things and to hear all things, and yet, nevertheless, not to be contained in space."

3

Irenæus, arguing with Gnostics, expressed similar ideas in positive terms (*haer.* 1.12.2). "He conceives that which He also wills, and wills when He conceives. He is all conception, all will, all mind, all light, all eye, all hearing, all fountain of every blessing." It is noticeable that the Gnostics, with the concrete imagery and picturesque metaphor which were characteristic of their thought, often introduce a positive presentation of ultimate principles which in part the Fathers tend to put negatively, though the importance attached in Gnostic circles, no less than in orthodox, to the conceptions normally expressed in negative forms is illustrated by the abstract and negative titles chosen even for some of their æons. It is more illuminating to observe how far removed from the truth is the assumption that a positive statement is necessarily clearer or more instructive than a negative statement. In point of fact, though the Fathers in speaking of the ineffable being of God tended to use abstract forms which are outwardly expressive of a negative meaning, nevertheless their minds were far from being bounded by merely negative conceptions. The negative forms are enriched with an infinite wealth of positive association.

This may be realised when it is seen that the negative prefixes so widely employed in words intended to describe the divine nature really testify to divine freedom and independence. When it is asserted that God is free from various limitations and controls, the effect is to assert His entire freedom to be Himself and to act according to His own nature and will. His absolute independence is a corollary to His absolute goodness and wisdom, as well as to His absolute capacity to create. Thus the emphasis, which will require fuller investigation at a later stage, on God being uncreated (ἀγένητος) implies that He is the sole originator of all things that are, the source and ground of existence; and the conception is taken as a positive criterion of deity. The insistence that God is uncontained spatially (ἀχώρητος) conveys a very necessary warning against Stoic pantheism. Though the created universe contributes an implicit revelation of God through His works, it is by no means a complete or perfect revelation of His being; He is infinitely greater than His creation. Thus Justin claims (*dial.* 127.2) that God is uncontained either in one place or in the whole universe, since He existed before the universe came into being. Stoicism exercised no little influence on Christian theism, but Christianity had to repudiate decisively the idea that the world is necessary to God's own existence, or co-extensive with Him.

Similar considerations account for the incomprehensibility and impassibility attributed to deity. Incomprehensibility is associated with infinity, as when Hippolytus refers (*ref.* 5.9.5) to "an incomprehensible (ἀκατάληπτος) magnitude" or (*ib.* 6.18.3) to "incomprehensible air, possessing neither beginning nor end"; or again (*ib.* 1.2.6), speaking of the Pythagorean theory of numbers, states that abstract number constitutes the primary originating principle, being indefinable and incomprehensible, including within itself all particular numbers which quantitatively reach to infinity. But infinitude, as well as being incomprehensible (*i.e.*, illimitable) quantitatively, is also incomprehensible intellectually. The idea expresses something that in the full sense lies beyond the measure of man's mind. Hence the Academic school is said (*ib.* 1.23.1) to have introduced the doctrine of "universal incomprehensibility," alleging that there is no truth to be found in the sphere either of mind or of sensation, and that the appearance of things is an illusion of human consciousness. So when God is called incomprehensible, it does not indeed mean that He is irrational—a conception which the Greek Fathers would have considered purely self-contradictory—but it does imply that His wisdom ranges infinitely further than human wisdom can compass, just as His power infinitely excels human creative capacity. "By His most all-magnitudinous might He established the heavens," observes Clement of Rome (*Cor.* 1.33.3), "and by His incomprehensible wisdom He set them in order." Or as Clement of Alexandria states (*strom.* 5.11, 71.5), He is beyond place and time and description and understanding.

Just as God is supreme in power and wisdom, so is He morally supreme, incapable of being diverted or overborne by forces and passions such as commonly hold sway in the creation and among mankind. The word chosen to express this moral transcendence is 'impassible' (ἀπαθής). Describing the incarnation, Ignatius remarks (*Pol.* 3.2.) that the Timeless and Invisible became visible for our sakes, the Impalpable and Impassible for our sakes became passible. It is invariably assumed and repeatedly stated that impassibility is one of the divine attributes. Human nature, on the other hand, is passible, because in men the rational mind is dependent on a fleshly instrument, and consciousness is mediated through physical senses. Perfect mental and moral stability is thus impossible to us in this life, though it is often stated, as by Athenagoras (*suppl.* 31.3), that Christians look forward to a future existence in which the redeemed will abide with God, indefectible and impassible in soul, not like fleshly beings, even if they retain their fleshly nature, but like heavenly "spirit."

Impassibility then implies perfect moral freedom, and is a supernatural endowment properly belonging to God alone. God, says Clement (*strom.* 4.23, 151.1), is impassible, without anger and without desire. God is impassible and changeless, he repeats (*ecl. proph.* 52.2); impassible and unalterable, says Methodius (*de creat.* 4.1), and proceeds to defend the position that the act of creation involved no change in the being of God Himself. It is clear that impassibility means not that God is inactive or uninterested, not that He surveys existence with Epicurean impassivity from the shelter of a metaphysical insulation, but that His will is determined from within instead of being swayed from without. It safeguards the truth that the impulse alike in providential order and in redemption and sanctification comes from the will of God. If it were possible to admit that the impulse was wrung from Him either by the needs or by the claims of His creation, and that thus whether by pity or by justice His hand was forced, He could no longer be represented as absolute; He would be dependent on the created universe and thus at best only in possession of concurrent power. Any such view leads straight to Manichæan dualism. But in that case God ceases to be the ground of all existence, τὸ ὄν. The Trinity, observes Epiphanius (*haer.* 76. 39.4, 968A), possesses impassibility and invariability, but everything subsequent to the Trinity is subject to passion, except the Impassible bestow impassibility, through immortality, on whomsoever He will.

In this connection certain difficulties had to be faced,

7

arising from the language of the Old Testament, in which the action of God had frequently been described in human language. No Jew would ever have imagined that certain of these metaphors could be taken literally; but the case was rather different with Gentiles, trained in a Greek tradition, accustomed to physical representations of divine forms, and prepared to dismiss Jews as intellectually barbarous, though they happened to possess a revelation of the true God. It certainly needed to be made clear to the Gentile world that the anthropomorphisms of the Old Testament were to be interpreted in a spiritual sense. And even those bred in the Jewish tradition were liable to misconception, when the anthropomorphic metaphors were derived from moral rather than from physical qualities. Clement makes the position clear by a statement of principle that is both acute and effective. He expressly denies mental variations to God, such as the emotions of joy or pity or grief (*strom.* 2.16, 72); to ascribe such physical passions to the impassible God is inadmissible. On the other hand, deity cannot be described as it really is, but only as human beings, themselves fettered to the flesh, are capable of hearing; the prophets therefore adopted the language of anthropomorphism as a saving concession to the weakness of human understanding. Or, as he argues elsewhere (*strom.* 5.11, 68.1–3), the majority of mankind are so wrapped up in their own mortal concerns, like some of the lower creation, that they are led to form suppositions about the blessed and incorruptible God similar to the experiences with which they are familiar in themselves. They forget, he says, that God has bestowed on us innumerable gifts in which He does not Himself partake—creation, though He is uncreated;

8

sustenance, though He has no such need; growth, though He remains in equipoise; a blessed old age and a blessed death, though He is immortal and ageless. "Therefore when the Hebrews mention hands and feet and mouth and eyes and entrances and exits and exhibitions of wrath and threatening, let no one suppose on any account that these terms express passions of God. Reverence rather requires that from these expressions an allegorical meaning should be extracted." As he says a little further on (*ib.* 71.4), "you must not entertain the notion at all of figure and motion, or standing or seating, or place, or right or left, as appertaining to the Father of the universe, although these terms are in Scripture;" each of them has its own meaning, which is capable of explanation as occasion arises.

Another line of thought which is expressed largely in negative terms is concerned with the indivisibility of God. He had originally been described as 'one,' more by way of rejecting claims of false gods than with a view to expounding His own essential nature. But it is a clear and recognised philosophical principle that the ground and author of the whole multiplicity of creation must present an ultimate unity. Hence Athenagoras argues (*suppl.* 8.2) that God is one; but, unlike a human individual, who is created and corruptible, composite and divisible into parts, God is unbegotten and impassible and indivisible, and therefore not composed of parts. Origen, again, contends (on *St. John*, 1.20, 119) that God is altogether one and simple; or in the words of Chrysostom (*de incompr.* 4.3), God is simple, without composition and without configuration. In the statement of the Thirty-nine Articles that God is without body, parts or passions the denial of parts is at least as important as the denial of material substance or of the control of what is spiritual by what is merely psychological.

The thought of ancient philosophers attached to the constitution of composite objects the idea of transience. Change and decay in all around they saw. The material universe was, by its nature, compound and corruptible. Objects which are constructed out of, and can be analysed into, different parts are plainly subject to instability not only in the parts but also in their mutual relations. Because the world was of composite construction it was therefore impermanent, liable to transformation and ultimate dissolution through the chances and mischances of perpetual variation. But deity, said Eusebius (c. *Marcell.* 1.1.19), is superior to any sensible and compound body. Bodily nature, said Gregory of Nyssa (*or. cat.* 7), is necessarily subject to passions and infirmities, because it is compound and flows into dissolution. Unbegotten substance, said Basil of Seleucia (*or.* 25.4), cannot form a natural compound with begotten substance; deity has no parts ($\dot{a}\mu\epsilon\rho\dot{\eta}s$). A phrase like "the divine uncompounded nature" is employed without explanation or discussion since it expresses what was taken to be an axiom of thought. The divine spirit, says the pseudo-Cæsarius (*resp.* 43), is one, of single form, single character, single substance, indivisible.

As might be expected, in connection with the doctrine of the Trinity, the character of God as being incomposite presented special problems to those who were concerned in the fourth century to maintain and expound the view that God was also three in one. But it was clearly recognised and definitely laid down that even thus the principle of the incomposite character of God must be maintained. Apollinarius may be quoted in illustration of this statement. Apollinarius maintained peculiar views on the incarnation. They rightly failed to find acceptance; possibly they were not wholly understood. He was nevertheless a thinker of exceptionally acute insight, and his writings were for long accepted as containing an orthodox exposition of the faith. The value of his works is attested by the strange fact that his followers were able to pass on many of them as examples of orthodox teaching, even after his condemnation for heresy, by publishing them under the name of other authors whose theological respectability was unimpeachable. "We maintain," wrote Apollinarius (*fides sec. part.* 18), "that the Trinity is one God; not that we recognize the one as proceeding from the composition of three (for every part that depends on composition for its existence is incomplete) but that, what the Father is as source and progenitor, that the Son is as image and offspring of the Father."

Parallel to the doctrine of divine unity is the equally important doctrine of divine self-consistency. This doctrine is also closely allied to that of impassibility and on it the latter logically depends. As has been stated already, there is no sign that divine impassibility was taught with any view of minimising the interest of God in His creation or His care and concern for the world that He had made. In fact, any such theory is manifestly absurd. Impassibility, though affording an obvious line of approach to the wider doctrine, is a department of the larger question of self-consistency. God is, in the fullest sense, the same yesterday, to-day, and for ever. As the ground and unifying principle of the multiplicity of experience must, on the Greek view, itself be conceived as single, so must it also be regarded as possessing a changeless identity. A relative sort of being can be ascribed to the universe of development and retrogression only because it is grounded in a being that is permanent and self-consistent.

The way in which such considerations were imported into theology may be illustrated by a quotation made by Eusebius (*prep. ev.* 11.10, 526B) from the Platonist philosopher Numenius, to the effect that Reality or Absolute Being (τὸ ὄν) is simple and unchangeable and in the self-same form (ἰδέα); it neither voluntarily abandons its identity (ταυτότης) nor is compelled to do so by external influence. The substance of this statement was derived from Plato (*Republic* 380D). Similar ideas were a commonplace of popular philosophy. Among the Valentinian Gnostics—inconsistent as the notion may appear to be with their theories of development in the divine Pleroma and of the creation having been occasioned by a pre-cosmic fall of one element belonging to the Pleroma—a firm distinction was made between the divine and the phenomenal. The earthly Saviour had to have his celestial counterpart in the Pleroma, in order to make his dispensation effective, and the Only-begotten, in accordance with whose uninterrupted power the phenomenal Saviour did his work, is described (ap. Clem. Al. *exc. Theod.* 8.3) as "the Only-begotten in the sphere of identity," that is, on the plane of permanent being.

Among orthodox Christians, Clement speaks (*strom.* 7.3, 15.4) of the real God who continues in identity of righteous goodness. Alexander of Alexandria refers to the one ingenerate Father, who owns no one as the cause of His being, immutable and invariable, always in the same identical mode of existence, and admitting neither progress nor diminution (ap. Thdt. *h.e.* 1.4.46). Epiphanius (*ancor.* 6.1.) observes that the deity exists in identity and requires neither increment nor dignity nor progress. The same thought appears in a more mystical if less simple form in pseudo-Dionysius (*div. nom.* 4.8): "the divine intelligences abide in identity, incessantly revolving around the moral ideal (καλὸν καὶ ἀγαθόν) which is the ground of identity." Here again, as in relation to divine unity, a special problem was laid up for the defenders and expositors of the doctrine of the Trinity. The differentiation implied in the plurality of the divine Persons had to be reconciled with a theistic doctrine which required not merely unity but identity in the divine being. The difficulty pressed heavily on Origen, who adopted more than one line of approach to the solution of it. Athanasius felt it too, and not until his successors was a really satisfactory method worked out by which to meet it.

Seeing that the unity of God is positive, intrinsic, based on an infinite incomposite identity, the Fathers denied the possibility of His physical configuration. God is not circumscribed in place, says Clement (*strom.* 7.6, 30.1), nor can He be represented by the schema of a creaturely organism (ζῷον). As the author of the Clementine Homilies had argued (17.3), "Does God possess form (μορφή)? If so, He is subject to figure, and if under configuration, how can He be otherwise than circumscribed?" The point of this somewhat cryptic and unfamiliar reasoning is that the Infinite cannot be subject to diagrammatic boundaries; boundaries are merely marks of delimitation, and therefore imply finitude. Configuration belongs to material objects alone. Design in this sense may properly be ascribed to such an object as a statue which, as 'Constantine' pointed out (*ad sanct. coet.* 4), is first conceived in the mind of the skilled craftsman, then brought into existence by application of the rules of art to the material. But if the sculptor next proceeds to worship his creation as an immortal God, he is exhibiting not merely inconsistency, seeing that he has the best reason for knowing that it is the creation of a mortal man, but also ignorance; for the divine "neither requires form by which to be recognized nor admits of figure as of an image or copy."

The figure and shape imposed on created objects are God's handiwork; He is the author not merely of matter but of design (as is repeatedly asserted by the Fathers), and disposes all according to His will. But the sculptor who designs, and executes his design, can also change his design; there is no intrinsic finality about his work. God alone is immutable. Hence, says Cyril of Alexandria (on *St. John* 305C), immutability exists in God by virtue of His nature, and by the same token does not exist in us at all; but we may arrive at a kind of security which configures us to His immutability through effort and sobriety. Of the nature of God Himself the advice of Nilus (*de orat.* 66) gives pointed indication: "Do not figure the divine within yourself when you pray and do not allow your mind to be impressed into any form, but approach the Immaterial immaterially." When the Epistle to the Hebrews says that Christ sat down on the right hand of the Majesty on high, the Bible does not confine God to a place nor does it configure, that is materialise, Him, but merely indicates the identity of Christ's glory with that of the Father (Chrysostom on *Hebr.* 2.3). The protest against the ascription of form and figure to the being of God is really simply a protest against all materialistic notions. Configuration is the corollary of existence in physical space. The denial of it to God means just that the divine being, though truly and concretely subsisting, is not subject to the rules of Euclid and the geometricians.

It is true that a form or μορφή of His own is commonly ascribed to God. He has glory and form ineffable, says Justin (*apol.* 1.9.3). But it is quite clear that the expression is used in no technical sense, nor does it imply that God is circumscribed by any physical characteristics. The fluid character of the whole conception may be illustrated by the different applications which a single writer makes of the term. Basil argues (*hex.* 9.6) the absolute necessity that the Son and the Father should possess the same form, adding that the word 'form' should be understood, of course, in a sense such as is applicable to God. Here, form is applied to the divine substance. In another passage (*c. Eun.* 2.28) the same author uses the word to describe the personal distinctions in the Trinity. "The individualities, which are observed so to speak as characteristics and 'forms' imposed on the substance, distinguish the common element by individual characteristics." In a disputed letter (*ep.* 38.8) he uses the word 'form' to denote Christ as a visible expression of the Father; "so that the person of the Son becomes, so to speak, a form and presentation (prosopon) of the knowledge of the Father."

In another connection it is repeatedly stated that the human race, or at any rate that section of it which serves and is conformed to God, has the form of God. "He stamped mankind with his own form as with a vast seal" (*hom. Clem.* 17.7). "That man in whom the word abides . . . possesses the form of the word, is made like to God" (Clem. *paed.*

D

3.1, 1.5). "The form of the word, expressed in similarity," is impressed on those who are baptized (Meth. *sympos.* 8.8, 190); and the disgraceful passion of anger does violence to "the divine form" in man (Greg. Nyss. *or. cat.* 40). So again in creation mankind, compounded of the dust of the earth, was "formed" by God by reference to Himself (Greg. Naz. *or.* 5.31).

The meaning of all such speculations is clear when it is recalled that very great attention had been devoted in Greek thought to the distinction between form and matter. Matter is unknown to experience except in determinate forms, and forms, though they can be distinguished in thought from the matter to which they give shape and expression, are in practice only known to the human mind in association with that matter. The idea of any really existing substance could not, therefore, be easily divorced from the conception of a form in which it had its being presented. In the case of God, the divine substance was conceived, not indeed materially, but concretely. Even the divine substance must be conceived to possess some form of its own. And this conclusion is wholly legitimate. If any positive statement at all is to be made about the nature of God, it can only be made in human language and in metaphors derived from the analogies of human thought. It is worth noting that form or 'morphe' is distinguished from figure or 'schema.' 'Schema' merely expresses the abstract relation of parts to one another and to the whole object: but the real meaning of 'morphe' is substance expressed in a definite and concrete shape. This is perfectly clear throughout the patristic writings, both orthodox and heretical. When, therefore, form is ascribed to the deity it is only in an attempt to emphasise that God's being is a concrete reality, not a fiction or abstraction. Even then, it is quite possible that the word would never have come into use in this connection had it not happened to have been so employed by St. Paul (*Phil.* ii.6)—"who being in the form of God . . . emptied himself, taking the form of a servant, being made in the likeness of men." Form and likeness here bear the same sense, and 'nature' could well be substituted for either.

The conception of divine form or stuff carried one great advantage. It enabled a positive description to be given of the constitutive elements of the divine nature. Thus the 'form' or substance of the deity is described positively as spirit (πνεῦμα), a term which further illustrates the habit adopted by early theologians of meeting their difficulties as far as possible by recourse to the language of Scripture. But the term 'spirit' was not without associations in popular philosophy. Following a Stoic tradition the idea was prevalent that 'spirit' was itself material, though its materiality was of the utmost conceivable refinement. Thus Hippolytus (*ref.* 1.20.4), in expounding Aristotle's theory of the soul, describes it as surviving the body, but after that as being absorbed into a fifth element, of which the philosopher conceives the existence in addition to earth, air, fire and water—the four generally recognized—but more subtle than these, "like spirit." And Origen refers (on *St. John* 13.21, 128) to the view that God is corruptible, being body, though a spiritual and ethereal body. It is in protest against such ideas that Tatian (*ad Gr.* 4.1), on stating that God is spirit, immediately adds that He is not extended in matter.

Spirit is an essential element in deity. Athenagoras

(*suppl.* 16.2) describes God as being all things to Himself independently of external relations—light unapproachable, perfect order, spirit, power, word (or rationality); and again in emphasising the unity of the Persons he states (*ib.* 10.2) that the Son is in the Father and the Father in the Son in unity and power of spirit. Callistus, a theologian of undoubted force but somewhat obscure principles, is accused by Hippolytus (*ref.* 9.12.16) of teaching that the spirit (by which apparently he meant the divine principle) is one and undivisible—everything is full of the divine spirit—the spirit that became incarnate in the Virgin is no other than the Father. Eusebius argues thus (*c. Marc.* 1.1.19): "If spirit, then obviously divine, transcending any sensible and composite body." Basil says (*de Sp. sanct.* 22) that it is impossible in connection with spirit to envisage a nature which is circumscribed or in any degree similar to the creation, but "it is essential to conceive of an 'ideal' (νοερός) substance, infinite in power, unlimited in greatness, immeasurable in point of time or age, unstinted in respect of the goods which it possesses." Finally, in the words of Cyril (*ad Calosyr.* 364 A, Pusey vol. 5.604), God is spirit, and if spirit, not embodied nor in bodily form.

It is in keeping with the conception of spirit as implying the nature or vehicle or principle of deity, that the divine Son is referred to as being spirit. The heavenly Logos, says Tatian (*ad Gr.* 7.1), became spirit from the spirit and Logos from the power of logos. Christ, says the author of the so-called second epistle of Clement to the Corinthians (9.5), was first spirit, then became flesh. Irenæus confutes the Docetists with this argument (*haer.* 5.1.2): if, not truly being man, Christ merely appeared human, then He did not in fact remain what He had been, spirit of God, since spirit is invisible. And again (*ib.* 3.10.3), He had the power of salvation because He was spirit. The Son of God also, says Eusebius (*eccl. theol.* 3.5.19), is in substance spirit, and indeed spirit most holy (ἁγίων ἅγιον), seeing that He is the image of the invisible. Athanasius (*ad Serap.* 4.23) says that good Christians "worship Him both according to His flesh and to His spirit," as Son of God and son of man. Basil of Ancyra and his confederates, in the document preserved by Epiphanius (*haer.* 73.16), assert that the Father is spirit, the Son spirit, and the Holy Spirit spirit. Apollinarius maintains (*de un.* 6) that Christ is spirit, even though by the union with the flesh He has been manifested as flesh; and (*frag.* 32) that the directive element (τὸ κύριον) in the nature of the Godman is divine spirit. "Being God by his own (ἰδίῳ) spirit and not having in Himself a God other than Himself," he repeats (*frag.* 38); and (*ad Jov.* 1), "the same, Son of God, and God, by virtue of spirit, and son of man by virtue of flesh." So too Epiphanius, writing of the ascended heavenly life of Christ, says (*haer.* 69.67) that He has united His flesh to one deity, to one unity, to spirit that is both divine and bodily—a strange and rhetorical sentence in which 'spirit' appears to stress not the specifically divine nature so much as any immaterial vehicle of divine being. With this may be compared his remark (*exp. fid.* 17) that Christ rose with soul and body and the whole vessel, and the vessel henceforth was united to the spirit. Epiphanius almost seems to teach post-Ascension monophysitism. But his words aptly show how fully 'spirit' was reckoned as the 'stuff' of the divine nature, since the bodily stuff of the glorified humanity could be fused into it. Theodoret, on the other hand, corrects any misconception by remarking (*dem. per syll.* 2.10) that the sacred body was not changed into spirit, for it was flesh; the body remains body even after the resurrection. And the usage persisted; Leontius of Byzantium says (*c. Nest. & Eut.* 2, Migne 1321 D) that when Christ was glorified, He merely took that, in respect of His flesh, of which He ever had possession in respect of spirit. Christ then in His own heavenly nature is spirit, that is to say, divine. The effect of the expression is the same as was produced by the Nicene use of the word 'homoousios'; the divine Son is of the same stuff as God.

A few other passages can be quoted, in which by 'spirit' the personally divine character of the incarnate Son, rather than His divine nature, is indicated. In them, the term 'spirit' is transferred from the substance to the person of the godhead. Thus, according to the *Epistle of Barnabas* (7.3), Christ was Himself on behalf of our sins about to offer as sacrifice the vessel (σκεῦος) of the spirit. Three fragments of Eustathius of Antioch, preserved by Theodoret (*Eranistes* 3.235–236), manifest the same usage. "The divine spirit of Christ has been shown impassible." "The man"— an expression which is by no means uncommon for the incarnate manhood—"lives by the power of God, dwelling, that is, in converse with the divine spirit." "The body was crucified on high, but the divine spirit of wisdom both dwelt within the body and rested in the heavenly places."

In the light of all such passages the sense is quite clear of the famous statement of Ignatius (*Eph.* 7.2) that Christ is one physician, fleshly and spiritual. It means just what is implied in the familiar modern phrase, true God and true man. And a fuller light is also thrown on the attribution of 'spirituality' to the Scriptures and their authors, to the sacraments, or to the saints and ascetics. It means more than merely mystical and more than merely inspired. It stamps them as belonging in a special sense to God, because God is spirit and spirit implies God.

Another most important set of positive associations attaches to the word 'holy.' Holy means, properly speaking, something set apart for the use or service of God. Thus frequent references are made to the fact that John the Baptist was holy from his mother's womb. Sacrifices, says Chrysostom (on *St. John*, 82.1), are all called holy, and the proper meaning of holy is a thing offered to God. The idea is worked out in an interesting way by Procopius of Gaza (on *Deut.* xxii.9). Holy is used in two senses, he says. First, of a good object, which it is unnecessary to discuss; but "even when people are impious but are set apart for some particular service, they are called holy, as Zephaniah shows" (*Zeph.* i.7).

It is interesting to follow out the sense in the cognate word 'sanctify.' Properly it means to set apart for sacred uses, as when *Barnabas* (15.7) claims that we shall be able to sanctify the seventh day when we ourselves are first sanctified. Clement (*strom.* 5.6, 40.3) recalls the action of the high priest in putting on the sanctified garment. The treatise *de virginitate* (14), which was formerly thought to have been composed by Athanasius, bids the nuns make their thanksgivings over their table, "and thy food and drink shall be sanctified." Chrysostom (on *St. John* 82.1) explains our Lord's words, I sanctify myself (*St. John* xvii.19), as meaning, I offer thee myself in sacrifice. Secondarily, it comes to mean to consecrate, or in some sense or another to charge with supernatural power. Thus, says Clement (*strom.* 7.6, 34.4), the sacrificial fire sanctifies not the meat but the souls of the worshippers. A striking instance occurs in Clement's *Excerpts from Theodotus* (82.1): "the bread and the oil are sanctified by the power of the name of God; to outward appearance they remain the same as they were when they were taken, but by power they have been transformed into spiritual power." So also in connection with various sacramental rites, the neophyte is anointed at baptism with created oil that is sanctified (Didymus Al. *de Trin.* 2.6.23), and Gregory of Nyssa (*or. cat.* 37) expresses the belief of the Church "that the bread which is sanctified by the word of God is transformed into the body of God the Word." Again, those who participate in the Eucharist are sanctified both in body and soul (Clem. *paed.* 2.2, 20.1). Gregory of Nazianzus (*or.* 21.27), referring to the power which emanated from the presence of St. Athanasius, speaks of some people being inspired at the sound of the Bishop's voice, while others, as was said about the Apostles, were sanctified by his mere shadow.

The word hagiasma (sanctified object) regularly refers to things which are consecrated to God. Thus it may mean a holy place such as the Jewish Temple (Origen on *Jer.* 18.5), or the altar or sanctuary of a Christian church (Eus. *h.e.* 7.15.4), or indeed, in a late passage (Eustrat. *vit. Eut.* 13), the church itself. In the apocryphal *protevangelium of James* (6.3) this word in its sense of sanctuary is applied to Anna's bedchamber, in which our Lady was born. Again, it is constantly applied to various consecrated objects associated with religious cultus and possessed of a mystical force, such as the sacrifices of the Jew or the Christian sacraments; it is employed regularly by Basil and Gregory of Nyssa, as well as by Gregory the Wonderworker, in this latter sense. In Theodoret (on 2 *Kings* xi.12) it is explained as referring to royal chrism, and in later writers more than once it is the title for the holy oil of unction (e.g. Dorotheus *doct*. 6.8). Once, in a late treatise (the penitential of pseudo-John-the-Faster, Migne 88.1913A), it means the holy water which it was customary to consecrate at Epiphany.

The second sense of holy is, of course, morally pure. He was holy, says Origen (on *St. John* 32.19, 247) of Judas Iscariot, but fell; and again (*ib.* 2.25, 162), the holy man is a light to the world. Instances are too frequent to need further quotation. A corresponding sense belongs to the verb sanctify, but again we are recalled to the close connection of the word with God, by such statements as (Ath. *c. Ar.* 2.18) that creatures are 'sanctified' by the 'Holy' Spirit, and (Clem. *strom.* 4.23, 148.1) that as we marvel at the creation we 'sanctify,' that is, ascribe holiness to, its creator. Expressions of this kind are common.

With so much said by way of preface, the applications of the word holy to God or what belongs to God would cause no surprise. Following the example of Scripture the early Fathers addressed all three Persons of the Godhead alike as holy. The Trinity itself is called the holy Trinity, apparently first by Clement (*strom.* 5.14, 103.1); and God is referred to simply as "the Holy One" by Basil. Secondly, holy is applied to everything that specially derives from God: heaven, the angels, the Jewish tabernacle, the Bible. Origen (on *St. John* 6.42, 217) uses holy in this connection as equivalent to canonical: "if anybody cares to accept the book as holy." Next the word is applied to what belongs to the body of Christ, the Church; to the clergy ("the holy presbyters," Ignatius *Magn.* 3.1.), synods and synodical definitions, the festival of Easter, and, from the third century onwards, to the sacraments, particularly that of the Eucharist. Again, God's people are repeatedly named the holy ones, without necessarily any discrimination of exceptional sanctity, though the word is also employed from the second century onwards of such special saints as David or the Apostles, and of "the holy martyrs." In the more modern sense of the word saint, Basil remarks (*ep.* 93) that it was customary to communicate four times in each week "and on the other days if there is a memorial of some holy one," and Gregory of Nyssa not only refers (*in laud. Bas.*, Migne 46.797C) to feasts celebrated over the saints, but mentions (*Macr.* init.) how Basil, "that power among saints," had been translated to God. At least from the time of Theodoret (*hist. rel.* 16) the word holy or saint is applied to living ascetics, and begins to occur in titles of honour addressed to bishops (e.g. *ep.* 113), who are normally addressed as "most holy." There is also mention made occasionally of "the holy emperor."

In all the cases which have been illustrated it is plain that the true and ultimate source of holiness is God, and that all the other objects to which it is ascribed derive such holiness as they possess by participation from that primal fount. The idea of God entertained by the Fathers would be illustrated very deficiently without reference to the whole body of associations which gather round the idea of the holy, as something that implies both awful purity and also, and still more, supernatural power. God is, in a current phrase, the 'mysterium tremendum.'

24

CHAPTER II

DIVINE TRANSCENDENCE

THE preceding chapter will have shown how early Christendom sought both to establish and safeguard the supremacy of God in ways appropriate to a people trained to think in the schools of Greek philosophy, from which modern European thought is derived, and also to present the truth of His spiritual nature and moral holiness, which had been taught by the Hebrew prophets as corollary to His divine power. God was firmly held to be supernatural in the deepest and truest sense. Philosophically, this idea was expressed by the word ὑπεροχή, which may fairly be translated transcendence. The word occurs in Irenæus: God, he says (*haer.* 5.2.3), is the source of immortality and incorruption, for "out of His transcendence, not out of our own nature, do we possess eternal continuance." But the context of thought in which the term moved can be more fully illustrated from the Clementine Homilies. Their theology may be peculiar, but their background of popular philosophy fully serves the purpose. "He who would worship God ought before all else to know what is peculiar to the nature of God alone, which cannot pertain to another, that looking at His peculiarity and not finding it in any other, he may not be seduced into ascribing deity to another. This is peculiar to God, that He alone is, as the maker of all, so also the best of all. That which makes is indeed superior in power to that which is made; that which is boundless is superior in magnitude to that which is bounded; in respect of beauty, that which is comeliest; in respect of happiness, that which is most blessed; in respect of understanding, that which is most perfect. And in like manner in other respects He incomparably possesses transcendence. Since then, as I said, this quality, to be the best of all, is peculiar to God, and the all-containing world was made by Him, none of the things made by Him can come into equal comparison with Him" (*hom. Clem.* 10.19).

Holiness and transcendence are expressly connected by Clement in a passage (*strom.* 7.5, 28.2) where he is arguing against idolatry. "What product of builders and masons and mechanical craft could be holy? Are not they better thinkers who regard the sky and the firmament, and indeed the whole universe and totality of things, as a worthy manifestation of God's transcendence?" The word recurs in the Alexandrine tradition. Origen (on *St. John* 2.17, 123) speaks of the superlative transcendence of the life of God. Alexander, in the letter to Alexander of Constantinople preserved by Theodoret (*h.e.* 1.4.29), speaking of Christ as God, says that His ineffable subsistence has been shown as excelling by an incomparable transcendence all the objects on which He has Himself bestowed their existence. The gist of such passages as have been quoted does not indeed amount to a fully formulated doctrine of transcendence as presented in modern philosophies, but it means at least as much as the divine transcendence taught by the Hebrew prophets, which is the main trunk of the Christian idea of God. It links moral and metaphysical qualities in the most definite manner, asserts most strongly the "incomparable" superiority of

God over all creatures, and while hinting that their relative excellence is derived from His perfection interposes an absolute gulf between the Creator and the creation.

Yet such transcendence by no means implies that God's relation with the world is one of Epicurean remoteness. References have already been made to the Stoic doctrine of a pervasive divine spirit contained in the material universe and itself of a quasi-material character. That conception was naturally repugnant to Christian thinkers, yet their thought was much nearer to the Stoic cycle of ideas than to the Epicurean, and, much as Christian philosophy owed to the schools of Plato and Aristotle, particularly the former, the contribution of Stoic tradition to the common stock of ideas is by no means negligible. Christianity was eclectic in its philosophy, though its choice was always controlled by Scriptural teaching and precedent. Allusion was made not unsympathetically to the world-soul of the Stoics, without, of course, any approval of its materiality. Thus Athenagoras remarks (*suppl.* 6.4) that if God is, as certain Stoics said, a creative fire embracing and implanting their fundamental principles into created objects, and His spirit pervades the whole universe, then they really represent God as one, in spite of the varying names suggested by different aspects of His operation. In particular, he appears to accept (*ib.* 24.3) the notion of a created spirit concerned with matter, who has been entrusted by the true God with the administration of material species. Tatian, again, observes (*ad Gr.* 4.2) that the spirit which pervades matter, being lower than the more divine spirit and compared as it were to a soul, must not be honoured on a level with the perfect God. It seems from this that the Apologists were quite prepared to accept the existence of angelic forces whose function was to control and direct the operations of nature, in a manner which presents obvious similarities with Stoic doctrine, though they were careful to reckon such beings among creatures, and declined to confuse them with the transcendent God of the universe. Such a theory combined the advantages of maintaining divine control and yet avoiding any taint of pantheism.

Christian theologians had to meet serious difficulties in considering the relations of God and the world. The type of problem that confronted them may be illustrated by a somewhat extended quotation from Methodius, the Platonist and bishop in Lycia. The passage comes from the treatise on *Free Will*, chapters 5 and 6, and the section is headed "Concerning God and Matter." The primary problem under discussion is that of the origin of evil. As Methodius points out, this question involves a nice philosophical dilemma. Either God is the author of all things and therefore of evil among the rest; or evil resides in matter, and matter, in order to keep God clear from any responsibility for the existence of evil, must be regarded as possessing an independent reality of its own. That is the way in which this problem commonly presented itself to the ancient mind during the early centuries of Christianity. The consequences either way are disastrous for theology, because in the first case God would not be morally perfect, and in the second case He would not be supreme. The argument which follows is designed to refute the second of the alternatives named, that matter possesses independent existence. It shows that there can be only one ultimate and absolute ground of existence, or as the Hellenistic philosophers called it, ageneton; and proceeds to reject the pantheistic solution that God and matter are mutually dependent.

"I imagine you recognise that two ageneta (ἀγένητα, uncreateds) cannot exist simultaneously, however firmly you decide, with that presupposition, to add the absolute necessity of accepting one of two alternatives—either that God is separated from matter, or that, on the contrary, He is inseparable from it. If you choose to argue that He is united to it, you will be arguing for a single ageneton; each factor will form a complementary part, and being parts of one another they will not constitute two ageneta, but one, compounded of different elements. Though man possesses different members we do not resolve him into many geneta (γενητά, createds) like small change for a pound; but if, as reason requires, we confess that God has made man a single complex geneton, so, if God is not separated from matter, we must assert that they constitute a single ageneton.

"But if it is argued that He is separated, there must exist some middle term between the two factors which indicates their separation. It is impossible that one factor should be ascertained to be at an interval from another, without a further factor to determine the interval between the two. This principle holds good not merely up to the present point but up to any number of factors. The principle that we have laid down for two ageneta must be extended similarly if it were granted that there were three ageneta. About these also I should ask, whether they were separated from one another or on the other hand each was united to its complement. If it were decided to assert that they were united, the same argument applies as in the first case. If, on the other hand, that they were separated, it is impossible to evade the necessary concrete fact of the separating factor." In other words, there must be either a single ageneton which is ultimate and unique, or else an infinite regress of ageneta.

"A third explanation might be advanced as applying to the ageneta, that neither is God separated from matter nor again are they united as parts, but that God resides locally in matter, or matter in God. The consequence is this. If we call matter the local extension of God, it necessarily follows that He is also contained" (χωρητός, that is, in effect, finite) "and circumscribed by matter. Similarly He must be driven about irregularly at the instance of matter—instead of remaining constant and continuing in His own control—according as the element in which He is present is driven. Further, it will be necessary to admit that God resides even in what is less perfect. For if matter was ever formless and God ordered it, by an act of will for its improvement, then time was when God resided in what was unordered.

"And I should justly like to ask whether God filled the whole of matter, or was resident in some portion of it. If the reply, is, in a portion, you make God immeasurably smaller than matter, seeing that a portion of it contains God entire. If the answer is that He was in the whole and extended throughout all matter, tell me how He fabricated (δημιουργέω) it. You must either admit a contraction of God, through the occurrence of which He fabricated that part from which He withdrew; or else that He fabricated Himself together with matter, if He had no place for withdrawal." In these paragraphs Methodius raises the fundamental theistic objection to all purely immanentist theories of a self-directed evolution, that, in effect, they reduce the divine principle to a mere function of the universe.

"If anyone argues that matter is in God, it must similarly be investigated whether this happens through the formation of intervals in God, as various species of animals are present in the atmosphere, in the sense that the air is separated and divided in order to receive the objects included in it; or by spatial extension, as moisture is contained in the soil. If we say, like objects in the atmosphere, it must follow that God is divisible. If we say, like moisture in the soil, and matter was unregulated and unordered and, more than that, included certain evils, it must follow that God is the seat of unordered and evil elements. Such a conclusion I consider even more fallacious than it is irreverent. For you assume the existence of matter in order to save making God the author of evil, and in your effort to avoid this you call Him the receptacle of evil."

Methodius thus considers and rejects the idea that God has only concurrent existence with matter or with anything else, on the ground that concurrent existence implies lack of finality, and that such lack has to be repaired by the discovery of some further principle which shall be fundamental to both factors. He then criticizes a pantheistic doctrine which has a strikingly modern ring, to the effect that God and matter are mutually involved in one another and that one or other affords the basis on which its complement is grounded. The details of his argument need not be accepted as final, but they are interesting as showing both the difficulty presented by the problem of the relation of God and the creation, and also the kind of pantheistic conception which Stoic teaching had made familiar and Christian theology had to meet. In

GOD IN PATRISTIC THOUGHT

no merely immanentist sense, theology retorted to the
pantheists, does God pervade the world. He is no more
enclosed in it as spirit in matter, than He is as a subtle and
refined pneumatic matter in a grosser material universe.

Nevertheless, though it is denied that God is extended in
the physical universe in any material or quasi-material
sense, it is affirmed that He pervades it as the control and
guide of its existence. There is express Biblical precedent
for this belief in the Book of Wisdom (vii. 22 ff.). "There is
in her" (that is, in Wisdom) "spirit, ideal (νοερόν), holy, only-
begotten, complex, subtle, mobile, clear, unpolluted," and
so on; "all-powerful, all-surveying, penetrating all spirits
such as are ideal, pure, most subtle. . . . Wisdom pervades
and penetrates all things by reason of her pureness . . . she
is an effulgence of eternal light and an unspotted mirror of
the operation of God and an image of His goodness."

The functions that the Book of Wisdom ascribes to the
divine Wisdom are accepted by theologians as true in
principle. Nemesius in the third section of his treatise on
The Nature of Man (Migne 40.608 A) presents the statement that the purely unembodied nature penetrates (χωρεῖ
διά) everything without obstacle, but is itself impenetrable.
But long before his time the doctrine of divine pervasion had
been implied in a form only slightly different verbally,
though with a distinct and wider meaning. The same verb,
χωρέω, was employed, but without a preposition following,
in the transitive sense with which it bears the meaning of
'fill' or 'contain.' The common non-theological sense may
be illustrated from Hermas (*sim.* 9.2.1), who imagines a
great rock higher than the mountains, four-square, so as to
be able to 'fill' the whole world. Again he says (*mand,* 5.2.5)

32

that some vessel will not 'contain' or 'hold' enough, but overflows. A metaphorical use occurs in the letter about the martyrs of Vienne and Lyons (in Eusebius *h.e.* 5.1.9), where a man is described as capable of 'containing' the consummation (pleroma) of love for God and for his neighbour. So in the theological sense it is claimed (Hermas *mand.* 1.1) that God 'contains' all things and alone is uncontained. God. repeats the *sermo major de fide* (29) of pseudo-Athanasius, 'contains' all things but is 'contained' by none.

It is true, as has been said, that this is not quite the same thing as penetration of all things. But the two ideas of pervasion or penetration, and of receptivity or content, are in fact closely connected. Man is 'receptive' ($\chi\omega\rho\eta\tau\iota\kappa\acute{o}\varsigma$) of evil (pseudo-Macarius *hom.* 11.11). The holy man is 'receptive' of the Holy Ghost (Origen *de orat.* 16.3). A pupil is 'receptive' of so much of his master's teaching as he himself can understand (Didymus Al. on ps. lxviii.6). The Father and the Son (Gregory of Nyssa [?] *c. Ar. & Sab.* 12) are 'receptive' of one another, for, as he quotes, "I am in the Father and the Father in me" (*St. John* xiv. 11). That this receptiveness ascribed mutually to the divine Persons, or to the disciple and pupil, is not to be sharply distinguished from the other sense and usage of the verb, seems to be implied not only by comparison with a passage such as that of Nemesius quoted above, but with a number of others. Thus Basil, speaking of the angels, says (*c. Eun.* 3.2) that they have holiness pervading their whole being ($\kappa\epsilon\chi\omega\rho\eta\kappa\acute{o}\tau\alpha$ $\delta\iota\acute{a}$): spiritual influence here 'pervades' as well as 'fills' its recipients. 'Gregory of Nyssa,' who taught that the Father and Son contain one another, meeting the objection that

33

if the Father fills all things there is no space left for the Son to fill, observes (*c. Ar. & Sab.* 12) that their mutual receptivity implies their occupation of the same space—an idea which seems to involve mutual penetration. Nilus says (*epp.* 2.39) that the Son is in all things like His own Father "so that the Father extends in (χωρεῖν ἐν) Him." And Gregory, in the context of the quotation just made, emphasises the special 'penetrative' property belonging to divine being by the negative claim that mankind is not receptive of others nor does one man extend into (χωρεῖν εἰς) another.

To sum up, it is not the world that contains an infusion of God, as porous matter contains water, but God whose support frames the world. At the same time, the relation between the two is not merely that of vessel and contents; but the divine presence everywhere and always pervades, as it sustains, the universe.

Considerable relief was brought by such ideas to the pressure of anti-trinitarian controversy, when it could be stated that the divine Persons penetrate and permeate one another after a spiritual and divine manner. But in connection with God and nature, the idea of the penetrative quality of divine being, as not only externally framing and supporting, but also permeatively sustaining the created universe, afforded yet more immediate assistance. It provided, in modern language, a theory that God is immanent as well as transcendent, the immanence no less than the transcendence being based on the actual nature of the divine mode of existence, or 'spirit.' It is significant that, of the three divine Persons distinguished in the godhead, the Holy 'Spirit,' to whom the title of Spirit was specially appropriated, is the one to whom immanental powers are specifically attributed by the speculative and philosophical Athenagoras (see below p. 88). As a result, little further difficulty seems to have been encountered in maintaining that God created matter *ex nihilo*, that the creation has a distinct, if relative, existence—from which the important conclusion follows that God is independent of it and not bound up with its continuance—and, further, that the whole creation is nevertheless directly dependent for its own existence on the being of its creator. That the background of the whole conception is physical and spatial is no drawback, so long as no such limitations are attributed to the deity. Full and adequate measures having been taken to guard against that danger, there was even some advantage in describing the relations of God with physical nature in terms such as are directly applicable to physical nature. The weakness of theism in its hold on the modern popular mind may in fact not unjustly be attributed to the lack of an equally simple and appropriate range of ideas in which to express its meaning.

Another distinction was maintained, which makes little practical difference to pure theism, but is worthy of notice. While it was said that God contains all things, it is more specifically the divine Logos who was held to be the immediate creative ground of the existence of the universe. This fact, and the general dependence of the doctrine in its details on the Book of Wisdom, may be illustrated at length from Eusebius, who writes (*dem. ev.* 4.13.2–3), that the Logos by His divine prerogative, altogether apart from the fact of the incarnation, "always continuously pervades the whole matter of the elements and of actual bodies; and, as being creator-word of God, stamps on it the principles (λόγοι) of the wisdom derived from Him. He impresses life on what is lifeless and form on what is in itself formless and indeterminate, reproducing in the qualities of the bodies the values (τὰ κάλλη) and the unembodied forms inherent in Him; He sets into an all-wise and all-harmonious motion things that are on their own account lifeless and immobile— earth, water, air, and fire: He orders everything out of disorder, giving development and completion: with the actual power of deity and logos He all but forces all things; He pervades all things and grasps all things; yet contracts no injury from any nor is sullied in Himself." This passage seems at first sight to concentrate all immanent divine action in the Person of the Logos, to the exclusion of the Holy Spirit. Indeed, no very sharp line was commonly drawn between their respective activities in this regard. But the general sense of theology would support the connection of the universal scheme and fundamental principles of the creation, regarding creation not as a finished product but as a continuous process, with the Logos, and that of its living growth and progress with the Spirit of life (cf. Athenag. *suppl.* 6.3, quoted p.88, and Iren. 4.38.3, quoted p.45).

Eusebius continues by pointing out the particular concern of the Logos with the rational race of mankind, conducted at first through inspired leaders and prophets. But long before his time the close relation between God and the human soul had been emphasized. The soul (psyche) partakes of life, says Justin (*dial.* 6.1, 2), because God wills it to live, and will cease to partake of life when God ceases so to will. Life is not necessarily inherent in the soul, as it is in God. Just as man's existence is not perpetual, and body does not always accompany soul, but when the time comes for the partnership to be dissolved the soul leaves the body and the man ceases to be, so when the time comes for the soul to cease to be, the spirit of life leaves it and it does cease to be. We are acquainted, remarked Tatian (*ad. Gr.* 12.1), with two kinds of spirit, of which one is called soul, and the other is greater than soul, the image and likeness of God. Yet the soul, he added (*ib.* 13.2), is not without resource, because it possesses an affinity with the divine spirit and ascends to such regions as the spirit leads it. Irenæus observes (*haer.* 5.12.2) that the breath of life which makes a man alive or animal (ψυχικός) is quite a different thing from the life-giving Spirit that makes him spiritual. As Cyril sums the matter up (*ador.* 9D), though he differs from Irenæus about the interpretation of the phrase 'breath of life' in Genesis ii.7, "the image of the divine nature was ingraven on man by the infusion of the Holy Spirit." Athenagoras centuries before had suggested (*suppl.* 27.1) that only in heaven could man be justly called spirit. Contrasting human life on earth with that to be enjoyed hereafter, he says that the soul looks downward towards earthly objects as being merely flesh and blood and not yet a pure spirit—which he calls elsewhere (*ib:* 31.3), when perfected for eternal life, and in contrast with the flesh, a "heavenly spirit."

Reference has already been made, in connection with the long passage quoted above from Methodius, to the conceptions expressed by the words 'agenetos' and 'genetos.' As these words contain and summarise ideas of the greatest importance in the Greek doctrine of God, it will be desirable to discuss them at some length. Derived as they are from γίνομαι, to become, their primary meanings of

'unoriginated' and 'originated' depend on the idea of
transition, particularly of transition from non-existence to
existence. But a wealth of philosophical associations had
gathered round them, which needs investigation. Moreover,
the problem is enormously complicated by their interchange
and confusion with the words 'agennetos' and 'gennetos,'
derived from γεννάω, to beget, and meaning 'unbegotten'
and 'begotten.' It will be obvious from the outset that the
two pairs of words, so nearly identical in form, are frequently
employed in senses that, if not identical, are at least practically
equivalent. The investigation may therefore well begin with
a passage in Ignatius which adopts the second form, based
on the idea of generation, to describe the Person of the
incarnate Christ.

Ignatius writes (*ad Eph.* 7.2), "there is one physician,
fleshly and spiritual, gennetos and agennetos, God in man,
. . . of Mary and of God, first passible and then impassible."
It is to be observed that there is here no discussion whatever
of the relationship of the Son to the Father. If his language
is to be taken strictly, Ignatius is emphasising, in connection
with the incarnation, two points—first, that Christ's human
nature came into existence through the processes of birth,
that is to say, it was real and not docetic; and secondly, that
there was in Him something more than human, and in fact
divine, which was pre-existent and therefore did not come
into existence through the processes of birth. This passage,
therefore, has a direct bearing on the subject in hand. Its
consideration, moreover, introduces the very important and
difficult problem of the spelling. The question of one n or
two nn is obviously one in which the manuscripts of our
patristic texts are likely to manifest confusion. That

confusion is often made much worse in the printed texts by the reckless way in which some of the very latest editors have altered the spelling of the manuscripts according to their own idea of what the author ought to have written. In order to reach a clear determination of the sense which the Fathers attach to agenetos as an attribute of God, full investigation will be required of agennetos also; and the point must be decided whether in fact any serious distinction was observed between the two terms.

Justin, with the exception of one passage, seems to apply agennetos solely to God the Father, and often in contrast with the Son. It would therefore seem at first sight natural to suppose that he meant by it simply "not-begotten." Nevertheless, his use of it in such a passage as "Son of the only and 'ingenerate' and ineffable God," indicates that he associated with the word something of ultimate importance. He does not use agenetos anywhere, and in one context (*dial.* 5) applies agennetos to supposed ultimate realities. It must be noticed, first, that he is confessedly using "Platon-istic" language; and, secondly, that he finally insists on the necessity of assuming that only one ultimate cause can exist, in the following terms: "for God alone is agennetos and incorruptible, and for that reason He is God; everything else after Him is gennetos and corruptible." It is therefore obvious that in fact agennetos to Justin's mind means 'underived' or 'ultimate,' and that gennetos means 'derived.' In other words, he is using these terms, at least to some extent, in a sense which would later have come to be expressed by agenetos and genetos. Indeed he actually states (*dial.* 5.6) that "there is not a plurality of agenneta . . . but as you cast your mind forward towards infinity, you will halt at the conclusion of your effort at some single agenneton, and that, you will say, is the cause of all things." Justin's agenneton is thus equivalent to Methodius' ageneton.

The manuscripts of Athenagoras are said to be all derived from one existing archetype. It is therefore an easy matter in treating of this author to follow the manuscript spelling. When editorial corrections are ignored, certain definite and important results emerge. In the first place, God is never referred to as agenetos in the *supplicatio*, though in Dr. Goodspeed's edition that is the form to which the manuscript spelling has been corrected in every case. Agenetos actually only occurs in one passage (8.1) where Athenagoras is dealing with the theory that an ultimate plurality of gods existed. "For if they are gods they are not alike: but because they are agenetos" (the reading is corrupt but this is the probable restoration) "they are unlike: geneta resemble their exemplars, but ageneta are unlike, since they proceed neither from anything else nor toward anything else." In the second place, in nine passages of the treatise the Christian God is called agennetos, and in six of them an opposition is expressed either with genetos or with some other derivative of γίνομαι. The references are as follows: 4.1 fin, 6.2 fin, 8.2 init, 10.1 init, 15.1, 23.2. These appear to be the earliest occurrences of this form of contrast, but we shall find it recurring in Irenæus, Hippolytus, and Origen. Thirdly, gennetos is twice applied to beings other than the true God, and implies the sense of 'created' in contrast to agennetos, or 'uncreated.' But it is worth noticing that in each case the reference is to personal beings in the Greek mythology. Athenagoras does not seem to apply gennetos to impersonal objects in any sense. And since personal beings are normally brought into existence through a process of generation, 'generated' and 'created' are equivalent for practical purposes, even though the former on a strict interpretation means not 'created' but 'procreated.'

The data to be derived from the Apologies are neither immense nor yet negligible. It is safe to say that the indications point to the use, in the second century, of the terms that by derivation imply generative process, and the terms that by derivation imply demiurgic process, in very much the same sense. The philologically privative terms connote ultimate self-dependency and universal responsibility, and their connotation is therefore positive rather than negative. The philologically positive terms imply the lack of these things, and are therefore to some extent logically tinged with a negation. (The fact is worth noting as a refutation, so far as it goes, of the statement commonly made that the Fathers defined the nature of God by negatives. The assertion contains greater substance grammatically than it does theologically.) In so far as God was thought of as the universal Father, there was little need to distinguish between generation and creation. From the standpoint of theism, the denotation either of agennetos (ingenerate) or of agenetos (uncreate) was identical. God was the only being to which either word could properly be applied. Since the Fatherhood of God was a cardinal point of Christian doctrine, the current terminological conventions were easily accepted by Christian writers, and He could be called agennetos or agenetos indifferently with perfect propriety. If the manuscripts can be trusted at all, the former spelling would appear to have prevailed, as was more natural in speaking of a personal being. On the other hand, since a large proportion of the finite creation consists of impersonal objects, it was more natural, though possibly not invariable, to refer to elements in the finite creation as geneta rather than genneta, particularly when the subject of the discussion was impersonal. Hence would arise what seems at first sight the strange contrast of agennetos with geneta.

A word on the fidelity of the manuscript tradition will not be out of place. Obviously it would be presumptuous to maintain that the manuscripts are always right. In a number of cases the manuscript readings of Hippolytus, for instance, are demonstrably wrong, as when they give us γένημα ἐγένησαν or γεννέσεως (*refut.* 8.9.2, 6.22.1, compare also γεννετήν, 6.23.1). Yet it may be concluded that the general tendency is to drop a genuine n rather than to add one which ought not to be in the text. ἐγένησαν (6.29.6) and γεγενηκότων (6.30.6) are further cases in point; and in 6.38.2, 6.42.8, and 7.28.4, it is quite clear that the single n of Hippolytus should be corrected to the double nn of Irenæus lat., supported in each case by other textual evidence. And the general consistency of their tendency, taken in the mass, constitutes a rather impressive body of testimony. It may, of course, be argued that this consistency represents the tendency of the copyists, many centuries later than the autograph, and not the habit of the original authors. But against this view lie two facts. Copyists, unlike editors, were normally unintelligent and more apt to create than to emend difficulties in their text. Their visual errors resembled the aural miscarriages of uneducated stenographers. To assume that they deliberately altered a familiar term like agenetos is to credit them with an unexpected operation of intellectual initiative. In the second place, the normal trend of intelligent emendation at a later age must have been in the direction of omitting one n from agennetos, rather than of adding a second n to agenetos. As soon as theology turned from theism to Christology, the spelling agennetos raised the most agonising difficulties, and in fact provided one of the main pivots of the Arian heresy. Christ was not agennetos: He was the Son of the Father; was He therefore to be reckoned among geneta? This problem seriously troubled Origen, and submerged Arius. The only solution lay in drawing the firmest distinction between agennetos and agenetos, and making the latter the pivotal term instead of the former. But the fact that the Apologists, according to the manuscripts, prefer to use the former term, is very strong evidence that the manuscript tradition is substantially accurate.

So far, then, it would seem that there is nothing much to choose between agennetos and agenetos, except a vague sense of the greater propriety of the personal term in connection with the personal being. We are dealing with alternative spellings of a single word, in fact, rather than with two separate terms bearing distinct connotations. This conclusion is borne out, on the whole, by a study of Irenæus. In Irenæus agennetos is much more frequent than agenetos, and is applied ordinarily to God, or at least to the ultimate Power or Father of the Gnostic sects. The Greek of Irenæus is often uncertain, being derived, where it survives at all, largely from quotations made by Hippolytus and Epiphanius. But when this is checked by the ancient Latin version, the conclusion emerges pretty clearly that the Gnostics habitually employed the double nn. Agennetos is translated sometimes by ingenitus, sometimes by innatus,

43

and at least once it is simply transliterated into Roman script (*haer.* 1.11.3).

On the other hand, there is some evidence that Irenæus, when writing in his own person, prefers the form agenetos. At *haer.* 1.11.1, if we may rely on the Latin text, the 'nati æones' are contrasted with the 'infectus pater.' This may be an accidental reflection into a Gnostic context of Irenæus' own preference. But in *haer.* 4.38.1ff. comes a long passage in which he develops his own views, not those of Gnostic heretics, and here the Latin, in every instance but one, gives 'infectus,' corresponding to the form agenetos. The Greek survives in the *sacra parallela* (text in Holl, *Texte & Untersuch.* XVI, new series I.1); one MS writes agennetos with almost entire consistency, while the others (said both to derive from a common archetype) with equal consistency write agenetos. It looks as if the 'two-nn' tradition must have been due to a deliberate revision, made in the light of conscious scholarship by some one who knew that the usual form in which the term appears in Irenæus had the double consonant; and that the other tradition, supported as it is by the Latin version, is to be accepted in this particular passage.

The passage is worth quoting for the useful notion which it conveys of the conception expressed by agen(n)etos. "If any one says, 'Could not God have exhibited man perfect from the beginning?' let him realise that, so far as concerns Himself, everything is possible to God, because He is unchanging and ingenerate (agennetos); but creatures (τὰ γεγονότα), since they subsequently acquired an independent beginning of temporal existence (γενέσεως), on that very ground are bound to be inferior to Him who made them. Objects recently created (γεγενημένα) cannot be agenetos. Inasmuch as they are not agenetos they are inferior to what is perfect." He continues to argue that as man was incapable of receiving God's perfection, being infantile, Christ came in the infantile flesh to train man up to the pitch of being able to contain in himself the Spirit, in the dispensation which follows that of the incarnation. He then continues: "The impossibility and deficiency did not then reside in God, but in newly created man, because he was not agenetos. In God are exhibited alike power and wisdom and goodness: power and goodness in His voluntary constitution and creation of beings that had no previous existence; wisdom in His making creatures harmonious and concordant. As creatures receive growth through His exceeding goodness and persist for an extended period, they will acquire the glory of the ageneton, since God bestows ungrudgingly what is good. In respect of their creation they are not agenetos; but in virtue of persisting through long ages they will receive the power of ageneton, God bestowing without price everlasting continuance on them. Thus God has the pre-eminence in all things; He alone is agenetos, and first of all, and author of existence to all. All else abides in subjection to God. But subjection to God is persistence in incorruptibility, and incorruptibility is the glory of ageneton. By this ordinance and such harmonies and such conduction, genetos and created man is rendered after the image and similitude of agenetos God. The Father's is the goodwill and command. The Son executes and fabricates. The Spirit nourishes and increases. And man gently progresses and rises towards perfection, that is to say, he approximates to the ageneton. For the

45

perfect One is the agenetos One, and that is God."

On a point of reading it may be noted that even the MS of the 'two-nn' tradition reads 'agenetos' with one n at the final occurrence of the term, just as the Latin version supports the double nn at its first occurrence. Apparently Irenæus follows the general tradition of the Apologists, treating agen(n)etos as embodying a single conception under either form of spelling: agennetos is the more appropriate form to use in reference to the personal deity, other considerations being equal; but when the term comes to be discussed in a more general and abstract way, it becomes more natural to spell it agenetos. The meaning is the same, but the spelling is governed by an unconscious sense of the greater propriety of the associations connected with one or the other distinct derivation.

But more important than the spelling is the meaning. The ageneton exists *per se:* its cause lies within its own being. As being independent of all other existences it enjoys perfection. Creatures, since their existence is not self-grounded, are necessarily imperfect. The difference between them and the ageneton is that which lies between the contingent and the absolute. Certain qualities may come to be enjoyed by creatures dependently and derivatively, provided they remain 'subject,' that is, by continuance in the imposed laws of their own being, and, of course, provided that those laws embrace such qualities in their scope. Thus man can attain to immortality, and enter in that degree into "the glory of ageneton," but only *per gratiam,* not *per se.* To the ageneton alone belong inherently omnipotence, perfection, creative power and goodness, glory, eternity, causation, and wisdom. It is not simply in God that all Goodness, Truth, and Beauty reside, according to this teaching of Irenæus, but in God by virtue of His being the ageneton or (as it may sometimes be written, in view of His personal being) the agenneton. However the word be spelt, by Christian, Gnostic, or Platonist, what it obviously means can best be described, not in a specifically Hegelian sense, but in general idea, as 'The Absolute.'

It has already been said that the text of Irenæus suggests the habitual use of agennetos with double nn by the Gnostics whom he quotes. This conclusion is confirmed by a study of the *refutatio* of Hippolytus. Except in the first book, the text of this treatise only survives in a single manuscript, which, in several instances, previously mentioned, can be convicted of dropping an n from words of the group cognate with agen(n)etos. In spite of this fact, agenetos seems to be applied to the personal God or to the Ultimate Aeon only in three passages. In one (7.32.1) the Irenæus lat. suggests that two nn ought to be read in the text. In the other two, in which Noetus and Heracleitus are under discussion respectively (9.10.10, and 9.9.4), the word occurs in conjunction with its opposite, in what appears to be a semitechnical formula—"genetos-agenetos"—intended to express the paradox of the Supreme Being existing at once as transcendent and as immanent. (Compare the phrase attributed to Callistus, *ref.* 9.11.3, γενητὸς καὶ παθητός, in reference to the incarnation of Christ.) Otherwise, all the writers whom Hippolytus discusses seem to use the double nn in speaking of personal deities.

In connection with impersonal First Principles, the double nn is still more frequent than the single, though the latter does occur in several instances. A striking case is that of

Hippolytus' discussion of Parmenides (*ref.* 1.11, where the text rests on four MSS). "Parmenides," he remarks, "supposes the universe to be one, everlasting, agennetos, and spherical." Reference to the eighth fragment of Parmenides (Diels, *poet. philos. fragmenta*) discloses that the poet actually wrote agenetos, the happy result of his adoption of hexameter verse to enshrine his philosophy being to put the question of the reading beyond all dispute. But so familiar was Hippolytus, in the course of his researches into more recent heresies, with the habit of employing generation-terminology in place of creation-terminology, that in summarising Parmenides he slipped into the same error. It clearly made no difference to the sense. A few more instances will help to illustrate the point further. In *ref.* 6.12.1, according to Simon, the gennetos world came into existence from the agennetos fire. In *ref.* 5.26.1, Justinus stated that there were three Sources of all things, agennetos; one of them was the father of all genneta. According to *ref.* 6.29.2, certain Pythagoreans and Platonists held the Source of all to be an agennetos monad. In *ref.* 5.12.2–3, the Peratae reckoned that transcendent agenneta were responsible for the existence of all genneta, and propounded a trinity of which the first part was agennetos and the perfect good, the second was good too, being self-generated (αὐτογενές), but the third was gennetos. Finally, in *ref.* 6.38.2 an unnamed Valentinian, after positing two ultimate æons, proceeds, "they projected, without projection, an ideal (νοητός) source over all, agennetos and invisible." In this last passage, which comes to Hippolytus from Irenæus, the object described as agennetos is not even strictly speaking ultimate, but a subordinate element in the primary tetrad of æons which the author conceived to be the source of all the rest.

It will scarcely have escaped notice that in several of the passages just quoted gennetos also occurs, and in the sense of 'derivative' or 'created.' A further instance may be taken from the *Letter of Ptolemæus to Flora*, preserved in Epiphanius. "This god will be inferior to the perfect god and below his righteousness, as being gennetos and not agennetos: the Father is the one agennetos" (*haer*. 33.7.6). It should be observed that here, as in the Peratic view quoted above, absolute moral worth is bound up with ingeneracy. Again, the Peratic author quoted by Hippolytus at *ref*. 5.16.1, observes that "anything gennetos also altogether perishes, as the Sibyl holds;" though the line quoted from the Sibylline Oracles (frag. 3, Geffcken p.230) reads "genetos." A further illustration occurs in *ref*. 6.23.1: "Pythagoras declared the unit (monas) to be the agennetos source of all, and the deuce and all other numbers to be gennetos. And he says the unit is the father of the deuce, and the deuce is the mother of all that are generated, she gennetos and they gennetos." We may compare *ref*. 4.43.4: "they said that god is an indivisible unit, which itself generates itself, and that from it all things are constituted; for this unit, he says, being agennetos generates the succeeding numbers." The last two illustrations extend the generation-terminology from the adjective to the verb. Similarly Simon is quoted, *ref*. 6.18.3, as saying that there are two suckers from the body of æons, "of which one appears from above, which is the great Power, the Mind of the whole, ordering all things, male; and the other is from beneath, the great Thought, female, generating all

49

things." Here, as elsewhere, the male element is regarded as giving the form, while the female produces the substance. Even gennesis is employed of creation, a usage of which it will be sufficient to quote a single instance, *ref.* 4.50.2. Hippolytus is criticising the practice of naming various constellations after animals and human beings: "these men and their names were generated," he says, "far later than the gennesis of the constellations occurred."

From the evidence put forward it is clear that the Gnostics frequently both thought and spoke of creation in terms derived from generation, and that sometimes such language passed over unconsciously into the vocabulary of their critics. Yet, in spite of their marked avoidance of agenetos, they also readily employed the derivatives of γίνομαι to express creation. Consequently, among Hippolytus' notes of heresies, further instances occur of the contrast between agennetos and genetos. In book I of the *refutatio*, of which, as has been said, the text depends on four manuscripts, instances occur at 1.19.4, and again in 1.19.6 & 8 (agennetos implies incorruptibility, genetos the reverse). In the later books, reference may be made to 6.29.5, 6.30.2, 6.30.7, 5.8.30 (the agennetos transcends time and space, enjoys perfection, and is the ultimate source of all), without mentioning a certain number of passages in which the contrast is made with some other derivative of the verb γίνομαι than genetos.

With Clement of Alexandria and Origen we begin to emerge from the confusion. Once Clement employs gennetos where genetos might have been expected (*strom.* 5.13, 83.1), but the next words refer to God under the title of 'the Father,' indicating that the metaphor of paternity is

in the writer's mind. Similarly Origen, once and only once
in the treatises edited and indexed in the *G.C.S.* corpus,
speaks of created things as genneta (*de orat.* 9.2), except
when he employs the word gennetos of specifically human
beings, with or without the addition of the word γυναικός
(i.e. 'born of woman'). It would be infinitely tedious to
pursue the question further in the course of the present
discussion, except in general terms. It must therefore
suffice to say that Clement and Origen both employ
agennetos in the sense of 'absolute,' implying eternity,
causation, and transcendence of finite limitations; but so far
as the present writer's observation goes (it is now possible
to speak with equal confidence about Clement as about
Origen, since the former has been fully indexed in *G.C.S.*)
they only apply the term to God. An apparent exception
to this statement may be noted. Origen (*c. Cels.* 4.30)
describes souls as agennetos, but the word here probably
does not mean 'ingenerate' in the ordinary sense. It is
employed rather as a strict negative, equivalent to 'not
brought into existence through the process of generation,'
since it is contrasted with the expression 'sown with the
seed of the body.' Souls, he means, are not procreated
like bodies. Twice the unbegotten Father is contrasted with
geneta. At *c. Cels.* 3.34 the reading is guaranteed by the
MS which is the parent of all existing MSS of that treatise.
At *St. John* 2.10, 73 both words are confirmed by repetition,
at 2.10, 75 and 2.11, 79 respectively. But Origen certainly
makes more frequent use of agenetos. The fog of Gnostic
metaphor is being steadily dispelled by the clear thinking
of the school of Alexandria.

Methodius, a strongly Platonist thinker, calls God the

Father agennetos when He is mentioned in distinction from the Son, but is otherwise strict in his employment of agenetos and genetos. The same statement can be made of. the author of the dialogue *Adamantius*. By the end of the third century the whole confusion in the use of these terms appears to have been cleared up, when everything was once more thrown into disorder by the Arians and their supporters. But the investigation of their peculiarities belongs to Trinitarian theology, and must be postponed to a later chapter in this enquiry.

Further light on the reasons for calling God agenetos may be derived from a brief investigation of the meaning of genesis. It occurs frequently in the sense of 'coming into existence' or 'origin.' Hence it sometimes means 'source,' as in such a phrase as 'the genesis of evil' or 'the root and genesis of every blessing' (Or. *c. Cels.* 4.65; Cyr. Al. *c. Iul.* 5, 158A). It is the ordinary word for 'creation,' giving its name, in that sense, to the Book of Genesis. It can mean 'birth,' though rarely except in the Alexandrine writers—"the divine character of His conception and genesis" (Or. on *St. John* 2.37, 224); "if John were the actual Elias who was taken up, now appearing according to Jewish expectation without genesis," that is, without re-birth (*ib.* 6.11, 71). In a number of passages it is practically equivalent to 'procreation' or even 'the generative organs' (cf. Or. *schol. in Cant. vii*.1). It had thus a close association with the idea of material and physical processes.

From such associations it was a short step to signifying 'the conditions of created or earthly existence,' in a word, 'nature' as opposed to God. None of those 'constituted in genesis,' says Hippolytus (*ref.* 5.16.2), can evade the influence of Cronos, according to the Peratæ. Clement (*strom.* 1.15, 67.4) speaks of 'sharing all the ills in genesis.' Celsus (ap. Or. *c. Cels.* 8.60) pictures the earth-bound demons as for the most part engrossed with genesis and riveted to such sensual delights as the blood and fragrance of sacrifices. On the other hand, as Cyril remarks (on *St. John* 504A), God moves on a plane superior to everything in genesis; and Athanasius (*ad Marcell.* 18) speaks of Christians as being baptized and redeemed from perishable genesis, and, as such, more valuable companions than physical relatives and earthly friends.

Hellenistic nature was not merely banished from God, but harnessed in some cases to the constellations. The Peratæ, as described by Hippolytus, were astrological determinists; they taught that things here below acquire their genesis and decline by an emanation from the stars, and are controlled thereby (*ref.* 5.15.3). So also Origen (*comm.* 3 *in Gen.; philocal.* 23.14) remarks that the astrologers, by fixing the positions of the constellations as they were at the moment of an individual's genesis or birth, professed to be able to state not merely his future, but the past, before the person in question was born or even conceived —extending the range of their investigation so far as to the finances, character, habits, and physical peculiarities of his father. According to astrology, the stars govern, or at least provide evidential signs of, the pre-determined course of genesis, or mundane, natural events. Hence the word genesis is also used for 'fate' or 'destiny.' There is neither God nor providence, it is said in the Clementine Homilies (14.3), but everything is subject to genesis; and two chapters later comes the warning to 'disregard genesis; I mean the science of astrology.' Christ Himself, says one of Hippolytus' heretics (*ref.* 7.27.5), was pre-determined under astral genesis, as the story of the Magi indicates! On the other hand, the *Excerpts from Theodotus* (76.1) of Clement claim that "the gennesis (birth) of the Saviour cast us loose from genesis and fate." Other instances too numerous to mention prove that the course of nature, whether genesis in general or human genesis in particular, was regarded by a widespread opinion as being under the dominating influence and direction of astral forces. To the conception of genesis as fatalism, as to that of genesis as materialism, the Christian replied by reference to the agenetos God and His redemptive power.

CHAPTER III

DIVINE PROVIDENCE

WE pass from consideration of the nature of God to that of His self-manifestation. Among other anthropomorphic metaphors of the Old Testament, which were all accepted and explained in a spiritual sense by the Fathers, such as the hand of the Lord, or His voice, or His word, there is one which merits rather more attention than it has received, namely the conception of God's face. The others mostly express a sense of the divine action, but this, though the same may still be said of it, contains a more direct suggestion of self-revelation.

The face is an obvious medium for self-expression, or presenting character. As it ceases to be used in pure metaphor, the sense which the word assumes is closely akin to that of 'presentation,' denoting the external aspect of an object, whether personal or impersonal, though with far greater frequency of personal or at least living objects. Its extremely important associations with the doctrine of the Trinity will fall to be discussed later, together with its application to Christ, who was called the prosopon of God with no less assurance (if with less frequency) than He was called God's Word or Wisdom. But at this point we are concerned with a different usage. Where the face of the Lord regards, there is peace and exultation, says Clement (*paed.* 1.8, 70.1). God is said to turn away His face, says

Basil (*in ps.* xxix.6), when in times of difficulty He leaves us given over to temptations. Gregory of Nazianzus, in a passage (*orat.* 31.22) in which he gives a spiritual interpretation to a number of anthropomorphic metaphors from the Old Testament, remarks that God's face means His oversight, as His hand means His bounty. Theodoret (on *Daniel* iii.41) interprets His face as His benevolence, His restoration of freedom and removal of care. John of Damascus, following pseudo-Cyril, connects the expression directly with what is more commonly understood by revelation, when he remarks (*fid. orth.* 1.11) that God's face means His display and manifestation through His works, on the ground that mankind makes its own manifestation through the means of the face.

The Fathers are emphatic that the revelation of the divine nature is not made directly to the mind of man, but is to be inferred from God's works, and apprehended thus by the exercise of rational faculties. We know Him, says Tatian (*ad Graec.* 4.2), through His creation. God cannot, says Theophilus (*ad Autol.* 1.5), be beheld by human eyes, but is seen and perceived through His providence and works. Origen goes still further. No kind of word or representation, he observes (*c. Cels.* 6.65), is capable of presenting the characteristics of God. Celsus had objected to the practice of assigning a name to God, and in so far as a name may be taken to express the full reality of His being, Origen agrees with Celsus. But human language is capable at any rate of giving certain indications of the matter. A name may in truth present some quality of God, and by a process of suggestion assist people to perceive certain of His characteristics; and in that sense, He can be described by name.

Again in another passage (*c. Cels.* 7.42), he observes that human nature has not the capacity in any manner to seek God and to find Him in perspicuity without assistance from the object of the search; but He reveals Himself to those of whom He judges it right for Him to be seen, to such extent as God can be discerned by man and man's soul can, while yet in the body, discern God. Human knowledge of God is thus represented as being limited and conditioned. Basil reverts to the earlier statement of the nature of those limitations (*ep.* 234.1): it is from His activities that we say we are acquainted with our God; we take no pledge to approach His very essence.

Since God is revealed in His works, it is a matter of some importance to consider the scope and manner of His providential ordering, or as the Fathers called it, His 'economy' (οἰκονομία). If the account here given seems unduly extended, or to cover more ground than is required for the immediate purpose of illustrating the theistic outlook of the Fathers, the reason is that the conception of 'economy' has a most important bearing on the doctrine of the Trinity, and a still more fundamental connection with the doctrine of the Incarnation.

οἰκονομέω means primarily to administer or oversee an office, such as a bishopric or a civil community (*hom. Clem.* 3.60; Ath. *c. Gent.* 43). Then it covers the administration of property; canon 26 of the Council of Chalcedon directs every church possessing a bishop to maintain also a treasurer, chosen from its own clergy, to 'economise' or administer the ecclesiastical property in accordance with the bishop's instructions. In this last sense it appears absolutely, meaning 'to be treasurer' (Chrysostom on

St. John 65.2: "Why indeed did He entrust to one who was a thief the treasury of the poor, or cause a covetous person to 'economise'?"). Next, it means to regulate or control in a general sense, as the natural forces of the body 'economise' the functions of animal life (Bas. *de ieiunio* 1.4), or as spiritual beings 'economise' their life on selective and prudent principles (Greg. Nyss. *Macrin.*, Migne 46.84A). From this usage the word comes to be applied to the penitential system in particular, meaning in the active 'administer penance,' and in the passive 'be subjected to penance,' as in Greg. Nyss. *ep. can.* 4 (Migne 45.229B), where it is stated that the person *administering* ecclesiastical *discipline* may shorten the time of penance in suitable cases, or Bas. *ep.* 217 *can.* 72, which directs that a person guilty of consulting diviners shall be *disciplined* for the same period as if for homicide. On the other hand, it also means to 'dispense' alms to recipients (*apost. const.* 2.25.2), and to 'supply' with the necessaries of life: instead of, "Your heavenly Father feedeth them" (*Matt.* vi.26), the *Acts of Thomas* (28) paraphrases with "God economises them," and pseudo-Macarius remarks, *hom.* 12.14, "he was nourished by God and his body was economised with other celestial food". The prevailing ideas, so far, are those of administration and provision for need.

But administration implies method, and thus 'economy' acquired the sense of plan and design. God, says the *Epistle to Diognetus* (9.1), had already 'economised' with Himself, together with His Son, the things prepared from the beginning. Dionysius of Alexandria (ap. Eus. *h.e.* 7.11.14) remarks that the reason for certain orders issued by the deputy-prefect was that "he was economising and preparing matters so that, whenever he wished to arrest us, he might find us all easy to catch." Epiphanius observes that a prophet saw future events as if they had already taken place, and was justified in announcing what God had economised as if it had been already completed (*haer.* 79.6). And since design involves practical methods of execution, 'economise' also means 'arrange' or 'dispose.' The mother's milk, says Clement (*paed.* 1.6, 41.1), "is economised in connection with giving birth, and is supplied to the off-spring"; and the creed of Sirmium (ap. Ath. *de syn.* 8) relates how Christ "descended to the regions below earth and economised affairs there," a possible reminiscence of Origen (*c. Cels.* 2.16), "that His soul should leave His body voluntarily, and after economising certain matters outside the body should return again."

A word with such a range of associations was extremely apt for adoption as an expression of the providential order. It covers either such gifts as God sends and supplies in a providential manner, or such events as He designs and disposes. The following instances include illustrations in which either *motif* predominates. In the *Martyrdom of Perpetua* (6 ad fin.) the phrase "as God economised" is exactly equivalent to the more modern expression, "by the mercy of providence." So it is said (*hom. Clem.* 20.21) that "God economises our affairs." On the other hand, in *test. Adam.* 37, "until that day which I am about to economise unto the world," the sense is rather that of supply than of manipulation. Origen claims (*c. Cels.* 4.69) that God economises not only the alternating seasons but whole cycles of ages, and pleads (on *St. John* 10.41, 286) that we should receive each statement of the Scriptures spiritually according to the will of Him who economised them to be written. The divine providence extends to particular actions of incarnate God. In what the incarnate Word economised unto men, he observes (*ib. frag.* 18), He did not operate with the godhead unveiled, but by assuming the form of a servant. He even speaks of persons as being economised, or divinely controlled and disposed of: what is the difficulty, he asks (*c. Cels.* 1.66), in accepting the story of the Flight into Egypt, for "why is it absurd that He who had once become incarnate should through human guidance be economised so as to avoid danger?"; and again he suggests (*de princ.* 4.3.10) that the dead are economised according to their actions in this life to receive various lots proportioned to their misdeeds.

To Eusebius (*prep. ev.* 8.1, 349C) the Septuagint version was an interpretation economised from God; and God had economised that the eldest son of Constantius should be present at his deathbed (*vit. Const.* 1.18.2). To the mind of Cyril of Jerusalem (*cat.* 14.24) the grace of God economised that certain lessons had fallen to be read on a certain day in the course of the lectionary. To Epiphanius (*haer.* 73.36) the bond of truth had been economised, in the Nicene formula of the homoousion, by the Spirit in the mouth of those who set it forth. Again (*haer.* 78.23), Mary was not divine but born of conception, though economised according to promise like Isaac; and Joseph had not received the Virgin on ordinary terms of wedlock, but she had been economised to him for him to protect (*ib.* 78.8). Chrysostom (on *Colossians* 12.7) bade his hearers, when they sought a husband for their daughters, to pray to God and say, 'Whomsoever thou willest, economise'—that is, providentially bestow. Pseudo-Macarius observes (*hom.* 15.29) that "there are some affairs that the Lord economises in order not to leave Himself without witness to divine grace; . . . and there are some that he economises by way of concession" (i.e. *permittendo*) "in such manner that man may be tested and practised." Allowance is thus to be made both for direct and primary, and for secondary and contingent providences. Further than this, enough has been quoted to show that divine economy was conceived as extending to things great and small indifferently—from the ordering of natural law on the widest scale to the particular disposition of unimportant details in daily life.

Certain other important senses of the word 'economise' occur; but for their bearing on the subject of providence it is only necessary to call attention to two. First, that of 'accommodation': as in Chrysostom on *St. Matt.* 6.2, where the star of Bethlehem "when they ought to proceed, proceeded, when they ought to halt, halted, economising everything to circumstance;" or (*ib.* 6.3) you might see many similar matters which God economises, or adapts to circumstantial needs, such as the employment of heathen prophets or the witch of Endor to convey a true message. Second, the sense of 'consideration'; as when Gregory of Nazianzus remarks (*ep.* 58) on certain action as being due to its authors economising, or 'studying,' their own cowardice, or pseudo-Basil speaks (*ep.* 8.6) of Christ economising, or 'studying,' two types of human frailty in His refusal to give knowledge of the day and hour of the judgment—encouraging the valiant to hope that his good fight might not be too prolonged, and the wicked to utilise the delay for repentance.

Before turning to the noun, 'economy,' it is worth noting

that Clement speaks of 'economic' prefigurement (*paed.* 1.6, 25.3); and Epiphanius of 'economic' incomprehensibility (*haer.* 77.25). In both instances the adjective means simply 'providentially ordained.' So we read that God caused the famine economically in order that the Israelites should go down into Egypt (Ath. *in ps.* civ. 16); that Shadrach and his companions were economically preserved from knowing that the fire would not harm them, which would have destroyed the merit of their firmness (Chrys. on *I Cor.* 18.4); and that when the Romans obtained universal dominion, it was because God economically assigned them that honour (Cyr. Al. on *Hosea* 51A).

The noun 'economy' bears in different connections the senses of charge or ministration, and (rarely) good management or thrift; business, occupation, or function, and hence, though apparently only in apocryphal literature, life's work or career or earthly course; arrangement, procedure, system; administration of alms, and so the alms themselves. A further sense, which becomes of notable importance in Tertullian's and Hippolytus' exposition of the Trinity, is that of the disposition of parts in relation to one another, organisation, constitution; instances of this meaning will be quoted in due course. In connection with the adaptation of means to ends, as practised in prudent administration, comes a whole class of passages in which the general sense is discretion, consideration, or concession, and sometimes reserve; in Chrysostom, with whom the word is a constant favourite, the sense of manœuvre can be illustrated by a number of instances; in Cyril seldom, if indeed ever, does the word bear this sense; but it sometimes recurs in later authors meaning policy, compromise, or even connivance in sharp practices.

Elements akin to many of these senses enter into the use of economy when it describes the management by God of mundane affairs. Thus it is stated in the Clementine Homilies (2.36) that a man who realises how the world is regulated by the good providence of God is not vexed at the occurrence of contrary circumstances, since events take their outcome advantageously under the economy of their Ruler. "If, then," says Clement (*strom.* 1.19, 94.1), "it is alleged that the Greeks gave expression to some aspects of true philosophy by accident, that accident depended on divine economy; for no one will be induced by the present controversy to deify Chance." Methodius claims (*de autex.* 2.8) that there exists "an economy and power" which we should do right even to call God. Eunomius, the super-Arian, couples economy with all providence (*lib. apol.* 27).

In particular, this divine economy may manifest itself in the form of providential over-ruling. Origen (*de princ.* 3.1.14) speaks of the economy of Pharaoh by God at the time of the Exodus. In Maximus Confessor economy becomes typical of one of three forms in which he recognises the expression of divine volition. "We must assume three wills in God—that of purpose (εὐδοκία), that of economy, and that of acquiescence (or concession)" (*quaest. et dub.* 20). He illustrates the first by the call of Abraham, the second by the ordering of Joseph's life towards the foreseen conclusion of his career, and the third by the trials of the patriarch Job. But divine economy is just as clearly manifested in the form of natural or spiritual law as it is in personal lives. The economies of God and the changes of the seasons are coupled together by the author of the *Epistle to Diognetus* (4.5). Clement asserts that to deprive the offspring of the economy of its mother's milk is to dishonour nature (*strom.* 2.18, 92.2); again (*ib.* 4.23, 148.2), the "created economy" is good, and all things are disposed aright. Origen (*c. Cels.* 5.16) speaks of those who have been created in the image of God, but by living in opposition to His will require for their chastisement the economy of punishment by fire. So too Chrysostom (*ep.* 125) remarks that this is the economy of the Master, that, as appears from the parable of Dives and Lazarus, He has ordained in opposite courses punishment for the impious and rest for the just. The proper use of alcohol is an economy to the author of the pseudo-Justin's *Letter to Zena and Serena* (12): the drunkard is like a craftsman who takes iron, and instead of fashioning it into a useful sickle or other agricultural tool, makes it into an offensive weapon, perverting the economy of God.

But above all, economy expresses the covenanted dispensation of grace. Ignatius (*ad Eph.* 20.1) promises that if possible he will set forth in a further tract the economy relating to the new Man Jesus Christ. Clement (*strom.* 3.17, 103.3), in connection with his discussion of attacks made on marriage by false ascetics, asks how the economy ordained through the Church could reach its fulfilment apart from the body. The Jews, remarks Origen (*c. Cels.* 5.50), once had the privilege of a special regard beyond other men, but this economy and grace, he observes, had been transferred to the Christians. Gregory of Nyssa (on *Cant. proem.*) refers to the economy relating to the covenants. Cyril (on *Hab.*, 563D) claims that the prophet's point is to indicate the superiority of the second economy to the ancient one. Economy in such contexts means simply dispensation or covenant.

The treatment of the subject would be incomplete without illustrating the ascription to 'economy' of particular instances of a dispensation of mercy or special divine interposition. Justin (*dial.* 107.3) calls the growth of the gourd to shelter Jonah from the heat an economy. A great economy of God took place, according to the letter of the churches of Vienne and Lyons (ap. Eus. *h.e.* 5.1.32), when the apostates who recanted after arrest were retained in gaol as evil-doers, thus heartening the perseverance of the confessors. Another such economy of God was experienced by Dionysius of Alexandria (ap. Eus. *h.e.* 7.11.2) in the course taken by his own trial before the deputy-prefect. "Lo, by economy of God they met a donkey-driver," is the phrase employed in the *Acts of Xanthippe and Polyxena* (31); and Eusebius (*h.e.* 2.1.13) asserts that an economy led the eunuch from the land of the Ethiopians to Philip. Elsewhere (*ib.* 2.2.6) he makes the remark, "The heavenly providence by economy put this into his head"; and again (*mart. Pal.* 11.28), ascribes to an economy of the providence of God the fact that the bodies of certain martyrs were not harmed by wild beasts, but were preserved for Christian burial. The apostles, according to Cyril of Jerusalem (*cat.* 15.4), were moved by divine purpose according to economy to address a question to our Lord. Epiphanius, with a somewhat morose reference to mania, says (*haer.* 78.3) that the Manichæans received their name by a just economy of God. Less of satire, but a no less profound sense of divine providence, attaches to Gregory of Nazianzus's ascription of sufferings endured to an economy and not to wickedness (*or.* 14.19), or to the remark of Diodore of Tarsus (on *Exod.* iv.24) that God intended to frighten Moses, and gave him as much as he needed of this economy. So, too, Chrysostom regarded St. Paul's conversion as an economy (on *Eph.* 6.2), and states (on *St. Matt.* 9.3) that God is accustomed to fulfil His own economies even through His adversaries' action. The monks in the desert had as strong a sense of the detailed guidance and overruling of events as had the Fathers in their studies. "God did us this economy," says one of them in the *apophthegmata patrum* (*Abb. Mac.* 2), "that neither do we freeze in winter nor does the heat do us injury in summer." "By economy it became dusk" says another (*ib., Eul. presb.*). "By economy of God the old man went to those parts," remarks John Moschus (*prat. spir.* 83). God's hand was recognised in the smallest things as in the greatest.

Just as economy means dispensation of grace in general, so is it used of particular sacramental operation. Origen refers (on *Jer.* 16.5) to the remission of sins and economy of the washing of regeneration; Gregory of Nyssa to the invocation by prayer which precedes the divine economy (*or. cat.* 34), and to the fact that the virtue of the sacrament is conditional on the disposition of the heart of him who approaches the economy (*ib.* 39). In Epiphanius 'The Economy' is used as a title of the Eucharistic service, just as 'Celebration' or 'The Sacrament' are sometimes employed in English: usually he adds the distinguishing words 'of worship' to the title. Thus (*haer.* 75.3) the bishop and the priest likewise perform the economy of worship; in some places, he says, the worship of economy (reversing the order and dependence of the terms) is performed on the fifth day (*exp. fid.* 22), and they perform memorials for the departed, making prayers and worships and economies (*ib.* 23).

But economy is a still more frequent description of prophecy and revelation. Certain economies of great mysteries were accomplished, as when an economy and proclamation was made in the marriages of Jacob (Justin *dial.* 134.2), by which were prefigured the relations of Christ with synagogue and Church. Irenæus (*haer.* 4.31.1) observes that an economy was accomplished similarly through Lot, without his knowledge, and that through his relations with his daughters the two synagogues were foretold. Origen claims (*de princ.* 4.2.2) that mystical economies are revealed through the divine Scriptures, and further remarks (on *Jer.* 18.6) that when the divine economy is involved in human concerns it carries a human expression in mind and method and phrase. No man, says Theophilus (*ad Aut.* 2.12), is able to express worthily the whole interpretation and economy of the Creation narrative.

Enough has been said to indicate the extent to which the Greek Fathers recognised, in principle and in detail, the providential activity of God in nature, human history, and the sphere of grace. It need only be added that the supreme instance of divine economy, whether in the sense of dispensation, condescension, or special providence, was exhibited in the Incarnation, for which the word 'oekonomia,' without any verbal qualification, is the regular patristic term from the third century onwards.

The world, then, was regarded as possessing both a spiritual basis and a spiritual government. It is therefore not surprising that the Fathers recognised in it the presence of subsidiary spiritual forces other than the Supreme Being

Himself, forces which, whether of good or of evil character, corresponded to the experienced tendencies of mundane progress or regression. Such forces held a wider cosmic significance than the angels of Jewish tradition, and required a more general title. One way of describing them was to call them 'powers,' or δυνάμεις. The powers of Satan are destroyed, said Ignatius (*ad Eph.* 13.1), by common prayer. Justin refers (*dial.* 125.4) to the power which is also called Serpent and Satan. With certain Gnostics astrological superstition entered. The stars and the powers are mentioned in Clement (*exc. Theod.* 71.2), as being beneficent and maleficent, right-handed and left-handed; fate, says the same document (69.1), is a congress of many diverse powers. Clement himself (*strom.* 6.16, 148.2) mentions the elements and the stars, that is, the directive powers. Hegemonius (*act. Arch.* 7) refers to the view that the good Father projected a power called the mother of life, while Epiphanius (*index tom.* 4, *haer.* 55) mentions the doctrine that Melchisedek was a power and not a mere man.

The word was naturally used of the angels, as in *mart. Pol.* (14.1), "the God of angels and powers and all creation"; and Justin (*dial.* 85.4), "angels and powers." Again (*ib.* 85.1) 'the lord of powers' is the translation for 'Lord of Sabaoth,' as Origen also notes (*c. Cels.* 5.45). The sacramentary of Serapion (1.3) prays that God will send angelic powers. Chrysostom uses the term collectively (on *I Tim.* 15.4) of the whole angelic power. Origen also appears to envisage the existence of minor spiritual beings (on *Jos. hom.* 20.1, quoted *philocal.* 12.1); there is in us a host of powers to which have been allotted our souls and bodies. God Himself is referred to as a beneficent and creative 'power' by the same writer (*de princ.* 1.4.3), a fact which emphasises the close connection of subsidiary spiritual forces with the supreme Governor of the universe, and indicates the similarity of function which they shared with Him. Hence, as we assert the existence of God, says Athenagoras (*suppl.* 24.1ff), Father, Son, and Holy Spirit, united in power, so we apprehend the existence of other powers functioning in and through matter: in particular there is one which is opposed to God, though created by Him just as were the other angels, and entrusted by Him with the control of matter and the forms of matter: for God made the angels in order to exercise providence over the things ordained by Him, that He might maintain a universal and general providence over everything, while the angels exercised a particular providence, according to their appointment, over their several spheres: certain of these angels had remained at the posts assigned them, while others had violated both the constitution of reality and its government. Eusebius has a lurid description of the infernal powers of various kinds (*dem. ev.* 10.8.73, 90ff).

Like God, the subsidiary powers were called spirits. Hermas speaks (*sim.* 9.1.1) of the holy spirit which had spoken with him. Origen (on *St. John* 2.31, 189) quotes a Jewish apocryphal writing entitled 'Joseph's Prayer,' in which a being bearing the name of Jacob claims to be an angel of God and a primary spirit. Eusebius (*dem. ev.* 6.15.12) refers to mystical mountains full of divine powers and holy spirits. Devils were no less spirits than were angels. Justin (*dial.* 76.6) asserts the Christian claim that demons and evil spirits were subject to the faithful by means of exorcism, and Irenæus speaks (*haer.* 1.9.5) of various spirits of deceit, which inspired the heathen; while Chrysostom (on *St. Matt.* 43.3) scornfully identifies the false prophets, demented and raving under the power of evil spirits, with the 'pneumatophoros,' or 'man that hath the spirit,' of Hosea (ix.7).

'Spirit' is the term by which was expressed supernatural being. Supernatural agency was similarly expressed by the word energeia, or 'energy.' In consequence the latter, like the former, is associated with the operation of the minor supernatural forces, particularly in connection with the illapse of that supernatural afflatus which is called 'inspiration' when it comes from God, and 'possession' when its origin is demoniacal. Justin speaks (*apol.* 1.60.3) of the inspiration and energy that is attributable to the influence of God. Origen (*c. Cels.* 2.51) argues the necessity of recognising that certain events in human life take place under the operation of divine energy, unless one is prepared to deny supernatural causation altogether. The events of Pentecost are ascribed in *Apostolic Constitutions* (5.20.4) to a similar source: "we were filled with His energy and spoke with new tongues:" while in the same work (8.1.3) it is said that the profit of exorcism does not accrue to the exorcist but to those who are thus cleansed by the energy of Christ. So too does Theodoret (on *Jer.* xxxii.1) refer to the receipt of the energy of prophecy.

But 'energy' is still more commonly employed to describe the activity of devils. By the energy of corrupt demons was death denounced against those who read prophetic books, says Justin (*apol.* 1.44.12). By the same energy were good men like Socrates persecuted (*ib.* 2.7.3). Clement (*quis dives* 25.3) repeats the accusation that the faithful were

persecuted under diabolic energy; Origen ascribes (*c. Cels.*
4.32) the rancour alike of governments and of peoples
against Christianity to the irrational and evil energy of the
demons; the nations, says Eusebius (*laud. Const.* 13.9)
were maddened by demoniacal energy. The power of Simon
Magus was derived from magical skill and the energy of
demons, according to *Apostolic Constitutions* (6.9.2).

The energy of the demons is an evil and hard fetter,
observes Chrysostom (*inc. dei nat.* 4.4), not without justice,
according to the universal assumption of the ancient world
that this life is a battle-ground of opposing spiritual forces
and supernatural agencies. Mankind, or at least Christian
mankind, had to contend with manifestations of supernatural
influence in the sphere of morals and physical action equally.
Disorderly sallies into the realm of nature were due to the
demoniacal movements and energies of the adverse spirit
(Athenagoras *suppl.* 25.3); the very stars accomplished their
energies (Clem. *ecl. proph.* 55.2); the names of Hebrew
patriarchs were employed in Egyptian incantations to evoke
an energy (Origen *c. Cels.* 1.22); and an unfortunate person
who had his face twisted round backwards had suffered this
injury, according to the *apophthegmata patrum* (*Poemen* 7)
"by energy." It is well known that those who were thus
regarded as being under the possession of demoniacal
influence were described in technical language as "ener-
gumens" (ἐνεργούμενοι).

In such circumstances it is easy to conceive how the false
gods of the heathen were commonly not explained away as
non-existent, but were accepted, though with some qualification, as subsidiary beings of evil propensity. Tatian
(*ad Graec.* 21.2) protests against the fashion of allegorising

the myths and the deities of whom they taught; either they are demons and, if of such character as the myths ascribe to them, are evil; or else, if reduced to physical agencies, they are not such as they are described. Athanasius says (*de incarn.* 15) that the heathen sought God in the natural creation and the world of sense, and feigned gods for themselves of mortal men and demons. Frequent reference is made to the absurdity of deifying men; but no less frequent is the accusation that the heathen deified supernatural beings of greater power and much less admirable character than kings and heroes. The prevalence of belief in the supernatural background of the world may be measured by the degradation of the word God, which not only permitted the customary bestowal of the title upon the deities of the heathen, but extended it to the evolutionary emanations of Gnostic fancy (e.g. Iren. *haer.* 1.8.5, Hipp. *ref.* 5.7.30), and enabled Arius to say (*thalia,* ap. Ath. *de syn.* 15) that the Son, though he had no being, for he existed at the will of the Father, was 'god only-begotten,' and that being a strong god he praises his Superior according to his degree. Such language was essentially polytheistic.

In fact, the word God came to be applicable in some sense to men, whose possession of a spiritual side to their nature ranked them in the hierarchy of supernatural beings. This result came about in consequence of two quite distinct lines of approach. In the first place, there existed certain Old Testament texts which appeared to ascribe divinity to men, and the Fathers were nothing if they were not sticklers for Biblical authority. The chief of these texts were psalm xlix.1 LXX, "God, the Lord of gods, hath spoken," and psalm lxxxi.1 & 6 LXX, "God standeth in the congregation of gods," "I said, Ye are gods and all sons of the Highest." There were others, and there was some uncertainty of interpretation whether men or angels were intended by the Old Testament writers. But in a number of instances the Fathers argue that the reference was either to all mankind, as children of the Most High, or at least to certain classes of men who performed such godlike functions as those of rulership or judgeship.

In the second place, a vigorous soteriological tradition taught that the destiny of man was to become like God, and even to become deified. Thus Origen (*comm. in pss. frag.* 1) quotes from the Stoic author Herophilus a definition of God as "an immortal rational being." According to this definition every rational soul is a god. If further particularisation is introduced, as some critics held that it should be, by adding the attribute "independent," human souls are not gods while encompassed with the body, but will be when released from its limitations. Such teaching had affinities with much of patristic thought. Thus pseudo-Justin (*or. ad gent.* 5, attributed to the second century) observes that the power of God trains mortals to become immortal, and humans to become gods. Irenæus (*haer.* 3.19.1), referring to those who would deprive man of his ascent to God, merely claims that the Word became man in order that man might become God's son. But Clement and Origen go further, the former observing (*strom.* 6.14, 113.3) that the soul, receiving the Lord's power, studies to be god—such a soul at no time ever is separated from God—while the latter (on *St. John* 2.3, 19) not only states that, apart from the true God, many become gods by participation in God, but further (*ib.* 20.29, 266) suggests that we should flee with all our power from being men and make haste to become gods. "Sons and gods by reason of the Word within us," is the phrase adopted by Athanasius (*c. Ar.* 3.25). Basil speaks of abiding in God, being made like God, and, highest pinnacle of aspiration, becoming god (*de Spir. sanct.* 23); and Gregory of Nazianzus (*or.* 29.19) dilates his rhetoric to write the words, "that I may become god to the same extent as He became man." Cyril prudently recalls the necessary limitations of such phraseology when he remarks that we have been called gods by grace (*de Trin. dial.* 4, 520C), and that in bestowing such a name on us God has not raised us to a sphere above our nature (*ib.* E).

All such expressions of the deification of man are, it must be remembered, purely relative. They express the fact that man has a nature essentially spiritual, and to that extent resembling the being of God; further, that he is able to attain a real union with God, by virtue of an affinity proceeding both from nature and from grace. Man, the Fathers might have said, is a supernatural animal. In some sense his destiny is to be absorbed into God. But they would all have repudiated with indignation any suggestion that the union of men to God added anything to the godhead. They explained the lower in terms of the higher, but did not obliterate the distinction between them. Not only is God self-dependent. He has also all those positive qualities which man does not possess, the attribution of which is made by adding the negative prefix to the common attributes of humanity. In addition, in so far as humanity possesses broken lights of God, they are as far as possible from reaching the measure and perfection with which they are associated in the godhead. Real power and freedom, fullness of light, ideal and archetypal spirit, are found in Him alone. The gulf is never bridged between Creator and creature. Though in Christ human nature has been raised to the throne of God, by virtue of His divine character, yet mankind in general can only aspire to the sort of divinity which lies open to its capacity through union with the divine humanity. Eternal life is the life of God. Men may come to share its manifestations and activities, but only by grace, never of right. Man remains a created being: God alone is agenetos.

CHAPTER IV

THE HOLY TRIAD

FROM the earliest moment of theological reflection it was assumed that Jesus Christ was true God as well as true Man. The Adoptionists, such as the elder and younger Theodotus at the end of the second century, who taught that Christ was a mere man, inspired by the Holy Spirit and deified only after His ascension, may have possessed a theological ancestry in certain obscure sects; but both they and their forerunners stand clearly outside the main stream of Christian experience. The problem which the Fathers had to solve was not whether He was God, but how, within the monotheistic system which the Church inherited from the Jews, preserved in the Bible, and pertinaciously defended against the heathen, it was still possible to maintain the unity of God while insisting on the deity of one who was distinct from God the Father.

Some of the earlier or more popular expressions of Christian writers, on the subject of our Lord, are so strong as to be susceptible of the theopaschite perversion which converts the divine nature into the subject of Christ's human experiences. The earliest occurs in Clement of Rome, before the end of the first century, and though it is not impossible to take the words in such a way as to avoid a mention of the 'sufferings of God,' that is the natural sense, and is accepted by Lightfoot. Clement wrote (*ad Cor.*

1.2.1): "Ye were all lowly in mind . . . more glad to give than to receive, and content with God's provisions; and giving heed to His words ye laid them up diligently in your hearts, and His sufferings were before your eyes." It is possible that 'His' words and 'His' sufferings glance back at the reference to the agraphon of Christ quoted from St. Paul's speech in the Acts, and overlook the intervening mention of 'God's' provisions. Consequently it is not wise to lay too great a stress on this one instance, the importance of which lies in its date.

But further instances could be multiplied from a date very little later. Ignatius, the prophet-bishop of Antioch, leads the way. "Our God, Jesus the Christ, was conceived by Mary" (*ad Eph.* 18.2); "by the will of the Father and Jesus Christ our God" (*ib. proem.*); "permit me to be an imitator of the passion of my God" (*ad Rom.* 6.3). Tatian (*ad Graec.* 13.3) speaks of the minister of the God that has suffered. Melito (*fr.* 7, Goodspeed p.310) says that God suffered at the hand of Israel. In the *Little Labyrinth* (ap. Eus. *h.e.* 5.28.11) we read that our compassionate God and Lord, Jesus Christ, did not wish that a witness to His own sufferings should perish outside the Church. Clement (*protrept.* 10, 106.4) cries, "Believe, o man, in Man and God; believe, o man, in the living God that suffered and is worshipped": and again (*paed.* 2.3, 38.1), "He washed their feet, girded with a towel, the prideless God and Lord of the universe." Naturally, such expressions are found in the popular literature of the apocryphal works, and survive in them to a later period than in more thoughtful or careful authors, as, for instance, *act. Thom.* 69, "the apostle of Christ the new God," and the later *act. Phil.* 74, "have mercy on me, o servant of the crucified God," and *act. Andr. & Mat.* 10, "He manifested to us that He is God, do not therefore think that He is man." There is thus considerable justification in Christian tradition for the attitude of late Monophysites such as Peter the Fuller, who (Theod. Lect. *h.e.* 1.20) anathematised anyone who would not admit that God was crucified, and added to the trisagion the words "who was crucified for us." And it is of interest to note that Tertullian —who is much closer to Eastern modes of expression than later Latin Fathers, and, unlike most of the Latin theologians, read Greek in the original—frequently employed similar phrases. Lightfoot (on Clement of Rome *ad Cor.* 1.2.1) collects references from the writings of Tertullian to such phrases as the sufferings of God, the blood of God, God crucified, God dead, the flesh of God, the murderers of God.

Less rhetorical expressions of the deity of Christ are common, and serve to fill out the picture. "There is one physician, of flesh and of spirit, begotten and unbegotten, God in man" (Ignatius *ad. Eph.* 7.2). "Thus ought we to think of Jesus Christ, as of God, as of the Judge of quick and dead" (pseudo-Clement of Rome *ad Cor.* 2.1.1). The Wisdom that spoke through the author of the Book of Proverbs is Himself the God begotten from the Father of the universe (Justin *dial.* 61.3); Joshua bestowed on the Israelites only a temporary inheritance, seeing that he was not Christ the God, nor the son of God (*ib.* 113.4). Tatian protests that he is perfectly sensible and rational in proclaiming that God came in the form of man (*ad Graec.* 21.1). Athenagoras speaks of "God the Father and the Son-God" (*suppl.* 10.3). Irenæus calls Christ Jesus our Lord and God and Saviour and King (*haer.* 1.10.1); and, he says

(*ib.* 3.6.2), no one else is called God except the God of all
and His Son Jesus Christ. Hippolytus quotes *Rom.* ix. 5 of
Christ (*c. Noet.* 6), "this is He that is God over all," and is
perhaps alluding to *I Tim.* iii.16 a little later (*ib.* 17 fin.)
when he writes, "coming forth into the world He was
manifested as God in the body."

Such language was not accidental. There were protests
against it, as in the Clementine Homilies (16.15), where it is
alleged that our Lord neither stated that Gods existed
beyond the Creator of all things, nor announced that He was
Himself God, but with reason blessed him who called Him
the Son of God. Yet the tradition remained firm. Clement
upheld it. "This Word Himself was manifested to men, who
alone is both, God and Man" (*protr.* 1, 7.1): "that man with
whom the Word dwelt" is made like to God, He "is the true
Beauty, for He is also God" (ὁ θεός); "that man becomes
God because He wills what God wills"; "the secret is
manifest, God is in man, and the man is God" (*paed.*
3.1, 1.5f). Even in his early and speculative work Origen
confesses the same: "when statements announced with such
authority have been fulfilled, it shows that God truly incarnate has delivered to men the doctrines of salvation"
(*de princ.* 4.1.2). Again, Christ's mortal body and soul, by
their union and commingling with Him, shared in His
divinity and were changed in quality to God (*c. Cels.* 3.41).
Whatever difficulties Origen experienced in explaining the
fact that Christ was truly God, he had no hesitation in
proclaiming the fact itself. He could not have done otherwise, without deserting the whole trend of Christian
tradition. Christ, as is plainly asserted in Gregory
Thaumaturgus (*exp. fid.*), was one Lord, sole out of sole,

God out of God, the impress and image of the godhead. Origen's own way of expressing His essential deity was to call Him "the agenetos and first-born of all created (genetos) nature" (*c. Cels.* 6.17 ad fin.). Agenetos, it will be recalled, is the title of absolute deity.

Down to the fourth century, the deity of the Holy Spirit came in for much less either of explicit assertion or of direct attack than that of the Son. Largely, this result was due to its raising no special problem; if the godhead was not unitary, it was as simple to conceive of three Persons as of two: hence the deity of Christ carried the weight of Trinitarian controversies without any necessity for extending the range of dispute, and as a matter of history, the settlement of the problems connected with the Father and the Son was found to lead to an immediate solution of the whole Trinitarian difficulty. A good fourth-century illustration of this fact may be found in a passage (quoted above on page 11) from Apollinarius. Apollinarius is there expressly giving his reasons for regarding the holy triad strictly as one God; but actually his explanation only extends to the relations between the Father and the Son; the argument for the unity of two Persons covers in principle the unity of three. An earlier instance occurs in Tertullian's treatment of the problem (quoted at length below in Chapter V), where amid copious emphasis on the 'trinitas' parts of the argument are in fact based on the unity and distinction of the Father and the Son alone. Such instances are quite common.

Another reason for backwardness in asserting that the Holy Spirit was God is to be found in the necessarily more subjective method of approaching the subject of His personality. Christ had appeared on earth and had made history; but the Holy Spirit was now dwelling in Christian hearts and now making history. The character of His operation as present and internal required time and distance to be achieved before it could present an equally objective appearance to consciousness. The being of God as transcendent and His action as creative are more readily objectified than His presence as immanent. Only when men could look back on historical results of His operation and correlate them with their own immediate experience did they become anxious to substitute such a phrase as 'God the Holy Spirit' for 'the holy prophetic Spirit' or 'the Spirit of God,' or to state explicitly that He was not only a gift or instrument of grace but its Giver. Theodore of Mopsuestia remarks (on *Hag.* ii.5) that the Old Testament writers did not know the Holy Spirit in His own person, but by 'holy spirit' meant His grace or His superintendence. This criticism definitely would not be true of early Christian writers, but it would be fair to say that they took time to reach a clear definition of the character which they did associate with Him. For the most part their doctrine of the Holy Spirit, though real, is rather implicit than scientifically formulated.

In its strictest sense, the word spirit itself implies the supernatural, as we have already seen, and is as such applied to God, and to Christ in His divine nature. A being called 'the Spirit' *par excellence*, and sharply distinguished from other spirits, could hardly fail to be associated with deity, even without the additions commonly made to His title, by which he became known as 'the divine Spirit' or 'God's Spirit' or 'the Spirit that is holy.' 'Holy' again implies a close association with God, as we have also seen. The adoption of the title 'the Holy Spirit' as a proper name, which occurs as early as Clement of Rome (*ad Cor*. 63.2), to say nothing of the New Testament, in itself therefore points towards an assumption of His divinity.

This impression is immensely strengthened by a consideration of the work ascribed to Him. He is the divine agent in the Incarnation. Ignatius says, in much the same sense, that Christ is "of Mary and of God" (*ad Eph*. 7.2), and that He "was conceived by Mary by economy, of the seed of David and the Holy Spirit" (*ib*. 18.2). (It would be interesting, but precarious, to connect the description of Jesus as "fleshly and spiritual" (*ib*. 7.2) on the one hand with His human mother, and on the other with the Holy Spirit; what other agency could better make Jesus 'spiritual'? But the reference is really to Jesus' own divine pneuma.) Again, in the divine work of salvation Ignatius makes the Holy Spirit take His place alongside our Lord. "Like stones of the sanctuary prepared beforehand for God the Father's building, raised to the heights by the mechanism of Jesus Christ—that is, the Cross—employing for cable the Spirit that is Holy; and your faith is the windlass," that sets in motion the operation of grace (*ad Eph*. 9.1). The Holy Spirit is thus conceived as the divine agent linking together Christ's redemptive work, done once for all on Calvary, and individual souls however remote in time and space from first-century Palestine. Sanctification is His special sphere. If a man is long-suffering, "the holy spirit that abides in him" will be pure, and not darkened by another and evil spirit; and enjoying ample room will rejoice with the vessel in which he dwells and serve God with much cheerfulness: but if any angry temper approaches, the holy spirit is straitened and has no pure place and seeks to retire, having no room to serve the Lord; for the Lord dwells in long-suffering but the devil in anger (Hermas *mand.* 5.1, 2–3). This passage is of particular interest, both because it makes so close an identification of the 'holy spirit' with the soul of the believer, and because it makes no attempt to draw the conclusion that this holy spirit, thus naïvely conceived, is equivalent to the personal presence of God in the human soul; yet the work which is described is clearly the divine work of sanctification, which no one else but God could undertake.

In Tatian, there appears again a close implication of the divine Spirit with the human soul, but alongside this a definite recognition of His divine character and personality. The devout soul, he says (*ad Graec.* 13.2), acquires a conjunction with the divine Spirit, and ascends to those regions to which the Spirit leads it. Originally the Spirit was the companion, or fellow-dweller, of the soul, but left it when the soul refused to follow Him. Hence (*ib.* 13.3) the Spirit of God is not present with all men; but descends on those of righteous converse and is implicated with their soul, and the souls that obey wisdom attract the Spirit to themselves as being akin to them; but those which disobey wisdom and renounce the Minister of the God that suffered are revealed as being God's enemies rather than His worshippers. This individualistic doctrine is supplemented by Irenæus (*haer.* 3.24.1), who writes that we receive our faith from the Church and preserve it; our faith renews itself through the Spirit of God, like a precious deposit in a fair vessel, and causes the vessel itself which contains it to be renewed. This gift of God has been entrusted to the

Church, like the in-breathing into the first man, to the end that all the members may receive it and be quickened; and therein has been distributed the communion with Christ, that is, the Holy Spirit, the earnest of incorruption, the confirmation of our faith, the ladder of ascent to God. In the Church has God placed apostles, prophets, teachers, (cf. 1 *Cor.* xii.28), and all the rest of the Spirit's means of operation; where the Church is, there is the Spirit of God; and where the Spirit of God is, there is the Church and all grace. Again he writes (*haer.* 5.8.1) that already we receive some portion from His Spirit, towards perfection and preparation for incorruption, as we are gradually accustomed to receive and support God. The earnest of our inheritance abides in us and is making us 'spiritual' even now, and what is mortal is being swallowed up by immortality—not, however, by discarding the flesh, but by communion of the Spirit. What then will be the effect of the entire grace of the Spirit? It will make man like God, according to His image and likeness.

Irenæus derived his doctrine from the New Testament, and on purely Scriptural lines built up an objective conception of the Holy Spirit and His work, related to the facts of Christian spiritual experience. Before him, however, such objectivity as was attained was mainly reached in connection with the phenomena of Scriptural inspiration, and of the Christian prophecy that carried on the prophetic tradition of the Old Testament. Here again, as ever, the first suggestion was derived from the Bible. "David himself said in the Holy Spirit," is the form recorded of our Lord's citation of the psalms in *St. Mark* xii.36, and the prophet of the Apocalypse "was in the Spirit on the Lord's day"

(*Rev.* i.10). So when Clement of Rome quotes the Book of Samuel, for instance (*ad Cor.* 1.13.1), he writes, "the Holy Spirit saith," and this is typical of his attitude to Scripture. Justin observes (*apol.* 1.44.1) that "the Holy prophetic Spirit taught us this through Moses"; and (*dial.* 25.1) "as the Holy Spirit cries through Isaiah." Athenagoras has a rigid view of Biblical inspiration: the prophets "uttered the message with which they were inspired (ἃ ἐνηργοῦντο) in a state of supersession of their rational consciousness, as the divine Spirit moved them, and the Spirit employed them as a flutist breathes into a flute" (*suppl.* 9.1).

In like manner, according to Clement of Rome, the apostles went forth preaching the gospel with the fullness of holy Spirit, and set aside the first-fruits of their converts as bishops and deacons after testing them by the Spirit (*ad Cor.* 1.42.4); and the directions which he himself gave to the rebellious Corinthians are similarly inspired: "be obedient to what we write to you through the Holy Spirit" (*ib.* 63.2). In the *Didache* it is "in the Spirit" that a prophet either gives utterance or directs the preparation of a banquet (11.7, 11.9). Ignatius, the champion of monarchical episcopacy, is a typical prophet; he does not argue, but pronounces; thus (*ad Philad.* 7.1) "although certain sought to lead me astray according to the flesh, yet the Spirit is not led astray, since it comes from God. . . . I cried with a loud voice, with God's voice, Pay heed to the bishop." "He is my witness, in whom I am in bonds, that I knew it not from flesh of man, but the Spirit was preaching, saying thus: Without the bishop, do nothing" (*ib.* 7.2). Ignatius had not made this exhortation to canonical obedience because of any report of foreseen schisms, but by inspiration of the Holy Spirit, as direct, it seems, in his sight, as if he too had been a flute to the divine breath. Hermas also emphasises the directness of inspiration. He attacks the practice of consulting false prophets, the delivery of whose message depended on enquiry being made of them: no spirit given from God, he says (*mand.* 11.5), needs to be consulted, but it possesses the power of deity and speaks all things of itself, because it is from above from the power of the divine Spirit. Thus the inspiration that possesses a true prophet directly represents, on Hermas's view, the Holy Spirit and acts with immediacy and authority. Prophecy was the one feature of the Spirit's personal action that from the first stood out concrete and clear-cut to the Christian mind, partly, no doubt, because the possession of prophetic gifts was a strikingly exceptional endowment, but mainly because it had an established historical background in the Old Testament Scriptures, so that Justin could declare(*dial.* 49.3) that the Spirit of God who had been in Elias came forth in John Baptist as herald of the first manifestation of Christ.

But the substance of primitive Christian thought about the Holy Spirit is by no means only to be deduced from the conceptions expressed about His operations. It simply is a fact that however well or ill, clearly or obscurely, the early writers approach the question of His essential deity—however far their statements may sometimes go, on the other hand, to suggest His subordination and the approximation of His being to created or impersonal forces—nevertheless, they actually draw a firm line between Him and all creatures. In practice, when a distinction comes to be made between that which belongs to deity and that which belongs to creation, the line is drawn below the triad of divine entities, and not below a dyad. The expression of divinity is threefold. The Holy Spirit may not be directly called God, but He stands unquestionably on that side of the border-line which belongs to godhead.

Why be at variance? says Clement of Rome to the people of Corinth (*ad Cor.* 1.46.6); have we not one God, and one Christ, and one Spirit of Grace shed upon us, and one vocation in Christ? Again, he adjures them to confidence with the words (*ib.*1. 58.2), As God liveth and the Lord Jesus Christ liveth and the Spirit that is Holy, who are the faith and hope of the elect. The threefold baptismal formula enunciated in the Gospel according to St. Matthew re-appears as early as the *Didache* (7.1), whatever may be the precise date of that perplexing and disputed document. Ignatius bids his readers (*Magn.* 13.1) be established in the ordinances of the Lord and of the apostles, that they may prosper in all they do with flesh and with spirit, by faith and by love, in Son and Father and in Spirit, in the beginning and in the end.

Justin three times reproduces triad-language in the course of the *Apology*. In refuting the ridiculous charge of atheism which was levelled at the Christian community, he observes not only that they acknowledged the Creator of the universe with entirely adequate forms of worship, but that they recognised as Son of the very God, and held in second place, that Jesus Christ who had taught them their worship and gospel—He had been born for that precise object— and held in third position the Prophetic Spirit: furthermore, he claims to prove that they honoured these two last with good reason (*apol.* 1.13.3). It is to be noted that this insistence on the honour due to the Spirit, as to the Son, is in answer to the charge of atheism. The implication is quite definite, that the triad thus formed made up the sum of whatever divine object or objects the Christians worshipped; and taken by itself the argument was far better calculated to make the heathen think that Christians were tritheists than to suggest that they were Unitarians or Binitarians. Later on (*ib.* 61.10–13) Justin describes the rite of baptism. No one would dare to name a name for the ineffable God, so He is invoked by the title of Father; the neophyte is washed in the name also of Jesus Christ, and in the name of the Holy Spirit who foretold through the prophets the things concerning Jesus. Once more, in describing the other great sacramental rite of the Eucharist (*ib.* 65.3), he says that the celebrant, taking the bread and wine prepared and presented to him, sends up praise and glory to the Father of all, through the name of the Son and of the Holy Spirit. Thus alike in the rite of initiation and in the liturgical worship observance is made of the same triad of divinity which appears in abstract doctrine.

Athenagoras carries the subject further than any other of the most ancient apologists. He asserts the place of the Holy Spirit as the immanent power in creation; God has created all things by His Word and holds them in being by the Spirit that is from Him (*suppl.* 6.3). He is equally insistent on the divine character of the Spirit's function of Biblical inspiration. The Holy Spirit that inspired the prophetic utterances, he claims (*ib.* 10.3), we assert to be an effluence of God, flowing forth and returning like a ray of the sun; how fantastic therefore it is to accuse of atheism people who hold God the Father, and a divine Son, and a Holy Spirit, and declare both their power in unity and their distinction in order. This conjunction of the triad, it may be observed in passing, is the more remarkable in that Athenagoras proceeds to enlarge his theistic system by the inclusion of angels and ministers distributed for the oversight of the universe, but emphatically distinguished from ultimate godhead. He returns again to the unity of the triad (*ib.* 12.2), in proclaiming the revelation of "the true God and the Word from Him, the unity of the Child towards the Father, the fellowship of the Father with the Son, the Spirit, the unity of these so numbered and their distinction though united, Spirit, Child, Father." Yet once more the subject recurs (*ib.* 24.1-2). He enumerates God and the Son, His Word, and the Holy Spirit: the Father, the Son, the Spirit, are united as to power, for the Son is Mind, Word, and Wisdom of the Father and the Spirit is an effluence like light from fire: and here again he proceeds to distinguish from this primary triad a host of "other powers" concerned with material nature. The actual word triad is not yet employed, but there is no doubt about the thing signified.

In two Fathers, Irenæus in the West and Theophilus in the East, an attempt is made to give definition to the doctrine of the Holy Spirit by identifying Him with the Wisdom of Old Testament thought, in the same manner as Christ was identified with the Word. It is a little strange that this attempt should have been made by authors so far remote, at almost the same moment—they both seem to have written during the ninth decade of the second century—and that in neither case does the suggestion appear to have been carried any further. Following psalm xxxiii.6 ("By his word the heavens were established, and all their power by his spirit") and *Proverbs* iii.19 ("God laid the foundations of the earth

by wisdom, and prepared the heavens by understanding"),
Theophilus takes Word and Reason to refer to the Son, and
Wisdom to represent the Spirit, summarising the act of
creation in the sentence, "God made all things through
His Word and His Wisdom," and the work of redemption
in the sentence, "God heals and quickens through His
Word and His Wisdom" (*ad Aut.* 1.7). Here the normal
distinction of function between the Son and the Spirit is
carefully preserved, Christ being the healer and the Holy
Spirit the quickener.

That this is the accurate interpretation of the passage is
proved by further statements in the second book of the work.
God begat His Word when He cast Him forth together with
His own Wisdom before the worlds (*ib.* 2.10); again (*ib.*)
there were no prophets when the universe was made, but
only the Wisdom of God that is in Him and His holy Word
who is always present with Him. The Word and the Wisdom
are distinct, in spite of the fact that just before Theophilus
ascribes "spirit of God" and "wisdom and power of the
Most High" to the Word, in token of the Word's divinity.
But the matter is put beyond dispute shortly afterwards by
the use of the actual word 'triad'—apparently its first
occurrence in relation to the godhead—with reference to
the same titles. He is expounding the significance of the
creation as described in *Genesis* i., and giving reasons why
the lights were only created on the fourth day. The celestial
bodies of different grades are held to represent the various
classes of mankind, and the three days before their creation
"are types of the triad, God, and His Word, and His Wisdom"
(*ib.* 2.15). The word triad simply means a collection of
three objects. It would be quite wrong to translate it here

by 'Trinity.' There are three days to be explained, and they represent the group of three entities or 'powers' that were to be reckoned on the divine side of the catalogue of existing beings. The problem of reconciling their recognition with the profession of monotheism was not in contemplation.

Irenæus in several places refers to the action of God in creation, in which He established all things by His Word and bound them together by His Wisdom (e.g. *haer.* 3.24.2). The title Wisdom occupies precisely the position filled by the title Spirit in Athenagoras (*suppl.* 6.3, quoted p. 88). God has no need of angels to assist Him in calling the creation into being, says Irenæus elsewhere (*haer.* 4.7.4); for "His offspring and His similitude minister to Him in all things, that is, the Son and the Holy Spirit, the Word and the Wisdom." The statement is repeated (*haer.* 4.20.1); the Father needed no angel or other 'power' remote from His own being, as though He did not possess 'hands' of His own; there are always present to Him the Word and the Wisdom, the Son and the Spirit, through whom and in whom He made all things freely and independently. He made all things by the Word and adorned them by the Wisdom (*ib.* 2). The Word, that is the Son, was always with the Father; that the Wisdom, which is the Spirit, was also with Him before all creation, is shown (*ib.* 3) by three texts from *Proverbs* (iii.19, viii.22ff., viii.27ff.).

The identification of the Spirit and the Wisdom failed to secure acceptance; already the title of Wisdom had come to be too closely connected with the Son. But the mere fact that it was put forward at all indicates that the being of the Spirit and that of the Son were felt to be associated and analogous, and that both needed some measure of definition of a similar kind. Both Son and Spirit belonged in some manner to the godhead, and though the exact relation of each to the Father (so far as it was as yet conceived with any precision) was clearly different, yet the difference was rather functional than qualitative. Father, Son, and Holy Spirit fell naturally and necessarily into a single group, and were described as a triad in fact, for a long time before the actual word triad was applied to them. This is the more noteworthy, in that the baptismal formula seems from the evidence to have played very little part in forming the conception of the threefold group of divine 'powers.'

One final quotation from Irenæus will further illustrate the recognition of the divine triad towards the end of the second century. Man, he says (*haer.* 4.20.5), cannot of himself see God, but God is seen by men according to His pleasure, by whom He wills, and when He wills, and how He wills: for in all things God is potent; He was seen of old through the Spirit prophetically, and through the Son adoptively, and shall be seen in the kingdom of heaven paternally, the Spirit preparing man to be a son of God, the Son leading him to the Father, and the Father bestowing incorruption unto eternal life. In this passage Spirit and Son in turn act as vehicles, in their degree, of the vision of God, in so far as prophecy can adumbrate it and the children of grace can experience it. The Spirit is treated as divine, in common with the rest of the divine group, though apparently He is not in set terms called God (as the Son is, frequently) by any Greek till Epiphanius (*anc.* 9.3). Tertullian (*adv. Prax.* 13) baldly states that the Father is God and the Son God and the Spirit God, and Lord each one. But the Greeks in general were content with such more indirect ascriptions of divinity as are implied in the practical recognition of the divine triad and of the divine character of the Spirit's operation; and their attitude, maintained until the middle of the fourth century, may not inaptly be summed up in the phrase of Athanasius (*ad Serap.* 1.12), that since the Spirit was among the Hebrew nation, God through the Son in the Spirit was among them.

It has already been said that the actual word 'triad,' with reference to the godhead, appears first in Theophilus. However, an allusion occurs in the *Excerpts from Theodotus* (80.3), preserved by Clement, which should be mentioned here, since it may be even earlier than the instance in Theophilus, and, though it does not positively call the godhead a triad, nevertheless implies a reference to it as such. The extract begins by saying that he whom his mother bears is brought into death and into the world; but he whom Christ begets again is transferred into life, that is into the ogdoad—the title for the body of the first eight æons. It then proceeds to state that for such a man death and corruption are overcome by the death and resurrection of Christ, "for being sealed through Father, Son, and Holy Spirit, he is invulnerable to all other power, and through three names has been set free from the whole triad that is in corruption." The "triad" of corruption is contrasted with the implied triad of immortal deity.

Tertullian, who called the several Persons of the godhead "God" in plain terms, also makes free use of the word trinitas. As with the early Greek theologians, trinitas bears a collective sense. It simply means triad, not tri-unity. 'Triad' also occurs in Hippolytus (*c. Noet.* 14). He quotes the baptismal formula, and says that anyone who omitted either of the three Persons failed to glorify God perfectly; for through this triad it is that the Father is glorified; the Father willed, the Son performed, and the Spirit manifested; the whole Scriptures proclaimed this truth. Clement (*strom.* 5.14, 103.1), quoting Plato from the *Timæus* and the *Letters* (he accepted their authenticity), says that he can only understand his author as signifying by his expressions "the holy triad." Rare as instances of 'triad' are until as late as Origen, Clement here slips in the reference to the holy triad, as if it were a term certainly easy to be understood, and possibly in common employment. Origen uses triad fairly freely, mainly in his commentaries. In that on *St. John*, which, unlike most, is preserved in the original Greek, he speaks of "the adorable triad" (6.33, 166). If his translator is to be trusted, he is apparently also the first to use the word of the godhead absolutely, without distinguishing epithet (on *Exodus* 9.3): "funis enim triplex non rumpitur, quae est trinitatis fides." What he understood by it may be indicated—subject to the limitation that the passage must be read mentally in Greek, and further, that the terms employed have not yet acquired their post-Nicene definition —by a passage from the (translated) commentary on *Canticles* (Delarue 84A): idem namque ipse qui ibi trinitas propter distinctionem personarum, hic unus deus intelligitur pro unitate substantiæ.

The word triad, then, did not originally express in any degree the unity of God. On the contrary, it emphasised the fact which constituted the main problem that Christian monotheists had to face. The term expressive of the principle of monotheism was 'monarchy.' Monarchy is naturally a metaphor from kingship. But it is not often employed of human kingship, simply by reason of the strong sense of absolute dominion which is attached to the word. The only ruler of everyday experience in the ancient civilised world, whose position approached that of monarchy, would be one of the most absolute of the Roman emperors. In practice therefore, the Fathers apply the word nearly always to the absolute monarchy of God, and its primary sense is omnipotence. But since the whole significance of omnipotence is that it can be wielded only by one ultimate power, it really comes to mean monotheism.

Thus Justin (*dial.* 1.3) observes that the philosophers are busy investigating the subject of God, and that their inquiries concern 'monarchy' and providence. Tatian (*ad Gr.* 14.1) taunts the Greeks with teaching polykoirania or plurality of lords (a reference to Homer) rather than monarchy; in other words, they believed in the lordship of a multiplicity of demons, not in monotheism. Theophilus (*ad Aut.* 2.4) argues against the Platonists that, if God is uncreate and matter is uncreate, according to their reasoning, God cannot be the Maker of the universe, nor is there any indication of the monarchy of God. The power of God, he goes on to assert, is shown by His creation of the world from the non-existent; any craftsman can manipulate existent matter. Again (*ib.* 2.35) he says that the Prophets pronounced by one and the same spirit (or inspiration) about the monarchy of God and the creation of the universe. And again (*ib.* 2.38), he contrasts monarchy with a plurality of gods, and observes that the speculations of heathen writers end with a recognition of monarchy, just as in fact those who had written against providence also used language which implied providence. Both Justin and Irenæus are

I

said to have written treatises, which have not, however, survived, "concerning monarchy." The kind of problem with which the latter attempted to deal is indicated by the full title—"concerning monarchy, or that God is not the Maker of evil." The problem of evil, in ancient no less than in modern times, always presented serious difficulties to the upholders of strict monotheism.

CHAPTER V

ORGANIC MONOTHEISM

THE recognition of divine monarchy and the proclamation of a divine triad were originally presented as independent facts, but they were facts which would clearly need a considerable amount of reconciliation in a philosophical mind, so soon as their contrasting truth was firmly held and fairly faced. This Tertullian attempted to achieve. Tertullian stands in a most interesting position in relation to earlier, as well as to later theology. He was very far, indeed, from being merely the father of Latin theology. His ultimate influence on Greek theological speculation was probably considerable, though it is extremely difficult to trace it very far in detail. But in certain respects the coincidence of his thought with that of Hippolytus is most striking, as will appear shortly. He is commonly accused by modern theological critics of having had the mind of a mere lawyer, and his thought is discounted as containing little more than a brilliant forensic presentation, clothed in supreme legalistic rhetoric. But, on a just appreciation, his place is secure as the last of the Greek Apologists. He was profoundly influenced by previous Greek speculation, and, unlike almost all of the Latin Fathers, he read Greek with facility, and actually composed his earliest works in that language. Though he owed an extensive debt to secular Greek philosophy, with which he was well acquainted, and in particular to the Stoics, his thought is in many points closely akin to that of the Apologists of the East, who had also drunk deep of the waters of profane learning.

The explanation which Tertullian proposes of the problem of 'monarchy', though expounded with forensic eloquence, is the common explanation accepted throughout the course of Greek theology, without much serious modification until a late period. Its nature appears in the treatise *against Praxeas*. He frankly admits (ch. 3) that the simple, who always constitute the majority of believers, are startled at 'the economy'—which, as will be shown later, is Tertullian's unexpected and somewhat startling name, accepted also by Hippolytus, for what modern theologians really understand by the doctrine of the Trinity. He points out that these people have been converted from polytheism to faith in the one, only true God, and entertain a not unnatural fear that the proclamation of a divine triad implies division of the divine unity. "They constantly accuse us of preaching two Gods, or three Gods, and take to themselves pre-eminently the credit of worshipping the one God." "We, they say, maintain the monarchy." But, replies Tertullian, appealing to his knowledge both of the Latin and of the Greek language, 'monarchy' means nothing else but individual and solitary dominion. "I maintain that no authority is so exclusively personal and individual or in such sense a monarchy, that it is incapable of being exercised through other proximate persons." He points out that monarchy does not automatically become divided when the monarch, to whom it belongs, assumes his son into a share of his own authority—as the Roman emperors, in fact, frequently did. Returning to the divine monarchy, he argues that its authority is administered by legions of angels, in their several degrees. How, then, can God be thought to undergo division and disruption in the Son and in the Holy Spirit, "who enjoy the second and third place," and are "tam consortes substantiæ patris," when such division and disruption are not involved in the exercise of the divine authority by the angels, who are "tam alieni a substantia patris"? "You must understand that the monarchy is overthrown when another authority, possessing its own principles and character, and therefore competitive, is brought in—when another god is introduced in opposition to the Creator."

This argument does not attempt to explain the basis of the divine unity. It merely rebuts the criticism that by acceptance of a triad of divine Persons the Church annihilated the unique, and therefore the ultimate and absolute, character of divine being. Its positive value lies in its recognition that the divine Father is the sole source from which the being of deity is derived. Tertullian's conception of divine unity, on the other hand, rests on his doctrine of 'economy,' that the unity constitutes the triad out of its own inherent nature, not by any process of sub-division, but by reason of a principle of constructive integration which the godhead essentially possesses. In other words, his idea of unity is not mathematical but philosophical; it is an organic unity, not an abstract, bare point.

When Tertullian employs economy, which he transliterates instead of translating, as a means of expressing the nature of the divine unity, the reference which lies behind this usage is mainly to the sense of interior organisation. The same word had been used in a somewhat similar sense by Quintilian in writing of literary craftsmanship. Quintilian (*inst. or.* 3.3.9) states that Hermagoras puts judgement, division, and arrangement, and whatever belongs to delivery, under the head of economy, which, he says, is a name taken in Greek from the oversight of domestic affairs and is here employed metaphorically; it lacks a Latin equivalent. Elsewhere (*ib.* 1.8.9), he contrasts economy with "sententiæ" or subject-matter, and again (*ib.* 7.10.11) he refers to the 'economic' arrangement of the presentation of a case. Clearly economy, as thus naturalised into Latin, was concerned with proportion and the co-ordination of constituent elements.

There is, however, no reason to conjecture that Tertullian derived the term from Quintilian or any other Latin author. As has been said, he both understood and wrote Greek, and transliterates other Greek words. Nor is it likely that he took it direct from the vocabulary of literary criticism, though Liddell and Scott give a reference to economy in this sense from Plutarch. Tatian (*ad Gr.* 12.2) observes that the composition of the body has a single economy, and refers, in the same place, to the arrangement of the hair, and the economy of the interior organs. In the *Martyrdom of Polycarp* (2.2) we find the statement that the economy of the martyrs' flesh was visible as far as the interior veins and arteries, in cases in which they had been punished by scourging. Irenæus, again (*haer.* 5.3.2), speaks of bones and sinews, and the rest of the human economy, signifying by this expression the whole complicated organisation which we commonly call the human frame. Clement (*strom.* 6.13, 107.2) relates the term 'economy' to the grades of the angelic and ecclesiastical hierarchies. There is therefore sufficient evidence of a standard Hellenistic usage of economy, in the sense of an organised system, corresponding generally with the more specialised literary sense, in which Quintilian employs it.

In Irenæus (*haer.* 1.16.2) there is preserved a reference to economy in what is not unlike a theological sense. It occurs in a passage in which he is dealing with the numerical speculations of the Marcosians, and the claim is made that certain representations form a figure of "the economy on high," by which is meant the system of æons. Whether Tertullian derived his usage from the Gnostics may, indeed, be doubted, for the word does not appear to be of common occurrence, and the reference just quoted seems to be made quite casually and incidentally. However, he claims (*adv. Prax.* 2) that, following the instruction of the Paraclete, Christians believe that there is one sole God, but subject to the following qualification, "which we call economy," that of the sole God there is also a Son. He denounces the heresy of thinking it impossible to believe in one sole God otherwise than by saying that Father, Son and Holy Spirit are the very self-same Person—as if, he continues with scorn, all three were not equally one, so long as they are all out of one, that is by unity of substance, and the mystery of the economy is preserved, which distributes the unity into a triad. He makes it clear that, according to his conception of economy, everything which is divine in the Father reappears unchanged, alike in worth, substance, and power, in the other Persons of the Trinity, in whom it is presented in different "degrees and forms and aspects." But what is thus presented in each instance is not merely something similar, but, he seems to imply, identically the same object.

He recurs again and again to the same conception of economy. His reference has already been quoted to the simple believers who were startled at the economy for fear of reversion to polytheism, not understanding that although He is the sole God, yet He must be believed in with His own economy. The numerical order and collocation (dispositio) of the triad, Tertullian says (*ib.* 3), was assumed by his opponents to be a division of the unity; whereas the unity, devolving the triad out of its own self, is not destroyed by it, but is 'distributed,' or dispensed, or organised, or methodised, or functionally constituted—Tertullian's term is literally untranslatable, but the paraphrases which have been used give some representation of its general sense. The actual words are, "quando unitas, ex semetipsa derivans trinitatem, non destruatur ab illa sed administretur." The last word is transparently the equivalent of the Greek 'economise' (οἰκονομέω). It implies, at least in some sense, that the substance of godhead is relayed in turn to each Person of the triad; in so far, the meaning is simply distributive. But, as dispositio expresses not merely distribution but also methodical arrangement, so economy carries a strong implication of constructive order and system. The instances quoted above prove this.

In this quotation, then, the idea of functional organisation is to be emphasised. The treatment recalls Tatian (*ad Gr.* 5.1), in his earlier approach to the same problem of the unity of the godhead. The Logos, he there says, was separated from the Father by a process of distribution (merismos), not by being cut off; for that which is cut off is parted from the original, but that which is distributed, while it acquires a distinction of economy, does not leave a deficiency in the source from which it has been taken. He goes on to use the familiar illustration of the torch, from which many lights are kindled without its suffering any diminution of its own original light.

This illustration is by no means wholly convincing to a modern thinker, because there is no limit to the number of new lights which can be kindled from the original torch, and, when all is said, the new lights are new, and separate, and no part of the original flame. But Tatian and the others who employ this metaphor quite definitely limited the number of fresh lights kindled from the source of divine being to two, and no less certainly regarded these as identical with, and not merely similar to, the original radiance. Thus Tatian, in the passage just quoted, proceeds to observe that, when the Logos proceeded forth from the power of the Father, He did not make Him who begat Him Logos-less. These early Fathers were groping after metaphors which should be capable of expressing unity in diversity, an organic unity, which should nevertheless not merely subsume the objects in which it was presented, as an abstract universal embraces all the separate objects in a particular classification, but be exhaustively expressed in them; a unity in which the distinction is merely a different aspect of the unity itself, and the diversity, though real, is in strict thought incapable of disjunctive enumeration. But they had no metaphors available to express such a conception with any degree of completeness. Modern philosophical thought, aided by the study of biology, and assisted, it may be, by a lingering enlightenment derived from the study of theology, has come nearer to success. But still the truth of the divine being, as understood in early Christian speculation, can only be expressed satisfactorily in a series of antitheses. Still more was this the case in the second and succeeding centuries. The history of Trinitarian controversy is really the history of the attempt to work out the necessary antitheses, after the primitive effort to construct a positive statement of the divine unity had broken on the rocks of Sabellianism. Strangely enough, it was Hippolytus, who shared Tertullian's conception of economy in the divine being, who also wrecked its application and wildly accused Callistus of heresy.

Tertullian's meaning may be further investigated in further quotations from the same treatise. He contrasts (*Prax.* 8) his own doctrine of divine emanations, according to the Christian gospel, with the emanations of æons such as Valentinus had taught. He indicates the features which make these two doctrines strictly incomparable with one another. He acknowledges that he would call God and His Word two objects, but only as the root and the tree are two distinct objects, or the fountain and the river, or the sun and its ray, which remain indivisible and coherent. Everything, he says, which proceeds from something else, must necessarily be in some sense second to that from which it proceeds; this does not mean that the two are separated, although the word 'second' implies two objects, as the word 'third' implies three objects. The Spirit is, indeed, third, just as the fruit of the tree is third from the root. The Christian doctrine of the triad, descending from the Father by coherent, interdependent stages, presents no obstacle to the monarchy, and preserves the character of the economy.

Again, (*ib.* 13) Tertullian ransacks the Scriptures, particularly those of the Old Testament, as being even more telling for his purpose than those of the New, to find illustrations of the ascription of deity to the Son and the Holy Spirit. But he challenges his opponents to prove, if they can, that this requires them, on the authority of the same Scriptures, to preach two gods or two lords. Illuminated by divine inspiration, he remarks, true believers make the assertion that two beings are God, Father and Son, and, indeed, with the addition of the Holy Spirit, three beings, according to the principle of the economy, which introduces numeration in order that the Father may not be believed Himself to have been born and to have suffered—a belief which was no part of revelation, and was not lawful. But he denies strenuously that a true believer had ever said that there were two gods or two lords.

A few lines lower down he accounts for the scriptural ascription of deity to Christ on the ground that, if Scripture had stopped its pronouncement short with the mere statement that there is one God and one Lord, it would have followed that the Father Himself should seem to have descended (seeing that He would have been the only God and Lord referred to in the Scriptures) and His entire economy would have been obscured. In this last mention of economy, the conception of function is becoming very prominent. But this should not be allowed to confuse the reader into thinking that the economy referred to is that of the Incarnation, even though 'economy' came in Greek to be the normal term for expressing the Incarnation. The economy of which Tertullian is speaking is not that of the Son, whether in redemption or in any other connection. It is expressly "His economy," that is to say, the economy of the being of God of which the Father is the sole source. The Father's economy would have been obscured if the idea had ever been conceivable that it was He who became man. In other words, the divine economy is not an economy of redemption, nor an economy of revelation, but an economy of divine being.

Tertullian was roughly the contemporary of Hippolytus, who uses the same conception of Trinitarian economy in his work against Noetus. The treatment certainly presents a more fully developed appearance in Tertullian; and force is added to the suspicion that he took the idea over from Hippolytus by the fact that the treatise against Noetus is now generally dated ten or more years earlier than Tertullian's work against Praxeas. Hippolytus accuses the followers of Noetus (*c. Noet.* 3) of having, with shameless and reckless audacity, pronounced that the Father is Himself the Son, was born, suffered and raised Himself from the dead. That is not so, says Hippolytus. The Scriptures tell us the truth, but Noetus has a different idea. Who will not acknowledge that there is one God, Hippolytus demands; yet one will not on that account demolish the economy.

Again (*ib.* 8), he argues that the unity of God is indicated by the fact that His power ($\delta \acute{v} \nu a \mu \iota s$) is one. It will be recalled how it was shown at an earlier stage of this inquiry that 'power' involves supernatural force which ultimately belongs to God, and that God Himself is regarded as a Power. So far, then, continues Hippolytus, as regards the power, there is one God; but so far as regards the economy, His manifestation is threefold. Once more (*ib.* 14) he proceeds to state that this economy is declared to us by Blessed

John, when he says, In the beginning was the Word, and the Word was with God, and the Word was God (*St. John* i.1). "If, then, the Word was with God, and was God, what follows? Would one allege that he mentions two gods? I shall not assert two gods, but one, and two presentations (πρόσωπα, Persons), and a third economy, the grace of the Holy Spirit." The idea of functional activity is probably here not absent, but in the light of what has gone before, the primary sense of economy is obviously that of co-ordinate distinction in the being of the godhead.

He repeats the claim that the Father, indeed, is one, but there are two presentations because there is also the Son; and then, he adds, there is the third, the Holy Spirit. The economy of harmony is conducted back to one God, for God is one. It is the Father who commands, the Son who obeys, and the Holy Spirit who gives understanding; the Father who is above all, and the Son who is through all, and the Holy Spirit who is in all (cf. *Ephesians* iv.6, "One God and Father of all, who is over all, and through all, and in all"). But we cannot otherwise think of one God than by believing in truth in Father, Son, and Holy Spirit. The Jews glorified the Father, but gave Him not thanks, for they did not recognise the Son. The disciples recognised the Son, but not 'in the Holy Ghost'; this explains why they denied Jesus. The Word of the Father therefore, knowing the economy and the will of the Father, namely that the Father seeks to be worshipped in none other way than this, gave this charge to the disciples after His resurrection, Go ye, and teach all nations, baptising them in the name of the Father, and of the Son, and of the Holy Ghost (*St. Matt.* xxviii.19). By this He showed that whosoever omitted any one of these failed in glorifying God perfectly. For it is through this triad that the Father is glorified. The Father willed, the Son executed, the Spirit manifested.

It will be observed that in these last passages (ch. 14) the word economy occurs both in the usual sense with reference to the internal relationships and systematised co-ordination of the whole godhead, and also with reference to the particular relationship of the Holy Spirit to the rest. In a similar way it is used (*ib.* 16) of the relationship of the Son to the Father. In reality, observes Hippolytus, the Power of the Father, which is the Word, came down from heaven, and not the Father Himself. What is it, he asks, that is begotten of the Father, but just spirit, that is to say the Word? (Again it will be recalled that spirit is a semi-technical term for divine being.) He proceeds to face the inquiry, how is the Word begotten? In your own case, he observes, you are unable to explain the process of causation by which you were begotten yourself, although you daily observe its human aspect; "neither can you explain with accuracy the economy in the case of the divine Son." Unquestionably, economy here refers to the heavenly generation of the Logos, and not to the Incarnation. Is it not enough for you, he asks a little lower down, that the Son of God has been manifested to you for salvation, if you believe, but do you also inquire curiously how He was begotten according to spirit? Only two people, he adds (referring to the authors of the first and third gospels), have been entrusted with the account of His generation after the flesh; are you then so bold as to seek the account of His generation after spirit which the Father keeps with Himself? The economy which Hippolytus has just mentioned, therefore, clearly refers to the relationship of the Son to the Father in the eternal generation of the Logos within the godhead.

We may now return to the explanation of a difficult passage in ch. 4, of which the exact interpretation is complicated by the fact that the Incarnation is under discussion. It will be seen that here also the word economy refers to the eternal relationship, and not to the specifically incarnate Sonship. Hippolytus quotes *Isaiah* xlv. 14, "surely God is in thee." But in whom is God, he asks, except in Christ Jesus, the Word of the Father, and in the mystery of the economy? Christ's incarnation, he continues, was indicated by a reference in the previous verse, with the words, I have raised him up in righteousness (*Isaiah* xlv. 13). "But in saying that 'In thee God is,' he indicated the mystery of economy, namely that, when the Word became flesh and incarnate, the Father was in the Son and the Son was in the Father, while the Son was living among men. This, then, brethren, was indicated, that this Word, by the Holy Ghost and the Virgin, fashioned one Son to God—a mystery, veritably, of economy."

What meaning, then, should be attached to this last phrase, "a mystery of economy?" At first sight it might appear to mean the mystery of the Incarnation. But against that interpretation stands the fact that it would be almost intolerable for the same term to be employed within a narrow compass, in the same treatise, and without a word of qualification or explanation, in two such widely divergent senses as that of Trinity and that of Incarnation. Economy in this passage must mean the same as it does in the remainder of the treatise. That this is in fact the case may be shown by a paraphrase of the argument of the whole passage.

That argument is not to the effect that a divine incarnation took place, which Noetus also admitted, but that the Person incarnate, while distinct from God the Father, nevertheless was one with God. The prophet Isaiah is quoted to show that God the Father raised up someone, and was in someone. The reference to raising up, on comparison with *Romans* viii.11, which Hippolytus quotes in full (the words, omitted from the extracts given above, are, "if the Spirit of him that raised up Christ Jesus from the dead dwell in you," etc.), proves that the person indicated is the divine Son in the flesh: it is therefore the incarnate sphere which is indicated, according to Hippolytus, by Isaiah's words, "I have raised him up in righteousness." But the Father can only be said to reside in the divine Logos by virtue of the mystery of the economy—"In whom is God, except in the Word of the Father and in the mystery of the economy?"— the mysteriously co-ordinated being of the godhead as a whole. Accordingly, after clearing up the reference to the resurrection, and noting that it belongs to the sphere of the incarnation, Hippolytus repeats that the words "God is in thee" refer to the mystery of the economy, by which he means, as elsewhere, the eternal relationship of the Father and the Logos.

It was precisely this mystery of the divine plurality which Noetus denied, and which Hippolytus was concerned to maintain. Hippolytus' main point is that the Father was in the incarnate Son simply and solely because He was in the eternal Son. In more modern language, the historical Jesus was the Son of God only because He is to be identified with the heavenly Christ, and because, further, the heavenly Christ is the Son of God. Therefore, even "while the Son was living among men," still the Father was in the Son, and the Son in the Father. The reason for this fact is that the Son of God incarnate, and the Son of God eternal, constitute "a single Son to God." That is how the mystery of economy is brought into relation with the incarnation. "This Word, by the Holy Ghost and the Virgin, fashioned one Son to God—a mystery, veritably, of economy." If Father and Son are distinct, though co-inherent, during the period of the incarnation, the same is true of them in the absolute, and it is only true in the incarnation because it is true in the absolute. The facts of the incarnation illustrate the eternal relationship of the godhead.

It must therefore be concluded that Tertullian and Hippolytus put forward a statement of the eternal relationships of the divine triad which is, apparently, unique in patristic theology. No other Father seems to employ 'economy' in this connection, and the precise relation between the theological ideas of these two thinkers might well repay detailed investigation. Their conception of economy might have proved extraordinarily fruitful, if it had been taken up and developed in subsequent theological thought. It provides a striking illustration of the importance of Tertullian's philosophical thought, and is in reality much more significant than his use of 'person' and 'substance,' which he employs far more nearly in the ordinary senses of contemporary Greek writers than in the highly specialised senses, either of later theology or of his modern interpreters. But this conception was apparently ignored and forgotten; it never reappeared in the whole course of subsequent theological development.

CHAPTER VI

THE WORD

GOD, Hippolytus had said (*c. Noet.* 10), subsisting alone, and having nothing contemporaneous with Himself, determined to create the world; it is sufficient for us simply to know that there was nothing contemporaneous with God; beside Him there was nothing; but He, while existing sole, yet existed in plurality. The substitutes for orthodox Trinitarian doctrine may take either of two forms. A doctrine of emanations lent itself with peculiar appropriateness, in the circumstances of the ancient world of thought, to a principle of subordinationism, according to which each successive emanation was not merely more remote from the source, but also further detached from the ideal substance of the divine original. This fact is obvious in the speculations of the Gnostics, which are parodied by Irenæus in the following passage (*haer.* 1.11.4): "There is a certain Pre-Source, royal, pre-inconceivable, a pre-unexistent power, a Pre-Free-Rambler; along with it is a power which I call Cucurbita: and along with this Cucurbita is a power which I call Utter-Vacancy. This Cucurbita and Utter-Vacancy, since they are one, projected, but without projecting, a fruit in every respect visible, edible, and delicious; a fruit which language entitles Cucumber. Along with this Cucumber is a power of the same potency as itself, which again I call Melon. These powers, Cucurbita and Utter-Vacancy and

112

Cucumber and Melon, projected the remaining host of the delirious Melons of Valentinus." Rambler and Cucurbita represent abstract or ideal conceptions; Cucumber and Melon are concrete and corruptible edible fruits, sufficiently remote (as the Gnostics thought) from the Pre-Source, or fountain-head of deity, to be brought into contact with the vile creation without involving the transcendent godhead in direct responsibility for its vileness. The fallacy of Gnosticism lay in the fact that, if contact with creation be indeed degrading, the degradation is just as great when it is indirect as when it is immediate. Their systems cannot meet the criticism that, at each stage of the descent from absolute deity, the divine principle is made to project an emanation inferior both to itself and to the previous emanation.

As an alternative, if such subordinationism were rejected, it was open to speculative thinkers to suggest, as the Sabellians did, that the three forms of divine presentation were mere forms and nothing more, that behind each mask there stood individually the same actor, portraying in succession the roles of creation, redemption and sanctification. It may be said at once, in passing, that no ancient Father until Basil uses the word prosopon in this sense of mask. When the word is employed to describe the Persons of the Trinity, it means, not a transitory and superficial presentation, but simply an individual. The alleged 'Sabellian' use of prosopon, in the sense of mask or character from a play, and the word's alleged consequent discredit in theology, with which modern text-books make so great a play, both seem to be pure legend.

But there is no doubt of the fact that Sabellianism existed, or that a vigorous and not illogical tradition of heresy taught the complete identity of Father, Son, and Holy Spirit. There are roots of this doctrine that may be traced even in a purely Gnostic context, since Irenæus (*haer.* 1.23.1) records of Simon Magus, the arch-heretic, that many people glorified him as God, and that he declared himself to be Him who among the Jews appeared as Son, and descended into Samaria as Father, and visited the other nations as Holy Spirit. It is difficult to gather a clear impression of the various Gnostic heresies, especially since the account of them is fragmentarily recorded by their more than unsympathetic opponents. But it appears from the statement quoted that Simon, whoever he may have been, might not have been averse from adopting a Sabellian attitude. The same can certainly not be said of the average Gnostic. Valentinus, according to Hippolytus (*ref.* 6.29.5), said of the only unbegotten Father that, when He became generative, He determined to beget and produce the fairest and most perfect element that He possessed within His own being; for He was no lover of solitude. For, says Hippolytus, quoting or purporting to quote Valentinus, He was all love, and love is not love except there be an object of the love.

There was, indeed, a third possibility, which was to deny the deity of the Son, and by inference that of the Holy Spirit, in any true sense. This bare unitarianism did not, however, exercise any wide appeal in the ancient world. The form in which unitarianism actually appeared was the Adoptionist compromise, which, while assigning to Christ the 'value' of God after His ascension, denied Him more than a merely human personality. Origen (on *St. John* 2.2, 16) recognises the existence of all three forms of error. There were some people, he remarks, who were afraid of proclaiming two gods, and on this account fell into false and impious doctrines. Others denied that the individuality of the Son was distinct from that of the Father, and confessed the deity of Him whom they addressed as Son, though in name alone. Others, again, denied the deity of the Son, but admitted His individuality and His being as distinct from those of the Father, though by way of limitation. The first of these classes are the unitarians, the second the Sabellians, and the third the subordinationists.

The Sabellians, though their doctrine seems to have gained some footing in Rome, were so handsomely refuted by Tertullian and Hippolytus, and by the historical and biblical commonsense of Christendom, that they did not continue to give very much serious trouble, at any rate until some species of doctrine possessing affinity with their thought was revived in the fourth century by Marcellus. Even then, the chief result of the revival was to damage the credit of the Nicene orthodox rather than to endanger the truth of the Trinity.

During the third century the unitarian school, which had been condemned in the person of Theodotus, experienced a notable revival in Paul of Samosata. Paul's teaching obviously owed much to the earlier Adoptionists, but was more consistent. He held, apparently, that Christ was an earthly man, indwelt impersonally by divine influences, to which He responded with obedience so complete that He was exalted to fellowship with God. His exaltation was the final stage in a moral progress. Paul was condemned by the Origenist Council of Antioch in 268. It is hard to say how far his opinions were really eradicated, and how far only driven underground. Robertson (*Athanasius* pp.xxvii, xxviii.) gives strong reasons for tracing a connection, through Lucian the Martyr, between Paul and Arius. But even when it has been granted that the eclectic system of Arius contained elements closely resembling Paul's teaching, the fact remains that Arianism, and presumably Lucianism, owed its distinctive character to its acceptance of an extreme form of subordinationism, which was undoubtedly derived from Origen, the teacher whose followers had condemned Paul. On Robertson's own showing, Lucian purchased immunity by identifying Christ with the divine Son and admitting that this Son was personal, even though not in the fullest sense God. This involved a profound change from the fundamental unitarianism of Paul of Samosata to a fundamental subordinationism, however much it exaggerated in practice the principles which Origen had sketched. The real struggle of the third and fourth centuries was with different forms of subordinationism.

Before turning to a full investigation of this subject, it will be necessary first to survey another doctrine with a special bearing on the problems with which subordinationism attempted to deal. The second Person of the Trinity was variously known as Son, Power, and Wisdom, but the title which came to exercise the greatest significance for theological discussion was that of Logos. The Greek word 'logos,' as is well known, may refer either to spoken expression, or to implicit rationality. In this latter sense of reason or understanding, it is commonly applied among the Fathers more particularly to the practical, as distinct from the speculative, reason. Prudent logos, or reason, forbids

one to follow those who act unjustly (Justin, *apol.* 1.2.1).
Athenagoras (*de res.* 24) refers to rational beings as those
who act according to the immanent law and logos. Clement
holds up as a model the man "who walks according to logos"
(*strom.* 5.3, 17.1), and mentions (*ib.* 2.11, 50.1) that human
nature possesses three measures or criteria: perception, for
objects of sense; logos, for spoken utterance and names and
terms; and intellect, for what is abstract.

The secondary senses of logos are almost innumerable,
and need not be set out here at length. But a reference must
be made to the Stoic conception of the 'logos spermaticos,'
or immanent germinative principle, not because it had any
influence on theology, but because it testifies to the general
belief in the rationality of the universe, and in the prevalence of immanent forces governing particular objects.
This doctrine is mentioned by Justin, Athenagoras, and
frequently by Origen, who seems to have understood the
term to imply a principle or character derived by physical
heredity, and contrasted with the fruits of moral effort.
Athanasius (*contra gentes* 40), when he comes to speak of the
Word of God who orders all things in reason, wisdom and
skill, carefully distinguishes this controlling divine Word
from the logos that is involved and inherent in all things
created, which some are accustomed to call the germinative
logos or principle, which has neither soul nor power of
reason and thought.

The associations of logos as a theological term may be set
out under three broad heads. In the first place, the Logos
is the interpretative revelation and expression of the Father.
Thus, Ignatius remarks (*Magn.* 8.2) that there is one God
who has revealed Himself through Jesus Christ His Son,

who is His Logos, proceeding forth from silence. With this may be compared his staggering appeal to his Roman friends (*Rom.* 2.1), to allow him to be martyred without any well-meaning intervention aimed at securing his release; for, he says, if you be silent and leave me alone, I am a logos of God. His martyrdom would prove to be an inspired and interpretative testimony to the truth of the gospel. So Justin (*dial.* 128.2) says that the power from the Father, who appeared to Moses, is called Logos because He brings to men the messages from the Father. Irenæus (*haer.* 2.30.9) states that the Father of our Lord Jesus Christ is revealed through His Logos, who is His Son; ever from the beginning does He reveal the Father to angels and archangels, to powers and virtues, and to all to whom God wills to be revealed. Again (*ib.* 4.6.5), he claims that the Father revealed Himself to all by making His Word visible to all; and adds (*ib.* 4.6.6) that through the actual creation the Word reveals God the Creator; by means of the universe, the Lord who made the universe; by the formation of man, the Artificer who formed him; and by the Son, the Father who begat the Son.

To Origen the Logos was so called because of His power of interpreting the hidden things of the universe to the rational consciousness of men. He argues (on *St. John* 1.19, 111) that in some sense Christ was the Creator and the direct source of existence to the things that are: this is in virtue of His being Wisdom. The title Wisdom, he adds, must be understood in relation to the constructive system of knowledge and ideas concerning the universe; the title Logos must be related to the association of the objects of knowledge with rational beings. Once again (*de princ.*

1.2.3), he observes that Wisdom must be understood to be the Word of God on this ground, that it discloses to all other beings the principle of the mysteries and secrets which are contained within the wisdom of God; and it is called Word because it is, so to speak, the Interpreter of the secrets of the mind. It is not without interest to observe that in Arian circles the idea was stressed of the remoteness of God, and that the function of the Logos was to reveal Him who was Himself invisible: Asterius has written, records Eusebius (*c. Marcell.* 2.3.24), that the Logos of God is the image of the unseen God.

A second group of passages emphasises the rational aspect of the Logos. We have been taught that Christ is the first-born of God, says Justin (*apol.* 1.46.2), since He is the Logos in whom the whole human race shares; and those who have lived with logos are Christians, even though they were reckoned atheists, like Socrates and Heraclitus among the Greeks, or like Abraham, the three holy children, and Elias among the barbarians. To Tatian's mind (*ad Gr.* 7.1) the heavenly Logos derived His 'pneumatic' character from the pneuma (spirit), and was Logos from the power of logos: and to Athenagoras (*suppl.* 24.1) the Son is the Mind, Logos, Wisdom of the Father. Tertullian, who held a doctrine of the Logos akin to that which will shortly be mentioned in connection with the distinction between the 'logos-immanent' and the 'logos-expressed,' thus expounds the matter (*Prax.* 5). Before the beginning of all things God existed alone, because there was nothing external to Him but Himself. Yet even then He was not alone, for He had with Him that which He possessed in Himself, that is to say His own reason. For God is rational, and reason

existed first in Him. This reason is His own consciousness
(sensus) which the Greeks call Logos, corresponding to the
Latin Sermo; and therefore it is now usual among Latin
Christians to say that the Sermo was in the beginning with
God. But it would be more suitable to regard Reason as the
more ancient, because God was not 'sermonalis' from the
beginning, but He was 'rationalis' even before the beginning,
and because Sermo itself, as it consists of Reason, indicates
the priority of Reason as being the substance of itself. Not
that this distinction, remarks Tertullian, is of any practical
consequence; for, although God had not as yet sent forth
His Sermo, He still had Him within Himself, in company
with, and included within, His very Reason, as He silently
planned everything which He afterwards intended to utter.

Hippolytus, again, observes (*ref.* 10.33.1) that the sole
and universal God first conceived (ἐννοηθείς) and begat the
Logos, not a logos of speech, but the immanent rationality
of all being; Him alone, says Hippolytus, did God beget
out of existent being (i.e. in contrast to creation 'out of
non-existence,' ἐξ οὐκ ὄντων), since the Father Himself was
existent being (τὸ ὄν), out of whom came that which was
begotten. Clement states (*protr.* 10, 98.3) that the Logos of
God is His image; the divine Logos is the true Son of Mind,
the archetypal Light of Light; and the image of the Logos
is the true man, the mind that is in man. Origen lays it
down (*de princ.* 1.3.8) that created beings derive existence
from God the Father, and rational existence from the Word;
that they possess holiness they owe to the Holy Spirit.
He amplifies this with the statement (on *St. John* 2.3, 20)
that the reason which exists in each rational being bears
the same relation (logos) towards the Logos who was in

the beginning with God, and was God, as God the Logos bears to God; both occupy the position of source, the Father being the source of deity to the Son, and the Son the source of reason (logos) to mankind.

The third group of passages which it is proposed to quote here, associates the Logos with the idea of divine fiat or will. There was ample precedent for this connection of thought in the Old Testament accounts of the creation, when "God spake and it was done." Justin comments (*apol.* 1.14.5) upon our Lord's teaching, such as is contained in the Sermon on the Mount and elsewhere, that His Commandments (logoi) are brief and terse, for the Logos of God was no sophist, but the Power of God. Hippolytus (*ref.* 10.33.2) calls the Logos the causative agency to the things that came into existence, because He bore in Himself the will of Him that begat Him; and maintains (*c. Noet.* 10) that God created by the Logos (creation was of course the supreme act of divine will) and disposed the creation by the Wisdom. Clement (*strom.* 5.14, 99.3), in expounding those elements of Christianity which he was able to detect in Plato, paraphrases the words of the writer Aristobulus in which he asserts that, when Pythagoras, Socrates, and Plato said they heard the voice of God in the course of accurate contemplation of the fabric of the universe, which was created and is incessantly maintained by God, they acquired the idea from Moses; Moses taught that He spake and it was done, thus describing the logos (word) of God as act. God's word was thus represented as an effectual expression of active divine volition.

In addition to the foregoing, several passages can be cited in which the Logos is directly associated with the 'thelema' (will) of the Father. By the will of His simplicity the Logos leaps forth, exclaims Tatian (*ad Gr.* 5.1). If, then, the Word is sent forth through Jesus Christ, argues Hippolytus (*c. Noet.* 13), Jesus Christ is the Will of the Father. Justin had already remarked (*dial.* 60.2) that the divine angel, identified with Christ, who appeared to Abraham at the judgement of Sodom, and to Jacob and on other occasions, was serving the will of the Creator of the universe; and a little later (*ib.* 61.1), justifies the variety of supernatural titles, among them that of Logos, which he assigned to Christ by the fact that under each title He served the Father's purpose, and by the further fact that He had been begotten of the Father by will. A similar process can be observed among men, he proceeds; when we project a word (logos) we beget a word, but in projecting it there is no such bisection as to diminish the logos within us. Both the existence and the action of the Logos are here clearly conceived by Justin as proceeding from the will of the Father. Clement states (*strom.* 5.1, 6.3) that He who imparted to us being and life imparted also logos, since He willed that we should live both rationally and well; for the Logos of the Father of the universe is not a 'word-expressed,' but Wisdom and Kindness most manifest of God, almighty Power which is truly divine and capable of perception even by those who do not confess it, all-potent Will. Origen (*de princ.* 4.4.1) asserts that the Word and Wisdom was begotten apart from any physical passion, just as will proceeds from mind; if He is called Son of love, why not in such manner also Son of will?

It is to be observed that the passages relating the Logos and the divine will, fall into two classes. In some the eternal generation of the Son, or His work of revelation, is said to proceed by reason of, and subject to, the will of the Father. In others He is Himself identified with the will of the Father. At an early stage of theological development this distinction seems to have passed unnoticed, and gave rise to no great doctrinal discrepancy. Later, it became of increasing importance in connection with subordinationist theory. When this occurred, the orthodox tradition laid stress on the identification which made the eternal Son the concrete expression of the will of the Father; on the other hand, the subordinationist school seized upon the suggestion of inferiority which seemed to be implied in the subjection of the Son to an external will, and the innocent speculations of Apologists came to provide support for the Arian school of thought.

Some references have already been made to an early speculation based on the distinction between 'logos-immanent' (ἐνδιάθετος) and 'logos-expressed' (προφορικός). Logos, in Greek, can equally well mean 'thought' or 'speech.' The idea was thereby suggested that the divine Logos had passed through two modes or stages of existence: from eternity, He was regarded as unexpressed, indwelling the being of the Father in the same way as thought and reason inhabit mind; but in the act of creation, of which He was the agent, He issued forth from the divine Mind and acquired external self-expression, as a thought does when it is uttered in speech. This speculation has an important bearing on subordinationism, because, if treated by unorthodox practitioners, it could easily be made to support the contention that the Logos was impersonal—a mere attribute of God—until the point in historic time at which He proceeded forth from the Father in the act of creation. Any such previous impersonality would derogate from the worth and even from the reality of His eternal existence, lending a spurious tone of Christian conviction to the cry of Arius that "the time was when He was not." Even apart from this conclusion, any theory of the kind tended to associate the Logos too exclusively with the act of creation and the continuance of the created universe. Thus when teaching of the same general character, though without any leaning to subordinationism—indeed, in conscious opposition to subordinationist tendencies—was revived in the fourth century by Marcellus, the evolution of a Trinity from the divine unity began with the need to satisfy the requirements of world-creation, and ended with their cessation.

Both the conception of the two kinds of Logos-existence and the terminology in which it was expressed were probably imported into theology direct from the Stoics. The suggestion that they came through Philo is unsupported by positive evidence, and is hardly encouraged by the fact that Philo's name is not mentioned in the Apostolic Fathers and is quoted only once (from Tatian) in Dr. Goodspeed's *Index* to the Apologists. Nor does it seem to occur in Theophilus. At its source, the doctrine appears to have manifested some association with Gnostic thought. At any rate, Irenæus detected an affinity between the Gnostic idea that God emitted a system of æons, including a Logos, and the common Stoic distinction, with which he was obviously quite familiar, of logos-immanent and logos-expressed. He argues (*haer.* 2.12.5) that it is impossible for Sige (silence) and Logos (speech) to co-exist in the same body of emanations; if the Logos is only 'immanent' speech, so also must the Sige be 'immanent' silence; the two are parallel and contradict each other; but that the Logos is not merely 'immanent' according to the Gnostic system, is proved by the order of the emission of the æons—in which Logos ranks subsequent to Sige, and is therefore clearly intended to represent the breaking of silence by utterance. A little later (*ib.* 2.13.8) he strongly attacks the Gnostics for applying to the universal Father a system of inadequate metaphorical inferences drawn from the production of human speech from human minds; "they transfer the generation of a human 'word-expressed' to the eternal Word of God."

All this language, however, is that of Irenæus' criticism, not of Gnostic formulation. The contrast of immanent and expressed logos would have encountered graver prejudice than it actually received, had it been formally adopted by the Gnostics. It was taken up by a few orthodox writers, in order to illustrate the perfect unity subsisting from the beginning between the Father and the Logos. But it was early opposed and soon repudiated. Yet there was this much further justification for its adoption: from the standpoint of the finite human observer, it is the external acts of creation and incarnation, by which the Logos presents in finite terms some likeness of the infinite Father, that have occasioned the historical recognition of the Father and the Logos in distinct perspective.

Athenagoras (*suppl.* 10.2-3), though he does not use the characteristic terminology of this theory, nevertheless expresses himself in terms which may possibly represent a similar notion. He says that the Son was the first offspring of the Father, though He was not a created being; for God, being eternal Mind, possessed from the beginning His own Logos in Himself, since He was eternally 'logicos'; but the Son was the ground and active force, on His proceeding forth, of created nature. It is Theophilus who first employs the actual language of Logos immanent and expressed. God, he observes (*ad Aut.* 2.10), possessing His own Logos immanent in His own heart, begat Him with His own wisdom when He "uttered" Him before the universe. (The reference in "uttered" is to psalm xlv.1, "My heart is inditing of a good matter," or in Greek, "My heart hath uttered a good word.") Again (*ib.* 2.22), he refers to the voice of God which Adam heard in the garden. What else can this voice be, he asks, than the Logos of God, who is also His Son? Not, however, Son in the manner in which poets and mythologists describe sons of God being begotten by intercourse, but as truth describes the Logos who was eternally immanent in the heart of God. For before anything came into being He had Him as His Counsellor, since He was His own mind and reason ($\phi\rho\acute{o}\nu\eta\sigma\iota\varsigma$). When God willed to create all that He had determined, He begat this Logos in utterance ($\pi\rho o\phi o\rho\iota\kappa\acute{o}\varsigma$), the first-born of all creation, not by depriving Himself of the Logos, but by begetting the Logos and continually associating with His Logos.

A passage has already been quoted (p.119) from Tertullian (*c. Prax.* 5), in which he argues that the divine Sermo existed before the creation, silently within the godhead and incorporated within the divine Reason, while God meditated and planned everything which, through the Sermo, He afterwards intended to utter. This passage involves the same cycle of ideas as those which have been quoted from Theophilus, though the adjectives 'immanent' and 'expressed' do not occur. The passage from Hippolytus (*ref.* 10.33.1), which was quoted in the same context, is also to be noted, stating, as it does, that God first conceived and begat the Logos, not a logos of speech, but the immanent rationality of all that is. It might be argued that a similar idea was in the mind of Ignatius when he wrote (*Magn.* 8.2) that God manifested Himself through Jesus Christ His Son, who is His Logos, coming forth out of silence. The reference, however, in this passage is not to the act of creation, but to prophetic inspiration and the Incarnation. The silence here intended is therefore not the absolute silence of the primordial void, but the relative silence in which, apart from special revelation, the mysteries of God are wrapped from the ear of man.

On the other hand, a series of theologians rejects the whole conception. Irenæus (*haer.* 2.13.8), as has been said, condemns the Valentinians for transferring to the eternal Word of God the generation of the 'word-expressed' of men. Clement, as we have also seen (*strom.* 5.1, 6.3, p. 122), denies that the Logos of the Father of the universe is the 'word-expressed'; on the contrary, He is the most manifest Wisdom and Kindness of God. Origen (on *St. John* 1.24, 151) calls special attention to the title Logos, as having not been employed by our Lord Himself, but derived from St. John. He refers to the gratification with which various people seized upon this title, particularly in connection with their incessant quotation of the psalm, "My heart hath uttered a good word," under the impression, as he says, that the Son of God was a paternal utterance ($\pi\rho o\phi o\rho\acute{a}$) practically expressed in actual syllables of speech, in consequence of which they denied Him any concrete individuality—at any rate if Origen had rightly understood them. What he is here dealing with, and opposing, is clearly some variation of the theory of the 'Word-expressed.' Eusebius once more opposes a very similar error in very similar language (*dem. ev.* 5.5.8): in another treatise (*eccl. theol.* 2.15.4), he denounces Marcellus for employing the conception of Logos-immanent and Logos-expressed, a denunciation which is apposite enough in substance, though the actual terms appear not to belong to Marcellus' own statement, but to Eusebius' comment. In the fourth century all but professed heretics seem to have repudiated the whole theory. The semi-Arians attack it in the *Macrostich* (section 5, ap. Ath. *de syn.* 26). The doctrine is anathematised in the eighth anathema of the Council of Sirmium (*ib.* 27). Pseudo-Athanasius (*exp. fid.* 1) describes the Logos as neither 'immanent' nor 'expressed,' not an effluence of the Perfect, not a division of the impassible being, not an emanation, but absolute Son. A succession of orthodox theologians repeats the condemnation.

CHAPTER VII

SUBORDINATIONISM

ENOUGH has been said to show that the doctrine of the Logos, great as was its importance for theology, harboured deadly perils in its bosom. In particular, the theory of 'word-immanent' and 'word-expressed' tended towards undue subordination of the Son by making Him fundamentally and primordially an impersonal function of the Father. This tendency was operative in Gnostic thought, in which a certain amount of play was made with the title Logos as a name for one of the many æons in the different systems of Gnostic speculation. Hippolytus, indeed, attributes a doctrine of Gnostic character, into which a Logos enters, to the Brahmins of India (*ref.* 1.24.2). Perhaps this suggestion is more fruitful in throwing light upon one possible line of Oriental influence on Gnostic origins than in actually elucidating the tenets of the Hindus. He also gives extracts (*ref.* 4.46.2) from an unnamed work, in which Gnostic allegories of an astronomical character were extracted from the poems of Aratus. In these extracts Logos appears to be a kind of rational cosmic principle controlling the evolution and fate of mankind. Several traces are found of a pagan Logos doctrine. Tertullian (*apol.* 21) says that the wise men of the heathen agreed that Logos, that is Sermo and Ratio, was the Artificer of the universe. Both Justin and Clement assign the name of Logos to Hermes the interpreter of the gods. The reference is probably in each case to Stoic allegories, by which the various pagan deities were resolved into one general element of divine power.

Valentinus reckons Logos as the fifth in his series of æons, and is also stated (Hipp. *ref.* 6.42.2) to have claimed a special revelation from Logos. It was not Logos, however, according to the Valentinian school, who became incarnate: Ptolemæus, indeed, said that it was the Logos of His celestial mother Sophia which descended on Jesus at His baptism (Hipp. *ref.* 6.35.6). Marcus involved the system of Valentinus in a complex series of alphabetical speculations, in which Logos played a crucial part as the instrument of divine self-expression (Iren. *haer.* 1.14.1). He also called all the æons indifferently by that name, and by other descriptions such as roots, seeds, and fruits (*ib.* 1.14.2, cf. Clem. *exc. Theod.* 25.1). In the system of the Peratic Ophites, the Logos is identified with the second of the triad of Father, Son, and Matter (Hipp. *ref.* 5.17.2). But in general the queer speculations of the Gnostics had little bearing on the development either of orthodox or of normally heretical theology.

Nevertheless, it was in keeping with the whole trend of thought which was most characteristically expressed in Gnosticism that the Son and the Holy Spirit should be definitely subordinated to the Father. And although the Logos doctrine was worked out, in some sense at least, as an answer to Gnosticism from the side of Christian philosophy, a certain subordinationist emphasis was imported into theology, and, once established in the tradition, though it was balanced by other elements, of which it will be necessary to treat in due course, proved hard to eradicate. Even

Hippolytus is capable of writing in such a strain as the following (*c. Noet.* 10, 11). As the author and counsellor and framer of the things that were being created, God begat the Logos; this Logos He possessed in Himself, and as it was invisible to the world then in process of creation, He made it visible, uttering His first voice; and begetting Him as light out of light, He projected Him as Lord to the creation. His own Mind, which was first visible to Himself alone, and invisible to the world then in process of coming into being, He made visible, in order that through its manifestation the world might see it and be capable of salvation; and thus a second stood beside Him. But in saying 'second,' Hippolytus is careful to add that he does not mean to imply two gods, but "as light out of light." For there is one Power which proceeds from the sum of things; the sum is the Father, out of which the Power is the Logos; and this is the Mind which came forth into the world and was manifested as the Son of God. Such a theory, transferred from the sphere of creation to that of redemption, would lend obvious support to the Adoptionist speculations of Paul of Samosata, though there is no evidence that he ever actually dallied with the jargon of 'word-immanent' and 'word-expressed.'

It has already been indicated that Eusebius denounced that theory, even before he found out its affinity with certain aspects of the thought of Marcellus. But in his own speculations he clearly represents a tradition which was strongly subordinationist, and it would not be impossible to make against him a colourable accusation of ditheism. His subordinationism was derived from Origen, the father alike of Arian heresy and of Nicene orthodoxy. Origen insisted most emphatically on the distinct and concrete individuality of the Son, and stressed no less emphatically the gulf which separates the triad of the godhead from all created beings. He nevertheless permitted himself to utter some extraordinarily strong statements of the subordination of the Spirit and the Logos. He says, it is true (*de princ.* 1.3.7), that his theory of the Father showering His benefits on all creation, of the Son extending His operations only to the world of rational beings, and of the Holy Spirit confining His grace to the sanctification of the righteous, must not be taken as implying that a higher worth attaches to the Holy Spirit than to the Father and the Son. It merely represents the special method adopted in the administration of grace. Furthermore, there is no greater or less (maius minusve) to be distinguished in describing the triad, since one fount of deity sustains the universe by His own Word and Reason, and sanctifies by "the Spirit of His own mouth" (psalm xxxiii.6) those that are worthy of sanctification.

Nevertheless, referring to the text, "the Father that sent me is greater than I," and to our Lord's refusal of the title "good," as addressed to Himself in distinction from the Father (*St. Mark* x.18), although he asserts that the Saviour and the Holy Spirit transcend all created beings incomparably by an illimitable transcendence, he proceeds to state that the Son is transcended by the Father in as great a degree, or even greater, than that by which He Himself and the Holy Spirit transcend the best of other beings (on *St. John* 13.25, 151). And he continues (*ib.* 152) that, though the Son transcends all thrones and dominions, and every name that is named in this world or the world to come, in substance and dignity and power and divinity and wisdom, yet He is not to be compared in any respect to the Father. For in relation to the Father the Logos is but an image of His goodness and an effulgence, not, strangely enough, of God, but only of His glory and His eternal light; faithfully as He mirrors God the Father, He is but a mirror. The only justification which can be made on orthodox lines for such an outburst, is that what Origen has in mind is quite strictly the 'monarchy.' In so far as the Logos enjoys and reveals the glory of the divine nature, He displays a richness which is not His own by origin, and to that extent He is incomparable with the Father, from whom the glory is derived. But this is not to say that the glory as derived is any whit less than the glory as exhibited in its source. The Logos is no less God by reason of the fact that He is not the source of deity. And so it is possible to square the assertions of this passage with the previous statement that in connection with the triad there is neither greater nor less.

Unfortunately the tale of Origen's indiscretions is not yet complete. It appears from a fragment of the *de principiis* (4.4.1, or according to the old enumeration 4.28), preserved with jealous orthodoxy by the Emperor Justinian and printed in the Berlin edition, that Origen positively called the Logos a created being ($\kappa\tau\iota\sigma\mu\alpha$). This Son, he says—and it is obvious why Rufinus softened the passage with a judicious paraphrase—came into being out of the will of the Father; He is the first-born of all creation, a created being, Wisdom; for Wisdom herself says, "God created me in the beginning of His ways" (*Prov.* viii.22). If this extract is genuine and literally accurate, the statement is, indeed, a serious matter; but even in the same context the erring Origen stoutly denies the truth of the formula which was afterwards adopted by Arius, that there was a time when He was not. Since this denial both occurs in the Greek fragment and is twice repeated in the translation presented by Rufinus, there is at any rate no doubt about its genuineness. We do not state, says Origen, in accordance with the views of heretics, that any part of the substance of God was converted into the Son, or that the Son was begotten by the Father from non-existent elements, that is to say, outside His own substance, in such manner that there was ever a time when the Son was not. Origen held a species of subordinationism, but he was most certainly no Arian.

His difficulty arose in some part from the attempt, which was universal both among the Fathers and among the heretics, to build his theology on literal texts of Scripture, which on a modern critical view would not be held to have any direct application to the matter in hand. The texts chosen were sometimes convenient in certain respects for the work of supporting orthodox arguments, while in other respects they presented decided difficulties. Origen was not the man to shrink from difficulties, and if Scripture said that the Lord created Wisdom, and ecclesiastical tradition identified Wisdom with the Logos, his bold speculative intellect was quite prepared to assert that the Logos was indeed created. This admission, however, would need to be taken in conjunction with other statements made else-where, of which the effect would be enormously to qualify the seriousness of the assertion. Origen might not flinch from admitting that the Scripture called the Logos a created being; but what the Scripture really meant by that expression is a highly complicated question, and what Origen thought the Scripture meant must be deduced from a general survey of the substance of his thought.

But the main source of his difficulty lay in the fact that no satisfactory distinction had as yet been clearly drawn between derivation and creation. So long as the ultimate deity was regarded as a unitary being, this deficiency led to no serious consequences, because every object to which an origin could be ascribed was also a creature. It was only when the deity came to be regarded as a triad, and a second and a third Person came to be distinguished within the divine being itself, that any problem of derivation, as distinct from creation, could possibly arise. This problem, therefore, is specifically a problem of Christian theology. How can the triad be reconciled with the monarchy, so long as the triad is a real and permanent triad?

We have seen that Origen, in a passage of not undoubted authenticity, expressly refers to the divine Son as a creature. The expression, however, if it is genuine, quite certainly did not arise from the theologian's own speculation, but was forced upon him by an inconvenience of Biblical interpretation. The term which he does in fact employ, with reference to the Son and the Holy Spirit, when his thought is independent of Biblical presuppositions, is not creature ($\kappa\tau\iota\sigma\mu\alpha$) but 'genetos.' Thus on *St. John* (2.28, 172), where he is discussing the depth of the mysteriousness of God, he remarks that the full knowledge of Him cannot be grasped by human nature, and perhaps not by any other geneta beyond Christ and the Holy Spirit.

This is a very significant remark to make. It is strongly monarchical in that it places the mysteries of the divine being in the Father alone. It is also strongly subordinationist, at any rate to this extent, that it ranks all beings, whether creatures or divine, in a hierarchy of existence, rising from rational humanity through the spiritual creation of angels and similar celestial beings to the Holy Spirit and Christ, and so to God the Father; the line between geneta and God is firmly drawn at a point which leaves Christ and the Holy Spirit on the same side as created ministers and human beings. On the other hand, it is assumed without a peradventure that Christ and the Holy Spirit stand by themselves, in a class in which their full apprehension of the being of God is unquestionable. It is possible that the angels may see into these mysteries, though by no means certain: but it is quite certain that Christ and the Holy Spirit can. So once more, even in this unpromising context, we are brought back to a firm recognition of the triad.

Again, the passage has already been quoted (*ib.* 13.25, 151), in which at one and the same time the Saviour and the Holy Spirit are said to transcend all geneta, though they are themselves transcended in an even higher degree by the Father. On a superficial view, it might easily seem that Origen meant to imply that the Son and the Spirit are creatures. The term geneton is, of course, regularly used to describe creatures in contrast to the agenetos, who is God. Not only is the term employed as a description of creatures, implying the secondary and contingent character of the creaturely nature: it is perhaps the most common title under which they are mentioned. Ageneton was so universally assumed to provide an accurate and sufficient equivalent of deity, that geneta, which strictly speaking ought only to convey descriptively a fact about the origin of creatures, acquired general currency as a common title for them. It is not therefore surprising that Epiphanius, with his anti-Origenistic zeal for orthodoxy, which recognised the ample provision that Origenism had made of munitions for Arian artillery, but not the equally important influence of Origen on the Cappadocian Fathers who had confuted Arianism, roundly asserts (*haer.* 64.8.3) that it is obvious that Origen, by calling the Son 'genetos theos,' meant to define Him as a creature.

But this inference was utterly false. In the second of the catena fragments of Origen on *St. John*, which are printed in Preuschen's edition, he even denies that the Logos was genetos. He quotes the text, "that which came to be in Him was life, and the life was the light of men." His comment is as follows. Just as God brought all things into existence, so those objects, whose nature it was to live, were made alive by participation in the Logos. No attention must be paid to people who hold, on the basis of this text, that the Logos is genetos. Anything which has 'come to be' is not in itself life. But the possession of life did not come upon the Logos from without, but "in Him was life." Unlike creatures, the Logos is Life intrinsically, in the same sense as the Father—not that the Father derives His life by participation in the life of the Logos, but God, who is Life, begets Life. Here we are clearly back again in the triad of absolute deity.

Once more, when Origen is again discussing the mysteriousness of the divine being (*c. Cels.* 6.17 ad fin.), and emphasising the fact that no one can grasp it who does not possess the Spirit that searcheth all things, even the deep things of God, he maintains that our Saviour and Lord, the Logos of God, alone rightly grasps and understands the vastness of the knowledge of the Father, though in a secondary sense it may be grasped by those whose minds are enlightened by God the Word Himself. No one, he quotes, knows the Son except the Father, nor the Father except the Son and those to whomsoever the Son shall reveal Him. For neither can anybody rightly know "the agenetos, and first-born of all genetos nature" as does the Father that begat Him, nor can anybody rightly know the Father as does His living Logos and Wisdom and Truth. It may be that, in here calling the Son the first-born of genetos nature, Origen intends to imply that the Son Himself falls in the same category of geneta, especially in view of the other passages which have been quoted to that effect. But it is undeniable that the inclusion of the Logos in this category is consistent with his inclusion, at the same time, in the category of ageneton, since that attributive of deity is expressly applied to Him in the same context of a single phrase.

It must be perfectly obvious that, if the Logos is both agenetos and genetos, the one word cannot imply just the plain negative of the other word. He is agenetos or uncreated because He belongs to the triad of deity, and uncreated life is the substance of His being. On the other hand, He is genetos or derivative because He is not Himself the source and origin of that being, but derives it from the Father. The two statements are thus not in the least inconsistent. What was needed in order to avoid any appearance of inconsistency was merely a clear definition of the terms, not in their philological sense, but in the logical sense in which they were employed in common usage. This task was in fact accomplished by Athanasius a century later. Origen's thought was sufficiently clear, as appears from an impartial study, but the absence of clear, formal definition left the subject still involved in some obscurity and difficulty.

Eusebius, permeated with the Origenistic tradition, but not possessed of so clear a head or such a powerful capacity for theological reasoning as his master, added nothing to the solution of the difficulty. Sometimes he distinguishes Christ from the geneta, sometimes he includes Him among them, sometimes he hesitates about the right method of classifying the Logos, or, while calling Him genetos, distinguishes Him from the remaining geneta, which derived their existence out of the non-existent. It will be remembered how firmly Origen had expressed, even among the daring speculations of the *de principiis*, his profound sense of the difference which was constituted by the derivation of the being of the Logos from the existing substance of the Father, in contrast to the creatures formed out of the non-existent.

In one of his later writings (*eccl. theol.* 1.8.2-3), Eusebius moves towards a solution of his difficulties in the statement that the Church believes in one God, Father and Almighty, the Father of the one sole Christ, but of all remaining beings the God and Creator and Lord. In proceeding to speak of the Son, he discards genetos as the term to express derivation, and, rather ingeniously, employs the term gennetos (begotten), which, apart from the forgotten heresies of Gnosticism, was free from the necessarily creaturely associations of the other word. So, he says, the being of the Son was not similar to that of the remaining genneta, nor did He live a life like that of those begotten through Him; alone He had been engendered out of the very Father, and was absolute Life. He even proceeds to distinguish the Son from geneta, when he observes that it befitted the supreme God to project this only-begotten offspring (gennema) before any geneton and before all ages. But his fumbling theology afforded great encouragement to the Arians.

The problem still continued to cause trouble for many years. The Son and the Holy Spirit had been regarded both as ageneta and also, in some sense, as geneta, by Origen. Origen's followers on the orthodox side were gradually compelled to deny the second half of this statement, particularly when the Arians seized upon it as a clinching reason for denying the first half of the statement. The fact still remained, however, that the Son and the Holy Spirit in one sense possessed an arche (source) and in another sense did not possess an arche (beginning). The universally accepted principle of the monarchy required that their arche should be found in the Father. In that sense arche means source. On the other hand, since they were God, they were eternal, from everlasting and to everlasting. They had no temporal 'beginning,' and in that sense they did not possess an arche. Gregory of Nazianzus (*or.* 25.15 fin.) states the situation very neatly. Writing of the Son and Spirit, he observes that they are not anarcha, and yet in a sense they are anarcha; which, he adds, sounds paradoxical. They are not anarcha in respect of causation, for they are out of God, even though they are not after God—like light from the sun—but they are anarcha in respect of temporality, for they are not subject to time.

Another form in which the problems of the monarchy exemplify themselves may be seen in connection with the Platonistic expression 'second god.' As soon as the triad was recognised in substance, and even before it came to be expressed in the formal term triad, it was inevitable that the words 'second' and 'third' should occasionally be employed with reference to the Son and the Spirit. Thus, Justin (*apol.* 1.13.3) had remarked that Christians recognised in the second place the Son of the very God, and, in the third grade, the prophetic Spirit. Elsewhere (*dial.* 56.4) he said that he would attempt to prove, on the basis of Scriptural authority, that there exists, and is acknowledged, another (ἕτερος, second) God and Lord in succession to the Maker of the universe, beyond whom there is no other (ἄλλος, different) God. A certain amount of arithmetic was inevitable in connection with a divine being who was only recognisable in a threefold presentation, however strongly the Fathers might assert that enumeration was out of place in reference to Him. Such language, inevitable as it was, could hardly fail to be linked by any devout Platonist with the speculations of his master. Plato, in the *Republic*, had designated the universe the "divine child" (θεῖον γεννητόν), and again, in the *Timæus*, he had called the world "the image of its Maker, only-begotten," and referred to it as being itself a "perceivable god" (θεὸς αἰσθητός). He did not actually call it a "second god," but Philo does apply this term to his Logos, and in doing so reproduces the meaning, if not the actual words, of the *Timæus*.

˙ Origen dallies for a moment with this conception (*c. Cels.* 5.39). Even if we assert a 'second god,' he says, let it be understood that the second god, which we assert, is nothing other than the Virtue which embraces all virtues, and the Logos which embraces all logos of whatsoever description in all natural objects. This expression was adopted by Eusebius and employed by him with considerable freedom. Thus in the *preparatio evangelica* (7.12, 320C) he writes that the Old Testament Scriptures introduce, after the anarchos being of the God of the universe, a second being and divine power, the arche of the geneta. It is worth noticing, incidentally, that in this passage, as frequently elsewhere, the word 'ousia' (here translated 'being') is used in a particular and not in a generic sense. The "second being," who comes "after the being of the God of the universe," is simply a second presentation of deity, not a lower grade of deity or demi-god-substance. In other words, Eusebius is merely calling attention to the fact that as the Father is the arche of the Son, so the Son is the arche of creatures, without reference to the respective likeness and difference in substance between the source and its product in either case.

He develops the subject of the Second God in the *demonstratio evangelica* (5.4.9-14). The true and sole God, he argues, must be one, and alone properly receives that title. The Second God achieves His association with the true God by participation; He is not reckoned God at all apart from the Father; He abides with the Father, and is made divine out of Him and through Him. He enjoys both His being, and His being God, not from Himself but from the Father. We have been taught to honour Him, too, as God, after the Father, on account of God dwelling in Him. Yet He is by nature both God and only-begotten Son, and is not adopted like those outside the godhead, who enjoy the title of 'god' only as an acquired privilege. Still, though He is dignified with the titles 'only-begotten Son' and 'our God' by nature, He is not the First God, but the first, only-begotten, Son of God, and only God on that account. For the one bestows, the other receives, so that, properly speaking, the former is the one God, both because He alone exists of His own nature and because He does not receive from another; but the latter enjoys second rank, and, since He receives from the Father the fact that He is God, He possesses this as Image of God. One godhead is discernible in both, as in the given illustration of an object and its image; but the one God is He who is of Himself, without arche and without origination (ἀνάρχως καὶ ἀγενήτως), and is contemplated through the Son as through a mirror and image.

Eusebius returns to the subject a little later (*ib.* 5.8.2). Although we confess two Lords, he says, yet we do not employ similar explanations of deity ('theologies') in the case of both. As piety requires, we place them in order. We have been taught that the supreme Father and God and Lord is also the God and Lord of the Second, and that the Word of God is the Second Lord, the master of all that is beneath Him, but not in like manner master of Him who is greater than He. For God the Word is not the Lord of the Father nor the God of the Father, but His Image and Word and Wisdom and Power. He is the Master and Lord and God of those that come after Him; but the Father is the Father and God and Lord of the Son. Hence they are referred to a single arche and the conclusions of a pious account of deity imply a single God.

This somewhat one-sided exposition is clearly to be connected with Origen's statement of the inferiority of the Son to the Father, but with this qualification, that in some measure Origen was led to his position by consideration of their operation or manifestation to creatures, while Eusebius appears to rest his argument more whole-heartedly upon the essential relations of the Father and the Logos. For

M

instance, after the lapse of time between Origen and himself, it is rather more significant that Eusebius should have committed himself to such a statement as the following (*dem. ev.* 5.6.4): the supreme God is not 'the first of the geneta,' since He has no conceivable arche and is beyond and above the 'first' of any numerable series; He Himself begat and gave substance to the numerical 'first'; hence it is the divine Word who is called the first of all the geneta. However, Eusebius' ultimate position is substantially orthodox (cf. *eccl. theol.* 2.17.1-3) though it is interesting to observe that Marcellus accused him in plain terms of precisely that combination of excessive subordinationism and ditheism which in fact constituted the heresy of Arius (ap. Eus. *c. Marc.* 1.4.40)—"he has dared to divide the Word from God and to call the Word another God, separate in substance and power from the Father." And he adds the caustic comment, that "the teaching of Eusebius is similar to that of Valentinus and 'Hermes.' "

In connection with the Second God theory, logically, and to some extent also historically, may be taken the distinction between 'God' (θεός, used without the definite article) and 'the God' (ὁ θεός, with the addition of the article). The difference may be indicated in English by contrasting the phrases "a divine being" and "the supreme being." This distinction also has its origin in Philo (*quod a deo somnia*, Mangey 1.655 line 20), and it is again Origen who takes it up and imports it into Christian theology. He distinguishes (on *St. John* 2.2, 17-18) between the supreme being, who is absolute God (autotheos), and the Logos. All that is deified, he observes, by participation in the godhead of the autotheos, ought more properly to be called not 'ὁ θεός' but 'θεός', and in that category the most honourable is the first-born of all creation, since He first, by being "with God," drew godhead unto Himself. The Logos who was "with God" is the archetypal image of all subsequent images. He was in the beginning, and because He was with God ever remains theos. But He would not have acquired that character had He not been "with God," and would not have remained theos had He not been abiding in the uninterrupted vision of the Father's profundity.

And again Eusebius takes up the tale, writing (*eccl. theol.* 2.14.3): when you hear the Logos called God by the evangelist, you are not to understand him as intending to imply that the Logos is anarchos and unbegotten like His Father, but that He was in arche. (Eusebius is taking the phrase, "He was in the beginning," as if it really meant "He was in a source.") What the evangelist meant by this reference to the arche, he continues, is clear from the form of the words that follow. He did not say, "and the Word was the theos," with the addition of the article, to avoid making Him out the supreme being; nor did he say, "the Word was in God," to avoid reducing Him to the human similitude (i.e. making Him out a mere 'word-immanent'); but he said, "and the Word was with God." Eusebius recurs to the subject later (*ib.* 2.17.2), saying that, if the evangelist had been composing his gospel in a sense agreeable to the mind of Marcellus, he would have been bound to write either "the Word was God's," or else "the Word was the theos," with the addition of the article; but as it is, he indicates that the Word Himself was God in a similar manner to the God with whom He was. There the matter rested; after the growth and overthrow of Arianism the speculation was not pursued further. But one rather interesting reference to it is preserved. Cyril (on *St. John* 1109C) recalls, quite accurately, the textual point that in *St. John* xx.28 our Lord is called 'the theos' by St. Thomas, when he said, after the Resurrection, "my Lord and my God" (ὁ κύριός μου καὶ ὁ θεός μου). This was written, Cyril claims, to prevent anybody thinking that Christ was Lord and God (without the articles) only in the same sense as that in which the holy angels are sometimes dignified by those titles.

Considering the large area of common ground which seemed to exist between Catholic subordinationists, like Origen and Eusebius, and the genuine Arians, and in view of certain close verbal resemblances between the forms in which they clothed their respective systems of thought, it is not at all surprising that an untrained and unphilosophical thinker like Constantine took the original quarrel between Arius and Alexander to be a mere question of words: "Having made a careful inquiry into the origin and foundation of these differences, I find the cause to be of a truly insignificant character and quite unworthy of such fierce contention," wrote the Thirteenth Apostle in a letter addressed jointly to Bishop Alexander and Presbyter·Arius (ap. Eus. *vit. Const.* 2.68). After all, Gibbon, who had vastly fuller opportunities than Constantine of discovering the real matters at issue during the controversies of the fourth century, thought that the whole difference between the two parties was merely a question of adding or subtracting a single letter of the alphabet.

Alexander and the orthodox said that the Arians were putting forward a theory which, in effect, combined the views of Jewish unitarians and pagan polytheists. Though the Church was, indeed, somewhat intolerant both of Jews and of heathen (not without good reason found by practical experience), this criticism of Arianism was by no means vulgar abuse. Arius, though he recognised the divine Son as an inferior deity, reduced the Logos to an impersonality; and by worshipping Christ, whom he regarded as a demi-god of different substance from that of the Father, he put himself in the same position as the polytheists.

Athanasius not only quotes some invaluable extracts from early Arian writings, but also gives some general indications of the kind of argument on which they relied. They asked, for instance (ap. Ath. *c. Ar.* 2.34), how the Son could always have existed with the Father; sons never are as old as their fathers; a father is thirty years old when he begets his son; it is true of every son that "he was not, before his generation." In other words, the Arians pressed the metaphor of paternity and sonship as rigorously as it was possible to press the statements of Scriptures conceived with Fundamentalistic literalism. Orthodox thinkers did much the same, it is true; but their Fundamentalism was tempered by their acceptance of allegorical methods of interpretation, and they showed a far profounder sense of the need to interpret the Scriptures as a whole by comparing one passage with another. The Arians on the other hand, like most people of schismatical temper, really neglected the Bible in order to concentrate on a few selected texts.

Asterius, a trimmer who had offered the heathen sacrifice during the persecutions and was equally ready to advance concessions to the Catholic party during the Arian controversy, though he seems to have been Arius' most indefatig-able and fertile pamphleteer, invented a distinction between

"Power of God" and "the Power of God" similar to that between 'theos' and 'the theos' (ib. 2.37): blessed Paul did not say that he preached "Christ The Power of God, or The Wisdom of God," but without the addition of the article, "God's Power and God's Wisdom." The apostle's meaning was, on this interpretation, that the proper power of God Himself, which is natural to Him and co-existent in Him ingenerately, is something else other than Christ, though, indeed, generative of Christ and creative of the whole world; there were many embodiments of this impersonal Power and Wisdom of God, and among them Christ was only the most prominent and most powerful; but the real and ultimate Power and Wisdom was an impersonal quality of the Father.

Again, we hear echoes of the 'Logos-immanent' theory. How can the Son be Logos, or how can the Logos be the Image of God? for the logos of men is composed of syllables, and only signifies the will of the speaker, and then is over and lost (ap. Ath. c. Ar. 2.34). This argument was formally developed by the later Arian Eunomius (ap. Cyr. on St. John 31A), who states that the Son is other than the Word-immanent or Word in ideal activity; the Son is the Word-expressed who is called Word because He participates in, and is filled with, the Word-immanent, and is declarative of the Father's being. (Again, it is very interesting to observe the absence of prejudice which enables Cyril, thesaurus 4, 31 D, E, and again ib. 6, 47 E, to employ this very conception in order to illustrate certain aspects of the orthodox doctrine of the Logos.) Once more, it was said (ap. Ath. c. Ar. 2.37) that, when the Son is called Logos, the title is a mere metaphor, just as when He is called Vine or Way or

Door; the only real Logos is the impersonal Logos. Further (*ib.* 1.9) Christ is not very God, but, like others, was made God by participation; the Son does not have exact knowledge of the Father, nor see the Father perfectly, nor exactly understand or know the Father; He is not the veritable and sole Word of the Father, but is only called Word and Wisdom in name. He is only called Son and Power by grace. As Athanasius comments, He is merely a partaker of the true Wisdom, and 'second' to it.

Eunomius, again, the systematic expositor of later extreme Arianism, develops on more formal lines the substance of earlier Arian argument in connection with the time relation and the eternal pre-existence of the Son (*lib. apol.* 13), maintaining that objects which are in existence do not need to be begotten, and that, if the Son existed before His begetting, He must have been unbegotten. The supreme contribution of Origen to the doctrine of the Logos, that the begetting of the Son was not an event in time, but represents an eternal process within the eternal being of God, no less actual at this moment than it was before the worlds were made, seems entirely to have escaped the notice of the Arians, who drew so heavily from other aspects of his thought when he was maintaining the principles of extreme subordinationist theory. All that Eunomius was concerned to emphasise was the qualification expressed in his statement (*lib. apol.* 27), "saving in all things and at all times the 'transcendence' and 'monarchy' of God, since the Holy Spirit is subjected with all else to Christ, and the Son Himself to God the Father." In support of this opinion he quotes the obvious and rather awkward text 1 *Cor.* xv. 28, "then shall the Son also himself be subjected to him that did subject all things unto him, that God may be all in all."

The Arians once again, in order to perfect their comprehensive acceptance of every aspect of subordinationist heresy that could be extracted from their predecessors, asserted that the Son originally was not, but came into being by the will of the Father (Arius ap. Ath. *de syn.* 15). It has already been pointed out how this conception, that the Son's being was dependent on an act of the paternal divine will, lent itself to exploitation by the more extreme forms of subordinationism, and how more orthodox writers avoided any such expression by a positive identification of the Logos with the paternal Will. Even the semi-Arians of the *Macrostich* (ap. Ath. *de syn.* 26) denounced those who should incautiously assert that the Son was begotten not by purpose nor will, because, in their opinion, such a conviction involved God in an act which was purposeless and involuntary, as if He had begotten the Son against His will, by an act of necessity.

Athanasius attributes this idea to Arian study of the Gnostics. He writes (*c. Ar.* 3.60) that Ptolemæus, the follower of Valentinus, ascribed to the agenetos a pair of attributes, Thought and Will; first He thought and then He willed, and what He thought He could not project, except when the power of the will was added. The Arians, according to Athanasius, took a lesson from this, and desired to prove that an act of will and a process of purpose preceded the Logos. He gives his own answer to this argument a few sections later (*ib.* 3.64), where he shows that, if the whole creation was made by an act of will "at God's good pleasure," and if, further, all things have come into being through the Logos, He is external to the things which have come into existence by act of will, and is Himself rather the Living

Counsel of the Father, by which all these things have come to be; how, then, he asks, can the Logos, being the Counsel and Will of the Father, come into being Himself by an act of will and purpose?

But the supreme scandal of Arian theology was its misuse of biological language to express the act of creation. It used to be thought, for instance by Dr. Robertson in his translation and edition of Athanasius, that the earlier Arians argued mainly from agenetos, though the later Arians, such as Aëtius and Eunomius, argued from agennetos. This view rested on the acceptance of Lightfoot's theory that a clear distinction had always been preserved between the two senses and two spellings of the word agen(n)etos. Reason has been given in Chapter II (compare also the full examination of evidence, by the present author, in *The Journal of Theological Studies* xxiv. p. 486 and xxxiv. p. 258), for supposing that Lightfoot was entirely mistaken in his belief. On the whole, the evidence, which is rather difficult and confusing, seems to indicate that from the first the Arians argued from agennetos.

There is considerable authority—which scarcely appears in the printed editions (even those critically edited in modern times) until reference is made to the notes recording the readings of manuscripts, unaltered by editorial correction —for a usage, according to which agennetos was contrasted with genetos. This usage fell in admirably with Arian preconceptions. It was common ground with all parties that the Father alone was agennetos, and Origen at least had attempted to indicate the derivative character of the Son's being by calling Him genetos, though he meant by this that the Son was not anarchos, not that the Son was a creature.

The Arians joyfully adopted this terminology, and used it to imply that the Father alone was uncreated, and that the Son indeed was a creature. To the Arian mind gennema (offspring) was exactly equivalent to poiema (thing made, or handiwork), and even gennetos (begotten) was exactly equivalent to ktistos (created). The early Arians, with the exception of Asterius, do not, indeed, seem to have called Christ directly genetos, though they call Him by every possible equivalent term. Asterius quite frankly called Him the first of the geneta. When Athanasius had argued against Asterius and his friends that there was a sense in which it was not only proper but necessary to call Christ agenetos, the later Arians did not trouble to attempt a proof that He was genetos, but instead made great play with the corresponding word gennetos.

The implication of their argument is this, that in opposition to Athanasius they denied the existence of any essential difference between the two senses or spellings of agen(n)etos, and in order to be logical, they had to extend the scope of their denial from the privative term agen(n)etos to the positive gen(n)etos. Aetius (ap. Epiph. *haer.* 76.12) reproduces, in a clearer form, the old Arian thought that agennesia (ingeneracy) is not a fact about the subject, but a quality of the substance. He asserts, for instance (*cap.* 4), that, if God persists continuously in his agennetos nature, and His offspring (gennema) is continuously an offspring, their respective substances are strictly incomparable, and the Son is neither 'of the same substance' nor even 'of like substance' with the Father; and (*cap.* 5) that it is blasphemous to maintain "the same substance to be both gennetos and agennetos." Consequently, agennetos and agenetos are more closely identified than ever, and the admitted fact that the Son was gennetos is proof positive that He cannot be uncreated, or anything other than a handiwork of God. The thought of Eunomius moves on a similar plane. He understands by agennetos everything that was involved in the agenetos of the philosophical schools, and for him the fact that the Son was begotten was final proof that the Son was a creature.

These facts make it plain why the Catholics were unable to accept without qualification certain formulæ proposed in semi-Arian quarters, such as the statement of the *Macrostich* itself, which seems superficially to be unexceptionable. The disingenuous ambiguity of such formulæ was at last observed by the semi-Arians themselves, as for instance in the joint manifesto of Basil of Ancyra and George of Laodicea, preserved by Epiphanius (*haer.* 73). The equivocal character of all such language as the Arians used is here clearly recognised, and the fact is emphasised that it was as entirely unscriptural as any of the technical terms adopted by the Catholics. It was at long last seen that if scriptural terms were capable of being expounded in diametrically opposite meanings, philosophical analysis was needed to define precisely how Scripture ought to be understood. In other words, theology does not consist in the parrot repetition of Biblical texts, but in rational thought about Biblical data.

The divine begetting of the Son had early been described, as for instance by Hippolytus (*c. Noet.* 10), in such terms as that the Father, begetting Light out of Light, projected It as lord to the creation. It will be noticed that the relation between Son and Father is compared to that between light and light· a continuous process is hinted at, if not expressly stated, since the projection of ray from sun (*ib.* 11 init.) is a continuous process. Origen takes up the notion (*de princ.* 1.2.4), pointing out that the difference between divine generation and human generation is as great as that between deity and humanity; therefore the Son's generation is eternal and everlasting, just as the radiance is continuously generated from the light. Again (on *Jerem.* 9.4), he illustrates from the divine generation of the Son the continuous generation of the just by God and of the unjust by the devil; in each case there is a process involved, which is continued by every act of righteousness or sin: and this is reasonable, because the Father did not once for all beget the Son and then dismiss Him from His generation, but He ever begets Him. The Saviour is the effulgence of divine glory; but it is not the nature of effulgence once to be begotten and then to cease to be begotten; so the effulgence of the glory of God continues to be begotten for as long as the light is creative of effulgence. So Eusebius recognises (*eccl. theol.* 1.8.3) that God was begetting the Son before all the things that were intended to be, like a ray from a light. It remained for Athanasius to point out the significance of such a gennema in terms of philosophy (*c. Ar.* 1.16). Necessarily, he says, the Son is that which is derived out of the being of the Father and wholly belongs to Him; it is all one to say that God is entirely participated, and to say that He begets. He contrasts gennema, therefore, with genetos (*c. Ar.* 1.31): if God is agenetos, then His Image is not genetos, but gennema. And (*ib.* 1.28) the Son is gennema belonging to the Father, wherefore the Father was ever Father; His fatherhood is not adventitious. In plain language, it belongs to His character eternally and unalterably.

To the Arians, on the other hand, gennema meant the same as ktisma (creature). It is worth recalling that gennema was constantly used in patristic writings of inanimate objects, and that the parellel word genema (product) hardly ever, if at all, occurs. Arius therefore (ap. Ath. *c. Ar.* 2.19, *de syn.* 16) called the Son ktisma, though not as one of the ktismata, and gennema, though not as one of the gennemata. Asterius (*ib.* 3.60) called Him the first gennema; on which Athanasius comments that Asterius had committed the blasphemy of making gennema and poiema identical, and regarding the Son as a mere specimen out of all existent gennemata. Aëtius (*cap.* 7, ap. Epiph. *haer.* 76.12) argued that if God is wholly agennetos, he cannot have begotten 'substantially' (i.e. have produced a gennema of His own substance); such a process would involve division of His substance; His 'gennema' therefore was brought into being by an act of creative authority. Finally, Eunomius (*lib. apol.* 17) describes the Son as the gennema and poiema of the Agennetos and Apoietos.

In fact, there was substance in the taunt of Athanasius that the Arians shared their ideas with the Gnostics. The Gnostics seem to have been the first people who consistently imported biological language into the discussion of theological facts. In sympathy with much which had appeared in Gnosticism, the Arians concentrated their attention largely on the cosmic functions of the Logos rather than on the nature of the being of God. The Son, says Eunomius (*lib. apol.* 27), was a most perfect assistant for all creative activity, for the constitution and continuance of the things that are, for divine dispensation and all providential process. The original Arian objection to the admission of the full divinity of Christ gradually developed, as it was bound to do, into the contention that He was not divine at all. And behind all expression of Arian thought lay the hard and glittering syllogism that God is impassible; Christ, being γεννητός, was passible; therefore Christ was not God.

CHAPTER VIII

INDIVIDUALITY AND OBJECTIVITY

THE point has now been reached at which it is necessary to make some investigation of the senses in which those terms were used, which finally became classical and technical in the theological exposition of Trinitarian doctrine. The first of these which needs to engage our attention is prosopon. Originally this word meant simply 'face,' and is sometimes expressly opposed to the sense of 'mask,' as when Clement (*paed.* 3.2, 11.2) inveighs against those women who by painting their countenances made their prosopa into prosopeia. From this sense various others were derived, such as the expression indicated by a person's face of his inner mind or motion, or the character which he might wish to assume, or the rôle which he intended to act. In Origen, in particular, certain mental or moral associations are sometimes implied as pertaining to the character portrayed. Later, but apparently not before the fifth century, the word comes to mean 'representative' or 'type.'

From such senses it comes to express the external being or individual self as presented to an onlooker, and of things, the expression or substance. It is fairly frequently used of particular individuals of a species, in much the same way as we speak of so many 'head' of cattle, or the 'poll' tax, and in this sense may be translated 'person' or 'party.' This usage is quite early, occurring in Clement of Rome (*Cor.* 1.1.1,

157

"a sedition which some few impetuous and rash prosopa had kindled," cf. *ib.* 47.6); Ignatius (*Magn.* 6.1, "in the aforewritten prosopa I loved the whole multitude"); Hippolytus (*frag. in Balaam*, Achelis p. 82 line 8, "it was necessary that Christ, as mediator between God and men, should receive a certain earnest from both, that He might be manifested as mediator between the two prosopa"); and elsewhere. And it persists to the end of the patristic period, John of Damascus observing (*dialectica* 43) that a prosopon means whatsoever is evidenced by its own proper activities and characteristics, and that the holy Fathers referred hypostasis (object) and prosopon (individual) and atomon (particular) to the same thing. Late writers use it with brutal impersonality of slaves; but from the time of Irenæus it is used of inanimate objects in the sense of a distinct item (*haer.* 3.11.9), the question under discussion being whether the prosopa of the Gospels might be either more or less than the orthodox four. Sometimes the qualitative aspect of the individual referred to is prominent, especially in connection with the vice of 'respecting persons' ($\pi\rho\sigma\sigma\omega\pi\sigma\lambda\eta\psi\dot{\iota}a$), which (be it said) has nothing to do with regarding their exterior, but means showing partiality to some particular 'individual'; at other times the aspect which is uppermost is purely numerical.

Passing to theology, we find that the 'face' of God, to which various Old Testament texts refer, comes to be interpeted of Christ. As Clement puts it (*paed.* 1.7, 57.2), the face of God is the Logos, by whom God is illustrated and made known. A similar thought is repeated by later writers, the idea underlying the conception being that the Son is an objective presentation of the Father. Occasionally, it is the Holy Spirit who is so-called, as by Cyril (*thes.* 34, 340C), who remarks that the Spirit is entitled the Face of the Father because He images forth, by means of His divine activity, the substance out of which He is.

The corresponding term persona is applied by Tertullian to the Persons of the Trinity, in the same sense as prosopon was commonly used in Greek. The 'persona' of the treatise against Praxeas is much more the concrete presentation of an individual than, as is commonly alleged, the holder of the legal title to a hereditament. Thus, we get such phrases as (ch. 7) "the Son acknowledges the Father, speaking in His own persona"; or (*ib.*, arguing for the substantiality of the Son) "whatsoever therefore the substance of the Word was, that I call persona . . . and while I recognise the Son, I assert His distinction as second to the Father." So again, after quoting various passages, Tertullian claims that they establish the existence of each several persona in its own special character (ch. 11 fin.); and remarks that it was because the Father had at His side a second persona, His Word, and a third, the Spirit in the Word, that He said, as recorded in *Genesis*, "let us make man in our own image," using the plural form (*ib.* 12).

Prosopon does not seem to have been used in Greek with reference to the Trinity earlier than by Hippolytus. In view of the relations previously shown to have existed between the thought of Hippolytus and that of Tertullian, it seems very probable that Hippolytus was the source from which his Latin contemporary adopted the term, though Hippolytus does not actually refer to three prosopa. But he does say (*c. Noet.* 7) that the use of the word 'are' in our Lord's saying, "I and the Father are one," must refer to two prosopa, though but to a single power. Again (*ib.* 14), he observes that he does not maintain the existence of two gods, but of one, though of two prosopa and of a third economy, namely the grace of the Holy Spirit; for, he continues, the Father is one, but there are two prosopa because there is also the Son, and there is the third (τὸ δὲ τρίτον—does he mean third prosopon, or simply 'the third item'?) the Holy Spirit.

The sense in which prosopon was in fact being used is shown in an interesting manner when he is criticising Callistus for his alleged adherence to the heresy of Noetus. After describing what he states to have been the doctrine of Callistus (*ref.* 10.27.4), his comment is: "This then is one prosopon, distinguished in name, but not in substance." By 'substance' (ousia) he here means, not generic character, but distinctive individuality, in the Aristotelian sense of 'primary substance.' Since therefore the Sabellians only admitted one such 'primary substance,' or concrete presentation, in the godhead, according to Hippolytus they taught a doctrine of a single prosopon. In describing more fully the doctrine of Callistus, in an earlier passage (*ref.* 9.12.18–19), he had said that that element, according to Callistus, to which the name of Son properly belonged, was simply the visible human nature, and that the divine pneuma incarnate in this Son was really the Father, who united the manhood to Himself and deified it and made it one, so that Father and Son can be called one God: the result, being a single prosopon, cannot be two, and thus the Father suffered with the Son. Obviously, by prosopon Hippolytus meant not 'mask' but 'individual.'

Origen is another of those who state that the Sabellians

taught the doctrine of a single Person. His words only survive in a Latin translation, where persona is the term employed; but there is no reason to think that it represents anything other than prosopon in the lost original. They assert, he says (on *Tit.* ed. Ben. vol. 4.695B), that the subsistence of Father and Son is one and the same, that is to say, it receives two names secundum diversitatem causarum; but that a single hypostasis [sic, Graece] subsists, that is to say, one persona underlying the two names. Basil (*hom.* 24.1), Gregory of Nazianzus and Chrysostom all say that the Sabellians reduced the godhead to a single prosopon, though it appeared under three names. Eusebius, indeed, states (*eccl. theol.* 3.6.4) that Marcellus maintained one hypostasis triprosopos (one object with three faces); but the phrase belongs to Eusebius' comment, not to Marcellus. Basil, again, in several of his letters, accuses the Sabellians of maintaining three prosopa, in the sense of masks or stage characters; but again the description is clearly part of Basil's own comment and criticism, and had not been used by the Sabellians themselves. Nobody in fact seems to quote any such language as representing the form in which Sabellian doctrine had ever been actually taught, and most of the critics of Sabellianism positively state that those heretics denied the existence of three prosopa.

Until the middle of the third century, however, the term prosopon is sparingly used with reference to the Trinity in any sense. It is worth noticing that Origen appears to use it in the ordinary sense of individual presentation, though again the passage is only preserved in Latin. He writes (on *Cant.* 3, ed. Ben. vol. 3, 84A) that the same being who in one passage is called a triad, on account of the distinction of personæ, is in another called one God by reason of the unity of substance; and this statement is the more noteworthy in that in this commentary Origen employs the word persona with some frequency in the sense of a character or speaker in a narrative or play. Eusebius revives its use in a rather different sense, observing (*dem. ev.* 5.13.3) that in the Prophets, though a man audibly spoke, the oracle which he delivered was from God, who used him as His instrument, the prosopon who truly delivered the message being in some cases that of Christ, in others that of the Holy Spirit, and in others that of the supreme God.

However, the word does not pass into common use in Greek theology until the Arian controversy brought up the whole subject in an acute form. From that point, while those writers who, like Athanasius, flourished before the 'Cappadocian settlement,' mainly avoided the use either of prosopon or of hypostasis, and preferred to speak simply of "three" and "one," those who flourished later usually employed either term without prejudice or partiality. There does not seem to be any evidence whatever for the view that the term prosopon was ever discredited in orthodox circles at any period of theological development. On the contrary, it provided a convenient non-technical and non-metaphysical expression to describe the permanent and objective forms or Persons in which the godhead is presented alike to human vision and to the divine self-consciousness.

We may now turn to the consideration of the word 'hypostasis,' which was ultimately accepted as the technical description in Greek philosophical theology of what the Latins called the personæ of God. Apart from theology, hypostasis was used in a great variety of senses, both in the Old and New Testaments and in other writings. A wide survey of the different meanings it could bear is made by Leontius of Jerusalem (*c. Nest.* 2.1). Broadly speaking, it may be said that the purport of the term is derived in one group of usages from the middle voice of the verb ὑφίστημι, and in another from the active voice. Thus it may mean either that which underlies, or that which gives support.

In the former sense it presents some exceptionally interesting features. It is used in the *Clementine Homilies* of a sediment or deposit (*hom.* 6.7). The author is discussing the legend of Kronos, and argues that, when the primordial substance was devoured by Kronos, it sank downwards; the heaviest elements sank to the bottom and were named Pluto; after these first dregs, the water which flowed together and floated on the first hypostasis (i.e. sediment) was called Poseidon; while the element of fire which rose highest and is the source of life was called Zeus. The historian, Socrates (*h.e.* 3.7), quotes Irenæus Grammaticus for the application of the term hypostasis to the dregs of wine in the cask. There is nothing new in this usage, since Aristotle and Hippocrates are both quoted by Liddell and Scott as using the term to denote sediment. However, it also occurs in a wider sense to denote the underneath or hidden part of any object. Thus Macarius Magnes (3.43) observes that counterfeit coins, when dipped in gold, present a bright surface, but their hypostasis is base metal. So to Epiphanius a purely metaphorical use does not come amiss, when he writes (*haer.* 66. 71) that with the process of the times the hypostasis of the power of the divine commands comes to be revealed; presumably what he means is that, in the course of progressive revelation, men come to realise the hidden purpose underlying the divine commands.

In the Septuagint hypostasis is the term employed to denote the encampment of the Philistines (1 *Sam.* xiii. 23 and xiv. 4). It is also quoted from the poet Sophocles (*frag.* 644) by Irenæus Grammaticus, in the passage to which reference has already been made, in the sense of ambush. Origen (on *St. John* 2.35, 215) remarks that the directive hypostasis of Christ extends over all the world in rational souls: this appears to mean that there is an occupation of the individual human rational consciousness by the Logos, and hypostasis should therefore be translated 'seat' or 'station.'

In the light of these passages, the true interpretation becomes apparent of a very troublesome statement in Clement (*strom.* 2.18, 96.2), of which the meaning has for long presented peculiar difficulties. Clement has been discussing the humanity of the Law, and finally illustrates his point by reference to the treatment of fruit trees. They are ordered, he says, to be tended and pruned for three years. To gather fruit from immature trees is forbidden; only in the fourth year is fruit to be plucked, after the tree has attained maturity. He then proceeds to argue that this figure of husbandry should teach us to be diligent in eradicating the suckers of sin and the barren weeds of the mind, which spring up alongside the productive fruit, until the scion of faith is matured and grown strong: for in the fourth year, since time is needed also for the person under firm instruction, the quartet of virtues (i.e. spiritual states) is consecrated to God, "the third μονή uniting the neophyte to the fourth hypostasis of the Lord."

The word μονη is accented in the manuscript, and is taken by Potter (the early eighteenth-century editor), as if it were the adjective, "only"; and Potter displays amazing ingenuity in his effort to make sense of the passage. It remained for Dr. Bigg to perceive that the accentuation was at fault, and that what Clement intended was the noun, which means 'halting-place' on the Imperial post road, 'stage,' or 'mansio.' Accordingly, he explained the passage as describing three stages or mansiones, which, joining on to the 'Person' of the Lord, in the fourth place, make up the quartet of spiritual states through which the neophyte has to pass before becoming a mature disciple. It seems, however, clear from the instances which have been quoted above, that the word hypostasis is not used in this comparatively early context for the Person of Christ. Hypostasis, in fact, is here simply a synonym for μονή: after the neophyte has passed through the three preliminary mansiones or stages, he reaches the fourth and final station, which is the goal of his journey, the bosom of Christ. We need therefore not concern ourselves to argue that Clement employed a characteristically post-Nicene phrase so long before Nicæa.

Connected with this intransitive sense is a further meaning, of which the root idea is that of basis or foundation. Hence hypostasis comes to mean the raw material, stuff, or 'matter' out of which an object is constructed, and on which its particular form is imposed by the designer or craftsman. Thus, in the *Epistle to Diognetus* (2.1), the reader is asked to consider of what hypostasis or of what form they are whom the heathen regard as gods; one is made of stone like the roads underfoot, another is made of bronze like the cooking-pots in the kitchen, another is made of wood which is rotten, another is made of silver which requires a guard for its protection, another is made of iron which rusts, and another is made of earthenware the uses of which are too dishonourable to mention. Or again, Cyril of Jerusalem (*cat.* 9.10) observes that in a single tree the same hypostasis, drawing on the same physical elements of rain and soil, produces one part designed for giving shelter and another for various fruits. Or Chrysostom (*ad Theod. laps.* 1.14), commenting on physical beauty, remarks that its hypostasis is nothing else but heat and blood and fluid.

Hence hypostasis comes to mean content or substance in general. Irenæus refers (*haer.* 1.15.5) to certain Gnostic alphabetical speculations, and says that the being and hypostasis of their divinity was botched up by them out of a multitude of letters, and they are no better craftsmen than Daedalus who constructed the labyrinth. Hippolytus (*ref.* 1.8.5) says that rivers derive their hypostasis from the rainfall. Origen questions (*c. Cels.* 6.71) whether the soul of man should be resolved into fire or into the hypostasis of angels. And Cyril of Jerusalem (*cat.* 9.5) interprets the Book of Genesis as meaning that God reared the sky like a dome and formed the stable hypostasis of heaven out of the fluid nature of the primordial waters.

In connection with theology, a certain use is made of this conception as applied to the content or substance of God, corresponding to what in the case of ordinary objects constitutes their determinate extension. The principal factor in causing the application of this conception to God was probably the text *Heb.* i. 3 ("who being the effulgence of his glory and the expression of his hypostasis"), which appears to have caused considerable exegetical difficulty as soon as hypostasis began to be defined as a theological term. Origen quotes it (*de princ.* 4.4.1), asking at what time the image of the ineffable hypostasis of the Father was not in existence. Athanasius (*c. Ar.* 2.32) inquires who dares to say that the 'expression' is different from the hypostasis, and the author of the Fourth Discourse against the Arians (ch. 33) says that the 'prophet' clearly proclaimed that the Father's hypostasis belonged to Christ. Elsewhere Athanasius (*ad Afr.* 4) lays it down that hypostasis means 'being' (ousia) and has no other significance than simply "that which exists"; the hypostasis and the being mean existence, for it is, and it exists.

Epiphanius, replying to the argument of the Arians that homoousios (consubstantial) was an unscriptural term, and to their question which of the apostles mentions the 'being' (ousia) of God, asks them (*haer.* 69.72) if they do not know that hypostasis and ousia have exactly the same sense; for in His hypostasis the Lord 'is,' and the effulgence of His glory and expression of His hypostasis likewise; and quoting the Tetragrammaton, "I Am hath sent me unto you," he adds, 'He that is' means the absolute being ($\tau\grave{o}$ $\mathring{o}\nu$), and absolute being means existent ousia. Again (*anc.* 6.5), he says that the term homoousios implies the existence of a single hypostasis, yet expresses the fact that the Father is enhypostatos (concretely individual) and the Son enhypostatos and the Spirit enhypostatos. In speaking of a single hypostasis, Epiphanius here is clearly not employing the term in the ordinary technical post-Nicene sense, but the use he makes of it is interesting as illustrating in what sense substance was ascribed to God. The 'substance' of God means the divine 'content,' whether the actual term employed is ousia or hypostasis. To the mind of the Fathers, down to the time at which the terminology became fixed and technical, the practical meaning of the two terms was substantially identical. They both indicated, to take the inevitable physical metaphor, the particular slab of material stuff which constitutes a given object; and neither term is used in a generic sense.

In the case of an ordinary object of experience, such as, for instance, the Matterhorn, the stuff or substance of which it is made is simply synonymous with the object itself. The certain weight of rock and glacier, with ascertainable height and shape and volume, is the Matterhorn; and nothing which is Matterhorn is anything else than Matterhorn. Complication arose in theology because, if Christianity is true, the same stuff or substance of deity in the concrete has three distinct presentations—not just three mutually defective aspects presented from separate points of view, in the sense that the Matterhorn has a northern face and an eastern face and an Italian face, but three complete presentations of the whole and identical object, namely God, which are nevertheless objectively distinct from one another. The theological problem of the Trinity was to stereotype terms which should give clear expression to this divine paradox which was also a Christian truth.

In the beginning, as has been said, hypostasis and ousia amounted to the same thing. There was, however, another and a much more frequent use of hypostasis, in which the emphasis was different. It is important to remember that this second is the normal sense. Ousia means a single object of which the individuality is disclosed by means of internal analysis, an object abstractly and philosophically a unit.

But in the sense of hypostasis to which we shall now turn, the emphasis lay not on content, but on externally concrete independence; objectivity, that is to say, in relation to other objects. Thus, when the doctrine of the Trinity finally came to be formulated as one ousia in three hypostaseis, it implied that God, regarded from the point of view of internal analysis, is one object; but that, regarded from the point of view of external presentation, He is three objects; His unity being safeguarded by the doctrine that these three objects of presentation are not merely precisely similar, as the semi-Arians were early willing to admit, but, in a true sense, identically one. The sum 'God+God+God' adds up, not to '3 Gods,' but simply to 'God,' because the word God, as applied to each Person distinctly, expresses a Totum and Absolute which is incapable of increment either in quantity or in quality. (Cf. Maximus Conf. *ambig.* 105(b).)

The ground idea of hypostasis in this connection is the active sense of support or resistance. Thus in a late document it is actually used to paraphrase $\sigma\tau\acute{\eta}\rho\iota\gamma\mu\alpha$ (buttress). Hesychius of Jerusalem (on psalm cv. 16) after quoting the verse cited ("he brake the whole buttress of bread"), remarks, "that is to say, the whole hypostasis of food," and observes that another translator gave the reading "staff." Hypostasis here clearly means that which props or stays, and this is pretty certainly its meaning in *Ruth* i. 12 LXX ("if I should say, I have hypostasis of getting an husband, and should bear sons; would ye tarry till they were grown?"), where it expresses hope or confidence. Patristic instances of this precise sense seem to be rare, but a very good one may be found in John of Euboea (*in SS. Innoc.* 2, Migne 96. 1504B) "I have no other hope or hypostasis except this babe alone."

Hypostasis occurs more frequently in the sense of firmness, obduracy, or persistence. In the New Testament this seems to be the sense in 2 *Cor.* xi. 17, "I speak foolishly in this hypostasis of boasting," and in *Heb.* iii.14, "If we hold fast the beginning of our hypostasis firm unto the end." In the Fathers we may quote the Epistle of the Churches of Vienne and Lyons (ap. Eus. *h.e.* 5.1.20), where it is said that the martyr Sanctus set the battle against his persecutors with such hypostasis that he refused even to state his own name; and the writer Apollonius (*ib.* 5.18.10), who states that, in exposing a disciple of Montanus, named Alexander, he also exposes the hypostasis of the 'prophet' his master. From meaning support or stay, hypostasis has come to signify endurance and stiffening, or, in the last instance quoted, brass-fronted impudence. It may be mentioned, in illustration of the extent to which this sense of the word hypostasis has passed without notice, that quite recent scholars have entirely missed the point of the passage last quoted.

The next sense to be distinguished is that of "objectification," as in *Heb.* xi. 1, "faith is the hypostasis of things hoped for": the R.V. margin, "the giving substance to," is not far from the mark. Thus Tatian (*ad Gr.* 21.3) says that the gods of the heathen, such as Hera or Athene, were not, in the opinion of Metrodorus of Lampsacus (who wrote a book about Homer that Tatian thought silly), in the least what those people thought who had established temples in their honour, but were mere allegories, 'objectifications' of Nature, and decorative representations of the elements. Nilus (*ad Eul.* 11), referring to the text in *Hebrews*, defines faith as the hypostasis of better things, made in hope of permanence, and Maximus Confessor (*quaest. ad Thal.* 57, 192A) remarks that the hypostasis (realisation) of prayer and petition is their fulfilment by the exercise of the virtues.

From this use the term derives the sense of productive or effective agency, source or ground. Tatian (*ad Gr.* 5.1) calls God the hypostasis of the universe; Irenæus (*haer.* 1.1.2) refers to the primogenerative ogdoad of Valentinus as the root and hypostasis of all things, and Origen (on *St. John* 2.24, 156) calls the true Life which is imparted to rational men the hypostasis of the light of knowledge. Hence hypostasis comes to be used in the sense of origination or creation. Irenæus (*haer.* 2.14.6) distinguishes between the sources of 'substitutio' (presumably a literal equivalent in Latin for hypostasis) and those of sensible and material existence. The passage is obscure, but it is possible that Irenæus is referring to the distinction recognised in the Valentinian system, and recorded by Hippolytus (*ref.* 6.30.8), between the male element in creation, which was responsible for the form of objects, and the female element, which was responsible for their material substance, and is contrasting the act by which objects are barely caused to come into existence with the process which gives them sensible content. Origen, in a fragment on *Genesis* (quoted by Eusébius *prep. ev.* 7.20, 335B), asks how it is possible to measure the vast extent of elemental substratum sufficient for the hypostasis (creation) of such a universe as this. Eusebius (*laud. Const.* 1.5) uses the phrase, "before the entire hypostasis of visible objects." Cyril of Jerusalem (*cat.* 7.5) says that God enjoyed the title of Father and the existence of His Son before all hypostasis and before all sensation, before times and before all ages. Basil even uses the term of the eternal processes which constitute the distinct being of the Holy Spirit and of the Son, arguing (*c. Eun.* 2.32) that the whole power of the Father has been set in motion for the begetting of the Son, and in turn, the whole power of the Only-begotten for the hypostasis of the Holy Spirit; and again (*ib.* 2.13), that there is no interval between the being of the Father and the Son, and that no thought is elder than the hypostasis of the Only-begotten. In the pseudonymous work, *de hom. str.* (2.1) which goes under Basil's name, the term is applied to the creation of mankind in the phrase, "our bodily hypostasis and formation."

Finally, from creation the term derives the sense of constitutive principle, the inherent law by which objects in their creation were designed to function. Thus Athenagoras (*suppl.* 24.4) says that the fallen angels insulted the hypostasis and origin of their being. Irenæus (*haer.* 5.13.3), in speaking of the resurrection of the flesh, refers to the transformation by which it, though mortal and corruptible, becomes immortal and incorruptible, not of its own hypostasis, but by the action of the Lord. Clement (*strom.* 7.17, 107.5) claims that the historic Catholic Church, as opposed to the plurality of heresies, was by its hypostasis and purpose and origin one. Origen (on *St. John* 20.21, 174) says that the devil is falsehood, not by his hypostasis, by constitution, but because he became such by a process of change and of his own will. And other instances could be quoted to much the same effect.

We now come to the sense in which hypostasis has its chief importance for theology. In contrast to imaginative conceit or picturesque unreality, it expresses the perdurability and objective resistance of solid fact. Like Dr. Johnson, hypostasis vanquishes Berkeley with a kick. It is used not infrequently in the phrase 'hypostasis of ousia,' which may be translated 'substantial objectivity,' or 'the reality of solid fact.' Irenæus (*haer.* 5.1.2) observes that certain things occurred, not in appearance, but in hypostasis of truth. The more usual phrase occurs in a passage of Methodius (*de res.* 3.6.4), where he is defining the different senses in which two objects may be said to be separated. An object, he says, can be separated from another object by process and hypostasis; or in thought, or in process, but not by hypostasis. The illustration he gives of the first is when wheat and barley are mixed together, and then separated out; they can then be said to be distinguished by the fact that they have been sorted out into separate piles, and by the fact that the piles are physically distinct objects. But things can be separated by process without being separated by hypostasis, when the element which is taken away has no 'hypostasis of substance.' The illustration that he gives is when the form of a statue, representing a man or a horse, is separated from the matter by the bronze being melted down: the form is abolished altogether, it has no 'objectivity of substance.' Eusebius discusses the theory (*c. Marcell.* 2.4.25) that the living Son of God operated in the incarnate Jesus by external action only (energeia) and not in hypostasis of ousia, that is to say, the Logos merely influenced a man, instead of Himself becoming incarnate in him. Later, hypostasis alone acquires the sense of 'reality,' or 'genuineness,' as in Epiph. *haer.* 69.61, "not in irony but in truth . . . that He may show the true hypostasis of the flesh;" Macarius Magnes 2.9, "he says this by way of indicating the hypostasis of His own godhead"; and pseudo-Athanasius *confut. propos.* 13, "showing that nothing in Christ should be taken as according to phantasm, but everything according to hypostasis and truth."

Hypostasis thus comes to mean positive and concrete and distinct existence, first of all in the abstract, and later, as will be seen, in the particular individual. According to Clement (*strom.* 2.7, 35.1), St. Paul laid it down that knowledge of sin had been revealed through the Law, not that sin had taken hypostasis by that means. Origen (*c. Cels.* 8.12) says that we worship the Father of truth and the Son who is the Truth, being two objects in hypostasis, but one in concord. Alexander of Alexandria (ap. Thdt. *h.e.* 1.4.38), quoting the text, "I and my Father are one," says that in these words the Lord does not proclaim Himself to be the Father, nor does He represent as one the natures which are two in hypostasis. Athanasius (*c. Gent.* 6) observes that certain Greek thinkers have erroneously maintained the existence of evil in hypostasis and of itself, in other words, have ascribed to it an independent and positive reality. Cyril of Jerusalem (*cat.* 11.10) says that the Word was not a word-expressed, but an enhypostatos Word, begotten out of the Father in hypostasis. Innumerable further instances could be quoted from writers of the fourth century, in which hypostasis expresses the character of concrete objectivity.

The adjective enhypostatos has a corresponding sense, meaning simply 'that which has an objective individual existence,' unlike an accident or attribute or other mental abstraction which is not a concrete object or thing. In the language of the mediæval Scholastics, an object would be enhypostatos which possessed both substance and accidents. It seems to occur first in Irenæus *frag.* 19, which is a comment on the command to Moses to take as his successor Joshua the son of Nun (*Numbers* xxvii.18). He says, if this is a genuine fragment of Irenæus, that it was necessary for Moses to lead the nation out of Egypt, but for Joshua to lead them into their inheritance; and that Moses, like the Law, should enter into rest, but that Joshua, as word, true type of the enhypostatos Word, should address the nation. The term here differentiates the divine Word, who is a substantive being, from the spoken word which was addressed to the people. It next appears in Origen's notes on *Deuteronomy* xvi. 19-20, where Christ is called the enhypostatos Wisdom and Word of God the Father. Cyril of Jerusalem (*cat.* 17.5) speaks similarly of the Holy Spirit as being not a spirit breathed from the mouth, but en-hypostatos. From this point the word is of common occurrence in Basil, Gregory of Nyssa, Epiphanius and other writers.

Hypostatikos is occasionally used in the same sense, apparently in connection with its earlier sense of 'tending to support,' or 'creative.' Some third and fourth century instances can occasionally be quoted of hypostatos with exactly the same meaning, the most telling example occurring in Hippolytus (*ref.* 7.18.1-2). Being, says Hippolytus, is distinguished under three heads, genus, species, and individual; as an instance of genus, he takes the word animal, and of species the word man, as being already distinguished from all other animal types, but still as yet unindividualised, and not yet formed into an 'hypostatos ousia'; to arrive at this result, he takes a particular man and

o

calls him Socrates; that is what he means by an individual (atomon), and that is what Aristotle "primarily and particularly and most properly calls an ousia."

As expressive of a concrete instance or substance, an object, thing or fact of presentation, hypostasis appears to occur first in a collective sense. Thus in Irenæus (*haer.* 1.5.4) there is a reference to the demiurge and "all the rest of the psychic hypostasis," including both the irrational beasts and man. In the same section he speaks of the devil and the demons and the angels and "all the spiritual hypostasis of wickedness." Cyril of Jerusalem (*cat.* 6.13), arguing about the problem of evil, puts the question whether God is powerful or powerless; if the former, how did evil come into existence against His will, and how comes the wicked hypostasis to arise? And Serapion (*sacr.* 13.2) addresses God as being incomprehensible to the whole created hypostasis. This use is admittedly rare, but sufficient instances have been collected to suggest that, in the cases quoted above, hypostasis means the totality either of existent things or of some particular class of existent things.

On the other hand, very many instances can be found in which hypostasis represents particular objects or individuals. Quoting the Gnostic Monoimus, one of the specialists of arithmetical cosmology, Hippolytus observes (*ref.* 8.13.2) that certain combinations of numbers became bodily hypostaseis. Clement (*strom.* 4.22, 136.4), speaking of knowledge, observes that apprehension extends by means of study into permanent apprehension; and permanent apprehension, by becoming, through continuous fusion, the substance of the knower and perpetual contemplation, remains a living hypostasis. This appears to mean that knowledge becomes so bound up with the being of the knowing subject as to constitute a permanent entity. Origen (*de princ.* 3.1.22) refers to individual rational beings as "rational hypostaseis," in contrast to the single lump of soul-matter out of which God has composed them. Eusebius (*prep. ev.* 11.16, 535A) mentions a composition of Plotinus on the subject of "the three primary hypostaseis" (facts or elements recognised in his metaphysics). It is very probable that the anathema of the creed of Nicæa against those who asserted that the Son came into existence from the non-existent, or from another hypostasis or ousia, means by these last two expressions, not generic substance, but individual objective source. At any rate, later condemnations by their turn of phrase suggest this inference—such as those of the Councils of Antioch, quoted by Athanasius (*de syn.* 25 and 26), which were directed against people who say that the Son was out of non-existent, or from some other hypostasis, and not from God; or the statement of the latter Council that He was not of any other pre-existing hypostasis beside the Father, but begotten out of God alone. Since "God" is obviously a hypostasis, in the sense of object, and not in that of generic substance, the "other hypostasis" may well be thought to indicate a similar object. Again, Basil (*de Spir. sanct.* 41) ridicules the idea that the supreme God is an abstract genus, such as may only be distinguished in thought but has no existence in any hypostasis.

Instances could be multiplied. But those which have been quoted are sufficient to show what the word hypostasis really means when it comes to be applied to the prosopa of the triad. It implies that the three presentations possess a concrete and independent objectivity, in confutation both of the Sabellian type of heresy, which regarded them all merely as different names, and of the unitarian type of heresy, which regarded the second and third of them as abstract qualities possessed by the first or impersonal influences exerted by His volition.

CHAPTER IX

OBJECT AND SUBSTANCE IN GOD

THE earlier instances in which Persons of the Trinity are referred to as hypostaseis, exhibit the term in a non-technical sense closely similar to that in which it was applied to any other object. It was by no means equivalent at this stage to the Latin persona. It was not even equivalent to prosopon, although in practice it amounted to much the same, inasmuch as it was applied to the same objects; but, strictly speaking, prosopon was a non-metaphysical term for 'individual,' while hypostasis was a more or less metaphysical term for 'independent object.'

Persons of the Trinity seem to have been described by the word hypostasis first in Origen (*c. Cels.* 8.12): arguing first for the unity of the Christian godhead, he turns to divert any suspicion of his thereby having deserted the belief that "Father and Son are two hypostaseis"; the sense is determined just below when he asserts that the Father and the Son "are two objects ($\pi\rho\acute{a}\gamma\mu\alpha\tau\alpha$, 'things') in hypostasis." Elsewhere he refers to three hypostaseis in the godhead (on *St. John* 2.10, 75). Dionysius of Alexandria is quoted by Basil (*de Spir. sanct.* 72) as saying that if, by reason of the assertion that the hypostaseis are three, the opposition should conclude that the three are separated asunder, still they are three, whether the opposition likes it or not. Eusebius accuses Marcellus (*eccl. theol.* 3.6.4) of maintaining a single hypostasis with three names, but himself remarks (*ib.* 1.20.40) that, when the Logos was dwelling in the flesh during His sojourn upon earth, He was other than the Father and He and the Father constituted two hypostaseis. He also refers (*ib.* 2.7.1) to the fear which was entertained by certain people that, by confessing two hypostaseis, they might be introducing two sources, and departing from the doctrine of divine monarchy.

Athanasius himself, in certain works, appears to adopt the term hypostasis for the Persons of the Trinity. Admittedly, he refrained from doing so in his major treatises. But an explanation was found for this restraint. In direct controversy with Arians or their sympathisers the use of hypostasis to describe the divine Persons might have given a handle to his opponents. Eusebius, who had some sympathy with the difficulties which were experienced by, at any rate, the milder Arians, had accepted the term. It is the fact that its use agreed well enough with the Arian position, since admission that the Son was a distinct hypostasis from the Father made a good opening for denying that He was of one substance with the Father: Arius himself was a distinct hypostasis, but not very God of very God. It was, indeed, the assertion that the Son was a distinct hypostasis from the Father which created the whole difficulty of conceiving His unity with the Father. This, therefore, was thought to be the reason why Athanasius, in his controversial works against the Arians, avoided the term hypostasis. It was always the way of Athanasius to concentrate on points of substantial importance and to avoid terminological side-issues.

However, recent researches by a number of patristic scholars have rendered the whole theory untenable. No doubt, the tract *in illud, Omnia* (6) says that the trisagion refers to the three hypostaseis of the Trinity, just as the word Lord, which follows the three Holys in that hymn, is indicative of the one substance. But unfortunately it has now been proved that at least the conclusion of this tract, in which the above passage occurs, has been interpolated. Again, the treatise *de incarn. et c. Ar.* (10) states that the Lord of Sabaoth is the Father and Son and Holy Spirit; for the godhead is one, and there is one God in three hypostaseis. But this work also has been shown to have received inter-polations, of which the reference quoted to the three hypo-staseis is one. In another treatise, *de virginitate* (1), there is again mention of Father, Son, and Holy Spirit, three hypostaseis, one godhead, one power, one baptism. This work, however, is almost certainly not the genuine treatise of Athanasius on virginity, which appears to have been rediscovered in Syriac and Armenian translations. There-fore no evidence remains that Athanasius himself, in giving expression to his own thoughts in his own way, ever applied hypostasis to the Persons of the godhead.

The meaning of the term was still theologically non-technical; it remained a philosophical rather than a theo-logical expression. Nor had it as yet been made entirely clear what was the exact relation between the three hypostaseis and the one ousia by which complementary definition was given of the nature of God. The state of development which had been reached by the middle of the fourth century may be illustrated by reference to the situation disclosed by Athanasius in the *tom. ad Antioch.* (5 and 6). The question under discussion was that of the terms on which Arians were to be readmitted to Communion, the recent accession of the pagan Julian to the Empire having happily resulted in the breakdown of official patronage for the Arianising party. Athanasius and his friends, in council at Alexandria, laid down that they rejoiced with all who desired reunion, and that concord might be established, for their part, without any further condition than that the Nicene definition should be accepted with an anathema against the Arian doctrine that the Holy Ghost was a creature.

At the same time, a statement of faith which was in circulation and purported, though incorrectly, to have been approved by the Synod of Sardica, was prohibited from discussion, as tending to prolong unnecessary controversy. This document vehemently attacked the conception of three hypostaseis; Sardica had merely decreed that the faith confessed by the Fathers at Nicæa was sufficient to safeguard the truth. Athanasius had discussed the matter with men of both parties. Of those who insisted on confessing three hypostaseis he had inquired whether they meant to convey the idea, maintained by the extreme Arians, that the three hypostaseis in question were alien in nature from one another, so that the first alone was in any true sense divine; or whether, like some other heretics, they had in mind three sources and consequently three gods. They assured him in reply that they neither meant to suggest either of these heresies, nor had ever held them. In answer to the question, what they meant by such expressions, they replied that they believed in a holy triad, not a triad in name alone, but one that really existed and was objective, a Father who really existed and was objective, and a Son who was truly real and objective, and a Holy Spirit who was objective and existent; but that they did not intend three gods or three sources, and held no truck with those who taught or thought thus, believing as they did in one godhead and one source, in a Son who was homoousios with the Father, as the fathers of Nicæa had said, and in a Holy Spirit who was no creature, nor alien, but proper to, and inseparable from, the being of the Son and the Father.

Having elicited this satisfactory reply, Athanasius had proceeded to make further inquiry of the other side, who insisted on speaking of a single hypostasis. Did they use the expression in the sense of Sabellius, which would make the Son and the Holy Spirit mere names, or did they use it in the sense that the Son and the Holy Spirit were merely unsubstantial and abstract qualities of the hypostasis of the Father? They, in their turn, assured him that they had neither used nor intended any such interpretation, but employed the phrase in the belief that hypostasis and ousia meant the same thing—as, indeed, was the case, as has been explained already, each term properly referring to a single concrete object, though envisaging it from a somewhat different angle. They therefore held that the godhead was a single object because the Son was out of the being of the Father, and because of the identity of the divine nature (διὰ τὴν ταυτότητα τῆς φύσεως)—it should be noted that 'identity' in God means not only unchangeability but that He cannot be duplicated or reproduced, except in a copy that is still in a real sense Himself, such as the Son. They believed that there is one godhead, and that it has one nature, and not that there is one nature of the Father and another alien nature of the Son or of the Holy Spirit. The conclusion at which Athanasius justly arrived was that those who asserted three hypostaseis and those who maintained a single ousia were in substantial agreement; the adherents of the single ousia were expressing the same faith as the other party, and even "in a sense giving an interpretation" of their opponents' doctrine. The manifesto of Basil of Ancyra and George of Laodicea (ap. Epiph. *haer.* 73.16) likewise recognised that when the Orientals spoke of more than one hypostasis they did so with the object of distinguishing the individualities of the prosopa as being concrete and existent. This was precisely the fact.

On the other hand, something must be said about those who were suspicious of a plurality of hypostaseis. Dionysius of Rome (ap. Ath. *decret.* 26) refers to those who divided the monarchy into three powers and "separate hypostaseis", and three godheads; dividing the holy monad into three hypostaseis alien from one another and altogether disjunct. Pseudo-Athanasius (*exp. fid.* 2) denied that he taught the existence of three hypostaseis mutually divided, in the way that individuals are physically separated in the case of human beings. We have already referred to the party interviewed by Athanasius at Alexandria in 362, who thought that hypostasis and ousia meant the same thing. The bishops of Sardica also had, in the synodical letter preserved by Theodoret (*h.e.* 2.8.38), denounced the Arian party for maintaining that the hypostaseis of the Father and the Son and the Holy Spirit were different and disjunct; the Catholic tradition, which they had themselves been taught, proclaimed that there was one hypostasis, which the heretics called ousia, of the three Persons; and in answer to the inquiry, what was the hypostasis of the Son, they would reply that it was one and the same hypostasis which was acknowledged as belonging to the Father.

The explanation of the terminology adopted in this letter is that those members of the Council of Sardica who remained to the end of the session and drafted the synodical letter were, with very few and insignificant exceptions, either Westerns or exiles in the West, and when Orientals quote their usage of the word hypostasis, it is likely that the term was understood, not merely in the same sense as the Greek ousia, but, what is more important, in the same sense as the Latin substantia, of which hypostasis is the exact philological equivalent. It was natural for the Latins to imagine that words philologically identical in the two tongues had precisely the same meaning, more particularly when the Latins, who were not deeply conversant with Greek philosophical thought, were unacquainted with the fact that hypostasis had two distinct ranges of meaning. Substantia corresponded in sense with the intransitive sense of hypostasis. A Latin could hardly be expected to realise that hypostasis had also an active sense, and that that active sense was in fact the sense in which the term was being applied to theology in the East.

The problem of understanding what it was that the Orientals were really trying to express was further complicated through the acceptance by Arius (*ep. ad Alex.*, ap. Ath. *de syn.* 16) of the doctrine that there were three hypostaseis. Arius, of course, by this phrase intended to convey the sense of three divided and substantially alien hypostaseis, such as Dionysius of Rome and Athanasius himself had repudiated. But the fact remained that Arius confessed three hypostaseis, and was perfectly prepared to confess three substantiæ, which no orthodox Oriental could have done. It is therefore impossible to be surprised at Occidental suspicion being directed against the three-hypostasis doctrine, and it was providential that in the exiled Oriental Athanasius the Latins had a man, who was not only a profound theologian, but was also willing to sacrifice all but the barest essentials of theological terminology so long as he was satisfied that the parties with whom he had to deal accepted the substance of the faith.

Additional extracts from the synodical letter of Sardica (which had met, it must be remembered, in 342, almost twenty years before the *tom. ad Ant.* was written) are worth quoting to illustrate the point further. The bishops affirmed that the Logos was truly the Son; not Son by adoption, in the sense that creatures can be called gods or sons of God, by reason of regeneration or merit but not, as in the case of Christ, in virtue of the one hypostasis which is the Father's and the Son's (Thdt. *h.e.* 2.8.43). Again, they observed (*ib.* 47) that the sacred words, "I and the Father are one," refer to the unity of the hypostasis, which is single, alike in the Father and in the Son. The same Occidental usage recurs in the synodical letter of Damasus to the Illyrians (quoted by Theodoret, *h.e.* 2.22.7), in a passage which deals with the definition of the faith originally made at Nicæa. That Council, says the letter, maintained that the Father and the Son are of one being (ousia), one godhead, one virtue, one power, one likeness ('character'), and that the Holy Spirit is of the same hypostasis and ousia. This was, as we have already seen, a possible interpretation of the phrase which the Nicene Fathers had used, though some grounds were given (p.177) for thinking it probable that they employed the term hypostasis in a particular sense, of the individual being of the Father, rather than in such a sense that the Holy Spirit could properly be said to share it.

In spite of modern assertions that the phrase 'one hypostasis' was the usual Oriental formula except at Alexandria, we may still doubt if it was normally used anywhere except as a Latinism. This view is supported by what Gregory of Nazianzus says in his *Oration on the great Athanasius* (*or.* 21.35). Speaking as an Oriental, he observes that it was normal to use, in a sense of pious orthodoxy, the terms one ousia and three hypostaseis. The Italians, he remarks, meant exactly the same thing; but, owing to the scantiness of the Latin vocabulary and its penury of terms, they were unable to distinguish between ousia and hypostasis, and were therefore compelled to fall back on the term prosopa (i.e. personæ) in order to avoid the assertion of three ousiai. The result, he says, would be amusing, if it were not rather a subject for regret, since the difference of terminology was taken to indicate a difference of faith. Orientals, when they heard the doctrine of three prosopa, were suspicious of a Sabellian intention being conveyed thereby. In point of fact, as we have seen already, the Sabellians never used this phrase to express their doctrine, and it was only through Eusebius (who had accused Marcellus of maintaining a single hypostasis triprosopos) and Gregory's friend and teacher Basil (who had criticised the Sabellians along such lines, though without ascribing to them the actual terms) that three-prosopon language had been brought into association with Sabellianism. Gregory is then probably reflecting merely recent and local opinion when he says that the doctrine of three personæ suggested Sabellianism. But he is on firmer ground when he continues by stating that Westerns smelt Arianism in the doctrine of three hypostaseis.

To Athanasius himself the assertion of one hypostasis was no impossibility either in the Latin or even in the Eastern sense. In this connection hypostasis might still retain its proper meaning of 'object,' the contrast lying between the single entity constituted by the divine being and the three entirely separated and disjunct entities, of unequal substance, dignity, and value, maintained by the Arians. On the other hand, he was fully prepared to accept the expression three hypostaseis, provided it were understood in the orthodox and not in the Arian sense.

To sum up briefly the relations of hypostasis and ousia, it may be said first that they are often, for practical purposes, equivalent. Nevertheless, they are probably never strictly identical in meaning, except in the Western instances quoted above, in which hypostasis may be regarded as a literal representation of the Latin substantia. Both hypostasis and ousia describe positive, substantial existence, that which is, that which subsists; τὸ ὄν, τὸ ὑφεστηκός. But ousia tends to regard internal characteristics and relations, or metaphysical reality; while hypostasis regularly emphasises the externally concrete character of the substance, or empirical objectivity. Hence, with regard to the Trinity, it never sounded unnatural to assert three hypostaseis, but it was always unnatural to proclaim three ousiai; although some writers, as will appear hereafter, occasionally use ousia in a sense approximating to that of hypostasis, definite examples of the reverse process are not often to be found.

Some sort of difference between hypostasis and ousia appears to be recognised by Irenæus (*haer.* 5.36.1): "neither

the hypostasis nor the ousia of the creation is to be abolished,"
he claims, but the 'fashion' of this world passes away (cf. 1
Cor. vii.31). He contrasts mere form with fact and content.
Origen also seems conscious of the distinction. He is
discussing (on *St. John* 1.24, 151) the use made of the
text, "my heart has uttered a good word," by people who
regarded this 'word' as a mere utterance, possessing neither
the substantive reality ascribed by the Catholics to the
divine Word, nor even the relative mode of existence
attaching to the Word when conceived as Word-immanent
and a quality of the paternal being. They think, he says,
that the Son of God is a paternal utterance simply expressed,
as it were, in syllables, and on this reasoning, if I understand
them rightly, they decline to ascribe to Him hypostasis,
nor do they recognize any ousia as belonging to Him at all;
I do not mean by this, he adds, that they deny Him some
particular form of being, but being of any description
whatever. Hypostasis here appears to mean, as usual,
substantive, concrete individuality; while ousia seems to have
a wider sense, which would include the existence proper to
a quality or attribute.

The distinction between metaphysical reality and empirical
objectivity comes out more definitely in a passage of Gregory
of Nyssa (*Macr.*, Migne 46.44B). Gregory is discussing
the nature of living bodies, and remarks that their hypostasis
is derived from a fusion of physical elements, but that, in
respect of their ousia, their physical grossness enjoys an
association with the simple incorporeality of the soul.
Hypostasis in this passage clearly has reference to the stuff
of objective presentation, while ousia no less clearly refers
to an analysis of abstract characteristics. The same dis-

tinction can be observed in pseudo-Justin (*quaest. Christ. ad Gent. resp.* 5 *conf.* 2), where the subject under discussion is the sky. The writer warns his readers against the danger of attributing deity to the sky from having regard to the vastness of its hypostasis ('concrete extension') and the incorruptibility of its ousia ('qualitative substance'). Macarius Magnes, again, in discussing (3.11) the difficulty created by a discrepancy between the Gospels of St. Matthew (viii.31ff.) and St. Mark (v.1ff.), observes that Matthew records the presence of two men, emphasising the number of the hypostasis, while Mark, who only records the presence of one man, disregards the number, and dwells on the ousia that was suffering from disease. Both words might be paraphrased by 'case,' in the one instance in relation to number, and in the other instance in relation to kind. Number is a matter of external presentation, and therefore hypostasis is the right word to use. Kind involves a question of quality, and therefore the right word is ousia.

It remains to give some detailed illustrations of the term ousia, as previously of hypostasis. It is well known that among the senses in which it commonly occurs are those of 'material substance,' as when Athenagoras (*de res.* 6) observes that the food which a person takes becomes an increment to his ousia; of 'secondary substance' in the Aristotelian sense, or element, as when Athenagoras (*suppl.* 22.2) says that, according to the Stoics, Zeus is the name given to the fervid ousia; or 'matter' in general; or 'property' (the close approximation of ousia to hypostasis is perhaps nowhere more strikingly illustrated than in the fact that hypostasis can also mean property, and is found in the papyri several times in the sense of valuation or tax assessment). It can also mean the principle, essence, or nature of an individual object, with reference to metaphysical analysis; or the element of form possessed in common by a number of individual objects, that is, logical universal or species. It may further express the result of metaphysical analysis in general, as perhaps when Justin (*dial.* 4.1) quotes Plato's doctrine that absolute being is beyond all ousia, and cannot be either defined or expressed; or as when Celsus (ap. Or. *c. Cels.* 7.45) says that ousia and genesis represent respectively what is intelligible and what is visible, for to ousia belongs truth and to genesis belongs illusion; or when Athanasius (*c. Gent.* 2) states that God exists beyond all ousia and human conception. In such instances, ousia appears to mean something like 'intelligible reality.'

But its most important meaning in relation to theology is that of individual substance, the 'primary ousia' of Aristotle's definition. Thus Athenagoras (*suppl.* 23.2) states that Thales defines demons as psychic ousiai; Clement (*strom.* 8.4, 9.1) discusses the question of knowledge of an object (ousia) in isolation, while its effects are totally unknown, instancing the consideration of plants or animals while in ignorance of their actions; and Methodius (*de autex.* 8.1) inquires whether evils are ousiai or qualities of ousiai. Turning to theological applications, we find Origen (on *Proverbs* viii.22) maintaining that the Wisdom of God is an ousia, He came into existence before the ages, and, before the creation, was eternal. Again, he states (on *St. John frag.* 37) that the comparison of the Holy Spirit to the wind blowing where it listeth signifies that the Spirit is, indeed, an ousia, and not a divine activity without individuality of existence. In the commentaries only preserved in Latin translations, he applies the conception of a single ousia to the divine triad. Thus he argues (on *Numbers* 12.1) for the distinction of three personæ in the Father, the Son, and the Holy Spirit; but contends that there is only one fountain head, for there is a single substantia and nature of the triad: and again (on *Leviticus* 13.4), he infers from the description of the shewbread (*Levit.* xxiv.5-6) a reference to a single will and a single substantia in the godhead, although the two rows in which the shewbread was to be arranged seemed to him to imply two individualities of personæ.

Pierius, who presided over the Catechetical School of Alexandria in the latter half of the third century, is alleged by Photius (*bibliotheca* 119) to have taught with pious orthodoxy concerning the Father and the Son, except that, in speaking of them, he used the expression two ousiai instead of the term hypostasis. According to Marcellus (ap. Eus. *c. Marc.* 1.4.39), when Hosius asked Narcissus whether he maintained two ousiai, like Eusebius of Palestine, Narcissus replied that, according to the Scriptures, he was induced to believe that there were three ousiai. And Marcellus further maintained (*ib.* 1.4.41) that Eusebius had positively written, word for word, as follows: "The Image, and that of which it is the Image, are not conceived as one and the same, but they are two ousiai and two objects and two powers."

Even after the Nicene controversy the word ousia not only continued to be used in general, apart from theology, of individual substances, but was still applied even to the Persons of the Trinity. Thus Basil (*hom. in Mamant.* 4) says that the text, "I am in the Father and the Father in me" (*St. John* xiv. 10), does not imply the confusion of ousiai, but identity of characteristics; and (*de Spir. sanct.* 46) calls the Spirit a living ousia, Lord of sanctification. And Chrysostom (on *Philippians* 7. 1, or, according to the old notation, 6. 1) observes that Marcellus and Photinus considered the Logos an activity of the Father, and not an objective (enhypostatos) ousia. It may be added, by way of further illustration, that the adjective οὐσιώδης is frequently employed with the meaning of 'substantive' or 'concrete,' in exactly the same sense as enhypostatos.

Ousia was applied by the Stoics, who were materialists, to their conception of the material content or substance of God. As early as Justin (*dial.* 128. 4) such a conception had been rejected from the Christian side, by the statement that the Son was begotten from the Father, but not by section, as if the ousia of the Father were cut in half. Origen (*c. Cels.* 3. 75) reminds us that the Stoics had taught the existence of a corruptible God and had described His ousia as a mutable body. Though rejected in this crude form by all Christian teachers, this kind of thought continued to have a certain influence on theology. The being or substance of God, without being considered as material, came to be regarded as something which could, at least by a sort of metaphor, be thought of as in extension; and Origen criticises (on *St. John* 20. 18, 157) those who so interpreted the text, "I came forth from God," as to make it appear that the Son was begotten out of the ousia of the Father, as a child is born of a woman, leaving the Father diminished and deficient in the ousia which He previously possessed.

The orthodox doctrine is expressed by Eusebius (*eccl. theol.* 2. 23. 1) when he maintains that the Church of God does not profess either two gods or two agenneta, nor two anarcha, nor two ousiai on parallel lines of march, but one arche and God. The whole ousia of the Father became by derivation the whole ousia of the Son, according to the old metaphor, as the radiance is derived from the light; Athanasius (*decret.* 25) quotes Theognostus, master of the Catechetical School of Alexandria towards the end of the third century, and an Origenist, as saying that the ousia of the Son is not one procured from outside, nor accruing out of nothing, but it sprang from the Father's ousia, like the radiance of light or the vapour of water; the radiance and the vapour are not the actual sun or water respectively, but neither are they something alien; the Son is an effluence from the ousia of the Father, which, however, suffers no partition in the process.

Athanasius himself seems to regard the ousia of the Father, out of which the Son was a true offspring, both in an external and in an internal aspect. Regarding it as an object or (so to speak) the empirical content of the deity, he says (*ad Epict.* 4) that the Son himself and not his human body was homoousios with the Father; the Son was born of the ousia of the Father, and His human body of Mary. This juxtaposition rather tends to suggest that what he has in mind, in speaking of the ousia of the Father, is the divine stuff of which the Father consists. With this passage may be compared the statement (*decret.* 19) that the Holy Synod of Nicæa pronounced the Son to be not merely from the Father, but from the ousia of the Father, in order that it might be believed that He alone is truly out of God; for there is a valid sense in which all created things come from God, as being His handiwork, though they are not formed of His substance.

On the other hand, there seems to be an internal reference to the essential character of the divine being in such passages as the following. Athanasius writes (*de syn.* 34): "if, when you name the Father, or use the word God, you do not signify ousia or understand by ousia Him that 'is' what He 'is,' but signify something else relating to Him, not to say inferior, then you should not have written that the Son is out of the Father, but that He is out of what is related to the Father, or what is in the Father." The point of the argument is that the Father's ousia is the Father Himself, and not an attribute of the Father, though it has an internal and qualitative reference; therefore the being of the Son, if He proceeds from the Father's being, must be the same as the Father's being, and not inferior. And the being of God which is here under discussion clearly seems to be not only a substance but a 'primary substance,' in other words, substance in the concrete, expressed in an individual. Athanasius rightly proceeded to comment that the Arians, holding the ideas they did, treated the Word and the title Son as representing, not an ousia, but simply a name; here again he means by ousia a primary substance.

In the next chapter he affirms that 'Father' and 'God' are simply and solely expressions of the actual ousia of Him that is; the Arians had admitted that the Son was out of God, that is to say, out of the ousia of the Father; and this expression was derived from the Council of Nicæa, the Fathers there assembled having considered that it was the same thing to say in a right sense "out of God" and to say "out of His ousia"; for creatures, though they may be said to have come into being out of God, yet did not do so in the sense in which the Son is out of God; for they are not offspring (gennemata) like the Son, but works. The word ousia is shown (*c. Ar.* 4.2) to be exhaustive of the whole being of God, and not to admit of distinctions into generic essence and qualities or accidents; but this need not be quoted, since this book was not composed by Athanasius himself. But the close connection observed in the word ousia, quite apart from all theology, between the concept of primary substance and the idea of metaphysical analysis may be illustrated from his *de incarnatione* (18): "what man, seeing the ousia of water changed and transformed into wine, can fail to perceive that He who did this is Lord and creator of the ousia of all waters?" The argument is that only He who had made water what it is could have been able to transform the particular measures of water, which filled the water-pots at Cana, into wine.

CHAPTER X

THE HOMOOUSION

THE true meaning of the ousia of God should now be fairly clear. But the crucial term in the creed of Nicæa and in the controversy subsequently ensuing was not ousia but the compound adjective homoousios (of one substance, consubstantial). This word demands full investigation, both in its secular meaning and, above all, in its long association with theological discussion.

The original signification of homoousios, apart from all theological technicality, is simply 'made of the same stuff.' 'Stuff' here bears a generic sense, necessarily, since no objects of physical experience are composed of identical portions of matter; it really means 'kind of stuff.' Homoousios seems to have been a fairly common expression in Gnostic writers. Ptolemæus writes to Flora (ap. Epiph. *haer.* 33.7.8) that it is the nature of the Good to beget and produce objects which are "similar to itself and homoousios with itself." According to the Valentinians (ap. Iren. *haer.* 1.5.1), Achamoth, the abortive and degenerate fruit of the final æon in the divine Absolute (pleroma), was homoousios with angelic ('spiritual') beings, and thus superior to the physical creation; she formed the Demiurge out of 'psychic' (animated) substance, in order that he might become "the Father and King" of all worldly creatures, "both those which were homoousios with himself, that is to say psychic (animated) objects, and those which sprang from passion and matter." Again (*ib.* 1.5.5), speaking of primordial man, "made in the image and likeness" of the divine, they say that his material nature was in the image, "having a resemblance to God, but not being homoousios with Him." In a similar sense, a piece of marble closely resembling Mr. Gladstone may be found at the National Liberal Club, but it is made of different stuff from that of which Mr. Gladstone himself consisted: it is in the image of Mr. Gladstone, but not homoousios with him. Hippolytus (*ref.* 7.22.7) describes another Gnostic conception, of a triple Sonship, homoousios in everything to the non-existent God, and produced out of the non-existent. Clement's *excerpts from Theodotus* (50.1) mention the creation of an earthly and material soul which was irrational and homoousios with that of the beasts. Similarly, the *Clementine Homilies* (20.7) remark that men washed the feet of angels (cf. *Genesis* xviii.4), as if they were homoousios with men; and that God projects an ousia that is homoousios, but not of identical function, when He changes a substance (as, for instance, the proper fiery substance of the angels who met Abraham) into something of a different form.

Coming to orthodox writers, we find Clement arguing (*strom.* 2.16, 74.1) that God possesses no 'natural' ($\phi\upsilon\sigma\iota\kappa\acute{o}\varsigma$) relation to mankind, unless we have the hardihood to claim that men are a part of Him and homoousios with God. Heracleon had said (ap. Origen on *St. John* 13.25, 148) that those who worship God in spirit and in truth are themselves spirit, being of the same nature as the Father: Origen paraphrases this (*ib.* 149) with the phrase "homoousios with the unbegotten Nature." Similarly, Origen (*ib.* 20.20, 170) accuses Heracleon of maintaining that some men are homoousios with the devil, being of a different substance from those classes which he and his followers called psychic or pneumatic. Methodius, once more (*de res.* 2.30.8), refers to a composition made out of pure air and pure fire, and homoousios with angelic beings. Eusebius (*dem. ev.* 1.10.13) says that the beasts are of the same genus and same nature and homoousios with the vegetable creation, since (*ib.* 1.10.11) they have no share in the rational nature of men, but their composition is of matter and physical elements, resembling that of the vegetable world. In just the same way, Basil (*c. Eun.* 2.19) observes that men excel their own products in skill, but, for all that, are homoousios with them, as the potter is with his clay; they are both similarly bodies. Diodore of Tarsus (*c. Synous.* 1 *frag.* 4, to be found in Migne 33.1561A) observes that mortal begets mortal according to his nature, and body produces that which is homoousios with itself. In this connection it is not without interest to notice that the expression οἱ ὁμοούσιοι is used more than once in the sense of "fellow-men," as in Diodore of Tarsus (on psalm liv.4), "I was grieved when I saw my homoousioi and homogeneis falling into the depth of wickedness"; Chrysostom (on 1 *Tim.* 16.2), "if we so serve Him that made us as our homoousioi serve us"; Macarius Magnes (4.26), "he enslaved his homogeneis by compulsion and might, not ruling his homoousioi by the ordinance of voluntary loyalty." It should also be observed that by a tacit assumption homoousios bears exactly the same sense as homogenes ('belonging to the same genus').

We may now turn to the use of homoousios in theology.

Origen (*frag.* on *Hebrews,* ap. Pamph. *apol.,* Migne 14.1308D) argues that certain analogies, which he has quoted, prove that there is communio substantiæ of the Son with the Father; for an emanation is homoousios [sic, Graece], that is, of one substance, with that body from which it is an emanation or vapour. This is substantially the same argument as was quoted above (p. 194) from Theognostus of Alexandria, who doubtless got it from his master. Dionysius of Alexandria (ap. Ath. *de sent. Dion.* 18) says that the charge alleged against him is untrue, that he had denied Christ to be homoousios with God; for even though he might argue that he had not found this term anywhere in the Bible, yet the illustrations which he had given of the relation between the Father and the Son were in accordance with its sense; thus he had given the example of a human birth, obviously on the ground that an offspring was "homogeneous" with its parent, and had referred to a plant, sprung from a seed or root, as being different from that from which it sprang, yet, at the same time, entirely ὁμοφυής with it. We note that homoousios is being explained once more, and this time in connection with the Persons of the Trinity, by reference to the terms homogenes and homophyes, which are both generic terms. Again, the author of *Adamantius* (1.2, 804C) professes his belief in one God and creator and maker of all, and in God the Word, who was out of Him, homoousios, and perpetual.

Dionysius certainly, Origen and the author of *Adamantius* probably, are here using homoousios in its ordinary secular sense, in order to insist that what the Father is, that also the Son is, without reference to the problem of the unity between them. It would appear that this problem was seriously raised by Paul of Samosata, though the obscurity of the form in which he actually raised it makes it necessary to set out the evidence at some length.

The work of Athanasius *de synodis* was written in 359, and in chapters 41ff. he deals with the position adopted by the semi-Arians, led by Basil of Ancyra, at the Synod of Ancyra, held in 358. In chapter 43 he accepts the statement of the semi-Arians, that the Synod of Antioch, which condemned Paul of Samosata in 268, described the Son as not homoousios with the Father. (He says that he did not himself possess the Synod's letter.) This repudiation of homoousios does not occur in the fragments which survive from the statements issued by the Synod of Antioch. But what does survive is not without significance. The fragments are collected in the third volume of Routh's *Reliquiæ Sacræ*, and reference will be made to the pages of that volume. In the *epistola ad Paulum* (290-1), the Council declares the Son to be Wisdom and Word and Power of God, and God, not by predestination, but in ousia and hypostasis. This means that He was ἐνυποστάτως Wisdom and Logos, and not an impersonal influence or attribute of God (cf. 293 lines 8-11); and ousia, like hypostasis, here implies that He was in actual concrete being. This is confirmed by the occurrence in the *epistola synodica* (310-311) of the accusation against Paul of teaching that the Wisdom was not conjoined with the human nature of the Lord substantively (οὐσιωδῶς) as Catholics believed, but as an attribute. Again (312) the Synod refers to Christ as an ousia substantified in a body. And this is in turn confirmed by Basil of Ancyra (ap. Epiph. *haer.* 73.12), who expressly states that the Synod of Antioch called Christ an ousia to guard against Paul's doctrine of an impersonal Logos, the sense they attached to ousia being that of primary substance and thus practically equivalent to hypostasis. So it is quite certain that the Synod of Antioch used 'ousia' as against Paul.

In what sense then, and on what grounds, did the fathers of Antioch reject homoousios, which was accepted by their friend Dionysius (who died in 265), and seems a natural corollary to the 'ousia' of the Son? Athanasius (*de syn.* 45) gives the following account. Paul (who certainly taught the Adoptionist theory that our Lord "from man became God," i.e. was originally a mere man who by response to grace was raised to the level of divinity) argued that, if this were not so, it must follow that He was homoousios with the Father; and that this involved the assumption of a third antecedent ousia, common to Father and Son alike, and prior to both. If Athanasius is correct, Paul reasoned about the Father and the Son from the nature of material substances, showing that in their case the existence of two articles, such as (let us suppose) two pence, alike made of copper, involves the presupposition of the substance copper—"a previous substance, and the other two derived out of it." Athanasius justly observes that the Council of Nicæa, when it decided to adopt the term homoousios, saw the fallacy of this argument, since homoousios does not apply in that sense to immaterial objects, and especially not to God. But he concludes, either by inference, since he had not the letter of the Synod of Antioch before him, or else on the information of his own correspondents, whom he is addressing, that the Antiochene Synod rejected the application of homoousios to Christ in the material sense which Paul had attempted to attach to it. In fact, their objection to its use was precisely the same as that of the people, unspecified, whom Athanasius quotes (*de syn.* 51), concerning whom he expressly states that he derived his knowledge from his correspondents.

There is some support for the attribution by Athanasius to Paul of this line of argument, in the following fact. In the letter of the Synod of Antioch to Paul, immediately after the statement that Christ is God in ousia, there follows (Routh 291) a repudiation of anyone who should oppose the doctrine, that the Son was God from before the foundation of the world, on the ground that this doctrine involved the existence of two gods (i.e. two ousiai). This is exactly the line of argument which in Athanasius' account of his position it is implied that Paul took: if Christ was pre-existently and personally God (i.e. an ousia), then there were two homoousios ousiai involved, in which case it was necessary to secure the unity of God by presupposing a unitary divine substance anterior to both Father and Son.

Athanasius' explanation of the repudiation of homoousios at Antioch in 268 is still more clearly reproduced by Basil (*ep.* 52.1, written about 370). It ought, however, to be recognised that Basil's account may not have much independent value. Part of the same letter (*ep.* 52.2) reproduces an argument obviously derived from Athanasius (*de syn.* 51); it is therefore possible that his account of Antioch may simply be derived from the version given in the same treatise of Athanasius (*de syn.* 45). This possibility needs to have attention drawn to it.

Basil illustrates the matter at issue by the instance of the copper coins, which has been borrowed above, and disowns the sense of homoousios thereby implied with the remark that the mere thought of a substance anterior to, or under-lying, God the Father and God the Son is an extravagant impiety. He further (*ib.* 52.2) alleges that homoousios was employed at Nicæa merely to express the view that, whatever the Father is, that the Son is also in identical measure. And further still (*ib.* 52.3), he hails homoousios as a safeguard against Sabellianism, since a unitary object cannot be homoousios with itself; the term implies plurality of hypostasis. The last point is not peculiar to Basil; it is also made by Epiphanius (*anc.* 6.4, written in 374).

To sum up, there is no definite evidence in the third century of a Sabellian or quasi-Sabellian sense of homoousios, either in theological or in secular usage. Basil and Epiphanius claim it as excluding Sabellianism. Athanasius and Basil give a different and perfectly reasonable explana-tion of its condemnation by the Synod of Antioch—an explanation fully consistent with expressions definitely employed by the Synod. We may therefore reasonably doubt the contention that its condemnation in 268 was due to Paul's having used it simply to convey the quasi-Sabellian sense of 'uni-personal,' which would be in direct accordance with his own teaching; and accept the view that he employed it in an indirect attempt to outflank the orthodox position.

There is one genuine difficulty, however, about this conclusion, not inherent in the facts, but due to Hilary giving an account of the Synod of Antioch divergent from that given by Athanasius and Basil. Hilary's version is presented in his *de synodis* (written in 358-9), and in the closing part of that work (77ff., cf. 68ff.) he addresses the semi-Arians of the Synod of Ancyra, which had recently been held. At the time of writing he had spent two full years travelling in Asia

Minor, and like Athanasius was attempting to reconcile the semi-Arians to the Nicene formula. Like Athanasius again, he had not the documents of the Synod of Antioch before him, but derives his knowledge of their condemnation of homoousios from a letter written by the semi-Arians (Hil. *de syn.* 81).

What he states is as follows. The semi-Arians declared against homoousios (*a*) because it might lead to the idea of a prior substance shared between the two Persons, (*b*) because at Antioch, in 268, the fathers rejected it as being Sabellian; Paul, they said, by this declaration of a single essence, taught that God was unitary and undifferentiated, and at once Father and Son to Himself. Hilary comments that the Church indeed considered it profane, through the employment of such terms, to reduce Father and Son to a bare unitary monad, by denying the personal distinctions in the godhead. Hilary himself appears to imagine that Paul of Samosata actually was a Sabellian (cf. section 82, what Christian can "follow the man of Samosata in confessing that Christ in Himself is both Father and Son to Himself?"). In this belief Hilary was almost certainly mistaken. Though it has been disputed, nearly all authorities are agreed that Paul was an Adoptionist, and believed, not that the Logos was a transient phase of the divine Person, but that it was a permanent and impersonal attribute of God.

Hilary's statement about Paul's teaching could be squared with the account of Athanasius, if it could legitimately be paraphrased as follows: "Paul taught that God was simple and unitary, and supported his teaching by an argument which involved the attribution (per reductionem ad absurdum) of homoousios to God; this affords an additional reason for declining to accept the term." Such an interpretation would obviously be forced, and it clearly is not what Hilary himself understood from the semi-Arians' letter. But since it accords exactly with what we have already been led to regard as the facts of the case, it might reasonably be taken as conveying the substance of what the semi-Arians had actually written to Hilary. The real anti-Pauline ground for rejecting homoousios is that expressed in objection (*a*). The Easterns would have mentioned Paul merely as an illustration of that objection, which was the true historical objection. It would then be necessary to assume that Hilary, believing, though incorrectly, that Paul was a Sabellian, mistook their mention of Paul for a second and distinct reason against the use of homoousios —'Paul employed homousios with a Sabellian intention.' The mention of Sabellianism would have been introduced for the first time by Hilary, who, for reasons unconnected with the statement of the Easterns, entertained the notion that Paul was a Sabellian and read this assumption into the facts laid before him.

Is there, then, any known fact which may help to account for Hilary's error, and to explain his ascription to Paul of the doctrine that Christ was "at once Father and Son to Himself?" There is a fact, which may throw light upon the matter, in the manifesto issued by Basil of Ancyra and his friends, which is reproduced by Epiphanius (*haer.* 73.12-22). If the second paragraph of section 22 (in the edition of Petavius, 869B to 870A) is part of the manifesto, it would appear to have been published in 359, and in that case it can only have been actually in Hilary's hands if the publication was really a republication of a document previously existing.

But it seems possible that this paragraph is a note by
Epiphanius, and not part of the manifesto itself (cf. Gwatkin,
Studies of Arianism p. 171 note 6); if so, Hilary may already
have had an opportunity to study it. In any case the man-
festo is evidence for the kind of utterance which Basil of
Ancyra must be supposed to have been in the habit of
making, and may therefore have delivered orally to Hilary,
altogether apart from the precise text of the manifesto.

In this manifesto, then, the semi-Arians begin (section 12)
by saying that Paul of Samosata *and Marcellus* had argued
from the first verse of St. John's Gospel to the effect that
the Logos was not a substantive Person, but an impersonal
Utterance of God: *consequently*, the fathers of Antioch
[seventy years before Marcellus], in judging Paul, had
insisted that Christ was an ousia. The name of Marcellus
is simply thrown in 'on general principles,' Marcellus being
an obsession with the semi-Arians, as well as being Basil's
deposed predecessor in the see of Ancyra. After this, without
another word about Marcellus, and without any mention of
Sabellianism, the pamphlet goes on to attack the extreme
Arians, and to defend, as against them, the use of the
unscriptural term ousia. Quite obviously the mention of
Marcellus is irrelevant. But he was notoriously accused
of advocating a modified species of Sabellianism. At the
same time, not only did he agree more or less with Paul
on the one point about which his name is quoted, but, in
addition, the term homoousios had been condemned,
though for completely different reasons, both at Antioch
in 268 (on Hilary's ground (*a*)), and also by the semi-
Arians of Ancyra in 358 (on the ground that it was equivalent
to ταυτοούσιος and implied Sabellianism, *ep. syn.*, ap.

Epiph. *haer.* 73.11, last anathema, i.e. on Hilary's ground
(*b*)). Consequently, it was easy for Hilary to gather—either
from Basil's manifesto, or from some similar tirade in which
Paul and Marcellus were lumped together, taken in conjunction with the known repudiation of homoousios in
connection with both heretics—the erroneous impression
that Paul and Marcellus taught wholly along similar lines,
and not only in respect of the pre-cosmic impersonality of
the Logos. It may be observed in passing that Marcellus and
Paul are also thrown together by Eusebius (*eccl. theol.*
3.6.4), who writes that Marcellus at one moment descends
into the utmost pit of Sabellius, at another moment attempts
to revive the heresy of Paul of Samosata, and at yet another
moment reveals himself as a downright Jew (that is,
Unitarian).

Hilary cared little about Eastern squabbles and per-
sonalities: he lauds the reactionary Council of the Dedication
of 341 (attended mainly by anti-Sabellian Conservatives,
later called semi-Arians), which confirmed the deposition
of Athanasius (Hil. *de syn.* 32 "congregata sanctorum
synodus"). He probably knew nothing detailed about Paul,
but can scarcely have lived in Asia Minor from 356 to 358,
in the society of semi-Arian friends, without hearing a very
great deal about the Sabellianism of their bogy Marcellus.
This is probably the explanation of his attribution of
Sabellianism to Paul of Samosata. And when allowance is
made for this mistake of Hilary, there is no reason to suppose
that the account of the Synod of Antioch and of its rejection
of homoousios, which was contained in Hilary's letters from
the semi-Arians, differed very widely from the account
given by Athanasius and Basil.

One alternative explanation might fit the facts—that Antioch never condemned homoousios at all. The Council of 268 regarded the Father and the Son as two real objects (ousiai), while Paul admitted only one ousia, the Father. Semi-Arian logicians, conscious that 'unius substantiæ' and homoousios were now being taken as equivalent, knowing that Marcellus's doctrine of the pre-cosmic Logos resembled Paul's, and obsessed with the 'Sabellianism' of Marcellus and consequently of the homoousion, may well have claimed that Paul's condemnation for insisting on a single ousia involved implicit repudiation of the homoousion in advance. That the word homoousios had actually been discussed in 268 would be a simple inference for any listener to make. Hilary could say, "The semi-Arians tell me that homoousios was rejected at Antioch because it is Sabellian"; Easterns who knew the proper meaning of the word, while accepting its alleged repudiation, would try to find a more convincing explanation in the argument about a prior substance.

We may therefore conclude that, down to the Council of Nicæa, homoousios meant 'of one stuff' or substance'; and that, when it was applied to the divine Persons, it conveyed a metaphor drawn from material objects, just as hostile critics alleged; with, however, that reservation imposed on the application of physical metaphors to the divine nature, which is claimed by Athanasius and Basil (pp. 202, 204, above), in order to safeguard the unity of God.

Arius and his friends also understood homoousios in a materialistic sense, writing, in the letter to Alexander (ap. Ath. de syn. 16), that the Son was perfect creature of God, but not as one of the creatures, and offspring, but not as one of things begotten, nor an issue, according to the

Valentinian conception of offspring, nor a homoousios portion of the Father, according to the Manichæan conception of offspring. (The Manichæans, apparently, regarded the divine substance as quasi-material, and held that the Son was begotten of the Father by cutting the paternal substance into two sections.) Later in the letter they argue that, if the words "from the Father" be understood to mean that the Son was a homoousios part of Him, then the Father is compound and divisible and changeable and material, and is subject to the consequences of corporeality.

The Nicene creed reaffirmed homoousios in the following terms: "begotten of the Father, only-begotten, that is out of the ousia of the Father, God out of God . . . homoousios with the Father." Now Eusebius of Cæsarea may have been slow-witted and irritatingly incapable of seizing upon the vital philosophical distinction at issue between Alexander and Arius; but unless he was also a fluent and ingenious romancer, the objections raised at the Council to the term homoousios, and met by the explanations which he records, have no relation whatever to Sabellianism, but are those which inspired the Synod of Antioch in 268. He wrote immediately from the Council to his flock at Cæsarea, to the following effect (ap. Ath. *de decret.* fin., Thdt. *h.e.* 1.12). The Emperor, after the reading of Eusebius's apologia, said that it expressed his own sentiments, and advised the Council to approve of it, with the addition of the single word homoousios. This word he interpreted, stating that homoousios was not intended in the sense attaching to the conditions of physical objects, nor as if the Son subsisted out of the Father by way of division or any sort of severance.

The imperial commentary was thus directed against a materialistic rendering of the term homoousios, exactly parallel to the reservations made by Athanasius and Basil; there is not a hint of any danger of a Sabellian interpretation.

Even with this explanation, the matter was not left without a full discussion (Eus. *ep. ad Caes.* 5). Questions and consultations took place, says Eusebius, and the meaning of the formula underwent close scrutiny. He summarises the result as follows (*ib* 7): on examination there is ground for saying that the Son is homoousios with the Father, not after the manner of physical objects, nor resembling mortal animals, for He is not Son by division of the ousia nor by severance nor by any affection or change or alteration of the Father's ousia and power, since from all such conceptions the agenetos nature of the Father is alien; the phrase, "homoousios with the Father," indicates that the Son of God bears no resemblance to the genetos creatures, but that He is in every way assimilated to the Father alone who begat Him, and that He is not out of any other hypostasis and ousia, but out of the Father. To 'the homoousion' (as it came to be called), thus interpreted, the Conservatives agreed, with the further reflection that the term had admittedly been employed by certain ancient "learned and distinguished bishops and writers"—presumably Eusebius is referring to the Origenist champion, Dionysius of Alexandria, and to Origen himself.

In all this there is not a trace of Conservative panic over any supposed Sabellian association or tendency of the term homoousios. So far as the evidence goes, such an idea had simply never occurred to them at the time of the Council. The term was officially laid down, with no suggestion of its being a definition of the unity of God, but solely as a definition of the full and absolute deity of Christ. Further, it is generally accepted that the early opposition to the Council was not theological in character so much as personal. The charge against it, that it countenanced Sabellianism, was not raised until Marcellus wrote a defence of it which could colourably be said to be Sabellian.

Marcellus' doctrine (ap. Eus. *eccl. theol.* 2.6.2, *ib.* 2.9.4, *ib.* 2.9.7) appears to have been that the godhead was originally a monad, which developed, of its own nature and character, by a process of active expansion into the triad; the Logos proceeded forth from God by an operative impulse in the beginning of world-creation; at the end of the world, when this operation of the Logos should be completed, His separate existence once more would be merged in God as it was in the beginning. It might be said of this theory that it maintained a Sabellian view of God before the creation began and after the creation should have ceased, and Eusebius attacked it with immense persistence.

All the same, Eusebius quotes with approval (*ep. ad Caes.* 10) an extremely questionable statement of his most religious Emperor Constantine that the Logos was in being, according to His divine generation, before all ages, since even before He was begotten actively, He was potentially in the Father ingenerately, the Father being always Father. (This declaration was not made with reference to acceptance of the homoousion, but to justify the pronunciation of an anathema against the Arian statement that the Son "was not, before he was begotten.") The implication recalls in an extraordinary manner the old idea of the 'Word-immanent,' of which the doctrine of Marcellus was a more highly developed type.

All such theories certainly helped to make it easier to preserve an ultimate grasp of the divine unity. Athanasius himself was a strong upholder of the divine unity, and it is well known that he could not at first be induced to repudiate Marcellus' doctrine. It may be conjectured that his reluctance was due not merely to the fact that Marcellus was a strong defender of the Nicene definition, which was one of the few theological formulæ that Athanasius regarded as crucial; but also to the fact that he was bound to regard with sympathy any legitimate theory which helped to maintain, as against Arius, the essential unity of the godhead. However, so far as the Council of Nicæa is concerned, the problem of the divine unity did not arise. The question which it had to settle was whether both the Father and the Son were God in exactly the same sense of the word God.

The official interpretation laid down by the Council of Nicæa left the problem of the divine unity unsolved. Nevertheless, there is no doubt that, from the first, the party which can later be designated Athanasian regarded the term homoousios as containing within itself the true and proper solution of that problem also. This may be seen by comparing with Eusebius' description of the Council's discussions the corresponding account in Athanasius of the motives which led to insistence on the homoousion. Athanasius, like Eusebius, states that the object of his friends was to exclude any description of Christ as a creature, or any other distinctively Arian formula. But in doing so he makes it perfectly clear that Christ's full and absolute deity involved identity, and not mere likeness, of substance with the Father. Eusebius does not so much as touch on the identity of content of the divine Persons: Athanasius treats it as an axiomatic correlative with the doctrine of the divine substance of Christ.

Thus he writes (*de decret.* 20) that, owing to the evasive attitude of the Conservative sympathisers with Arianism, the bishops were compelled to go outside the word of Scripture in order to enforce its substance, and to say that the Son is homoousios with the Father, in order to indicate that the Son is not merely similar to the Father from whom He proceeds, but identical in similarity, and to show that the similarity and immutability of the Son imply something different from the imitation which is attributed to men and which they acquire by means of virtue. Again, the generation of the Son from the Father is different from human processes, since He is not only similar to, but also inseparable from, the Father's ousia, and He and the Father are one, and the Logos is ever in the Father and the Father in the Logos, reproducing the relation of the radiance to the light, for that is what the phrase indicates [this is a most significant claim, because the metaphor of radiance and light was the traditional expression of divine unity, *de decret.* 23]: for these reasons the Synod, with that understanding, rightly wrote homoousios, in order to manifest that the Logos is other than the geneta. It is impossible to read this long statement carefully without observing that the unity of the godhead and the identity of the Son's ousia with that of the Father are as strongly in the mind of Athanasius as is the doctrine that the Son is God in the same sense as the Father is God.

Whether this correlative doctrine safeguarding the unity of God, which the dominant party understood to be also involved in the homoousion, was actually expressed at the Council, may well be doubted. Probably, if it had been

expounded with any fullness, Eusebius and the Conservatives would have taken fright at once and raised a
great anti-Sabellian outcry, not recognising the fundamental difference between the Sabellian doctrine and the
orthodox, that the latter for all its insistence upon unity
recognised the distinctions in the godhead as being absolute,
permanent, and real, while the former made them accidental,
transitory, and subjective. It was reserved for Marcellus'
speculations to reveal the possibilities of error which lay in
an intensive and unbalanced attempt to press the unifying
element in the Nicene conception of the homoousion.
However, it was enough for the orthodox party at the
Council to secure the term as against Arius, and to leave the
development of its full implications to the future.

None the less, the two sides are seen perfectly balanced
in Athanasius' own mind; homoousios implies 'of one stuff'
as against Arius, and 'of one content' as against the retort,
already as old as Paul of Samosata, that thereby was implied
the existence of two gods. It is worth quoting a few more
passages to illustrate this balance. In the *de synodis* (53),
he argues that homoousios is equivalent to homophyes;
one man is 'like' another man in appearance or character,
but not in ousia; in ousia men do not merely 'resemble' one
another, they are homophyes; 'likeness' refers to appearances
and qualities, but in discussing ousiai we speak not of
likeness but of sameness. Athanasius has not here abandoned
his claim that the homoousion involves divine unity of
substance; he is simply showing that 'likeness' is an inaccurate phrase to describe the equality existing between the
Father and the Son. He is therefore content for the moment
to let ousia stand generically for 'secondary substance'

or 'species.' The point is important, because the Cappadocians afterwards argued that the fact of men being homoousios with one another was analogous to the consubstantiality of the divine Persons; they contended, not very convincingly, but as the best illustration which occurred to them, that the solidarity of mankind afforded an analogy to the unity of God. That, however, is not the point with which Athanasius was concerned in this passage. His argument is directed towards exposing the error of calling the Son homœousios (of like substance) instead of homoousios.

He writes again (*ad Serap.* 2.3): we are homoousios with those to whom we are similar and with whom we possess identity; men are homoousios with one another, since we all share the same characteristics, such as mortality, and so forth; similarly, angels are homophyes with one another; and so every other class of beings. In other words, homoousios of itself, and apart from the special circumstances of theology, means, as it had always meant, 'of the same stuff.' In the *de synodis* (51) he shows very ably that the term cannot be confined to collaterals (ἀδελφά), but applies equally to derivation and derivative. This is a frankly philological cut at the theory that, if homoousios, the Father and the Son must be collateral, with an antecedent common source. It is worth remarking also how he says (*de syn.* 42), in effect, Do not try to press metaphors too far, when you argue from material analogies to God; just as, in saying 'offspring,' though we know God to be a Father, we entertain no human or material ideas about Him, but in listening to these illustrations and terms we form our conception in a manner harmonious with deity, so also, when we use the term homoousios, we ought to transcend all physical notions.

But again and again, having laid down the homoousion as a barrier against ktisma and geneton, he advances to the substantial identity of Christ with God. Thus he argues (*de syn.* 48) that, if the Logos is a work of God, He is separated from the Father and has a different nature, and cannot be called homoousios with Him, but rather 'homogeneous' in nature with the works, however far He exceeds them in grace; but if we confess that He is not a work, but a true offspring out of the ousia of the Father, it follows that He is inseparable from the Father, sharing His nature, and should be called homoousios. Further, if the Son be not such by acquisition, but is Logos in ousia, and this ousia is the offspring of the Father's ousia, and the Son says, "I and the Father are one," and, "he that hath seen me hath seen the Father," how shall we preserve the oneness of the Father and the Son? Not, he says, by mere moral community of outlook, as the Arian theory demands, for then any creature who conforms to the divine will could equally say, "I and the Father are one," which is ridiculous: but the Son, "being offspring out of the ousia, is by ousia one, Himself and the Father that begat Him."

Again he maintains (*ad Afros* 8) that the Son possesses the divine prerogatives of creating, eternity, immutability, and therefore cannot be a creature; for He possesses them, not as a reward of virtue, but as belonging to His ousia; as Nicæa had said, He is not out of another ousia, but out of that of the Father, to which these prerogatives belong of right. But, Athanasius continues, if He thus belongs to the ousia of the Father and is offspring out of it, what can He be, or by what other term could He be described, but homoousios? for all that can be discerned in the Father,

217

can be discerned also in the Son, and in the Son, not from acquisition, but by ousia; and that is the meaning of the texts, "I and the Father are one," and "he that hath seen me hath seen the Father." Proceeding, he argues that, if the Son had acquired these prerogatives as the consequence of moral progress, He would not be one with the Father, but merely similar to the Father, a conclusion which would make God a compound being. But, he replies, God who compounded everything else to give it being is not Himself compound; He is simple ousia ($\dot{\alpha}\pi\lambda\dot{\eta}$ $o\dot{v}\sigma\dot{\iota}\alpha$), in which no question arises of attributes as distinct from the substance itself; and the Son is impropriate to that ousia ($\ddot{\iota}\delta\iota\sigma$ $\tau\hat{\eta}s$ $o\dot{v}\sigma\dot{\iota}\alpha s$). What then can He be called—this offspring that is impropriate and identical with the ousia of God, and proceeds out of it—except on this ground also homoousios?

At the same time, Athanasius is no Sabellian. The Son is a presentation of the divine substance by derivation and in real distinction. He agrees with his pseudepigrapher: "We do not hold a 'Filiopater' like the Sabellians, nor do we assert the term monoousion instead of homoousion, and thus destroy the being of the Son" (*exp. fid.* 2). Still less would he trifle with the appalling docetic or pantheistic doctrine which tended to fuse the humanity of Christ into the godhead: "what Hades emitted the statement that the body out of Mary is homoousios with the godhead of the Logos?" (*ad Epict.* 2). Finally, it may be noted, before we pass on, that Athanasius extended the homoousion expressly to the Holy Spirit: the Spirit is one, but the creatures and the angels are many; the Spirit is not of the many, but is one; or rather, He is impropriate to the Logos who is one, and impropriate to God who is one, and is homoousios with Him (*ad Serap.* 1.27).

CHAPTER XI

IDENTITY OF SUBSTANCE

THE employment of homoousios by Athanasius to express substantial identity was a new development in the Greek language. Philologically, it was a pure accident, arising from the peculiar circumstances of the object to which the term was on other grounds applied; the special sense which it acquired was derived simply from theological associations, which belonged to the realm of thought rather than to that of language. But there were precedents in another tongue. It has been well observed that Athanasius did not invent the term, nor set great store by the word itself, as distinct from the truth which it was meant to convey. The same is true of the Nicene fathers; they found it the most apt expression for their purpose of excluding Arianism. The only bishops, present at Nicæa, to whom the word antecedently implied unity as well as equality in the godhead, were the five or six Westerns, of whom Hosius was chief; and there seems every reason for attributing to his influence the selection of, and insistence upon, the term homoousios. To the Westerns the philological history of the term, and any bad odour which it had possibly contracted in connection with Paul of Samosata, were of little or no interest. They knew, perhaps, that it had been propounded by Dionysius of Rome to Dionysius of Alexandria. But what was of far greater importance, they perceived that it was a convenient translation of their own formula 'unius substantiæ.'

This phrase was first set forth by Tertullian: "tres autem non statu sed gradu, nec substantia sed forma, nec potestate sed specie, unius autem substantiæ et unius status et unius potestatis" (*Prax.* 2); "alium . . . personæ, non substantiæ, nomine, ad distinctionem, non ad divisionem," "unam substantiam in tribus cohaerentibus" (*ib.* 12). It may be argued that to Tertullian substantia did not exclude the notion of secondary substance. This question may be studied in the following passage (*de anim.* 32), in which he distinguishes between 'substantia' and 'natura substantiæ.' Substantia belongs to the individual object, but its natura may be shared between a number of objects; for illustrations he takes stone and iron, as expressing substances; it is not absolutely clear whether he means 'stone' and 'iron,' or ' a stone' and 'a piece of iron.' The natura substantiæ in these cases he illustrates by the quality of hardness, and he observes that their hardness brings the objects concerned into union, whereas their substance, being individual to each object, is in itself a fact of estrangement; thus cattle resemble mankind in nature, but not in substance. In this account of substance, even if secondary substance is not excluded, it is not regarded as expressing a generic abstraction, but denotes substance as individualised in a particular instance, "propria est rei cuiusque."

Again, replying (*Prax.* 7) to the question of an imaginary inquirer, he claims that the Word is a substantia, "spiritu et sophiæ traditione constructa," and he retorts that his opponent does not wish to recognise the Word as "substantivus in re per substantiæ proprietatem," for fear that He should be admitted to be "res et persona quædam," a particular object and presentation. This collocation of res and persona is in itself sufficient evidence that Tertullian's thought, when he talks of three Persons, has a real philosophical basis in the tradition of Greek thinkers, and that his doctrine of Person is definitely not derived from the forensic abstractions of the Roman law. So the expressions 'unius substantiæ' or 'una substantia,' as applied to the Trinity, involve unity and identity, as well as equality, of substance. This is again well brought out by Novatian (*de Trin.* 31), "a quo solo [sc. patre] haec vis divinitatis emissa, etiam in filium tradita et directa, rursum substantiæ per communionem ad patrem revolvitur."

The Athanasians, then, may be regarded as having learned the full implications of the homoousion from the West, where the divine identity of substance had already been thought out and found expression; insomuch that Hilary writes (*de syn.* 76) that the one substance of Father and Son is not to be denied because it is similar in each case—on the other hand, the reason for asserting the similarity is "quia unum sunt"; and again (*ib.* 64) "non unum subsistentem, sed substantiam non differentem"; and (*ib.* 88) that with this previous conception in his mind, he had been in no small degree strengthened in his conviction by the term homoousion.

It is convenient at this point to refer to Athanasius's extension of his teaching concerning the Son to the third Person of the Trinity. The Holy Spirit, he says (*ad Serap.* 1.2), has the same unity with the Son that the Son has with the Father, although, as he scornfully points out, the Arians regarded the Spirit as a creature; or, he inquires, are we to conclude that the Trinity is not a triad but a dyad, and after that the creation? Just as the Son who is in the Father, and in whom also the Father is, is not a creature, but belongs to the ousia of the Father, so the Spirit who is in the Son, and in whom also the Son is, must not be reckoned among creatures (*ib.* 1.21). Again, if the Son, since He is out of the Father, belongs to His ousia, it necessarily follows that the Spirit, who is said to be out of God, also belongs in ousia to the Son (*ib.* 1.25). Athanasius rests his argument, apart from ample Scriptural quotation, largely on the fact that the Holy Spirit exercises divine functions in His own Person, particularly in creation and sanctification; he had used similar arguments in defence of the deity of the Son. He sums the matter up (*ib.* 1.33) by saying that our Lord Jesus Christ Himself taught the woman of Samaria, and through her taught us, the perfection of the holy triad as being an indivisible and single godhead.

Within ten years of the Council of Nicæa, the Conservative Origenists were in uproar against the homoousion. They had been persuaded to accept the term as expounded at the Council, but Marcellus, one of the foremost supporters of the Nicene formula, published a work which laid him open to the charge of Sabellianism, and, as a result, the Conservatives were thrown into the arms of the Arians for thirty years. They had now more than adequately grasped the connection of the term homoousion with theories of divine unity. What made matters even worse was the fact that certain Marcellians apparently combined their master's speculations with the confession of a perfectly orthodox statement, subjecting to anathema (ap. Epiph. *haer.* 72.11) those who did not admit that the Holy Trinity is three prosopa uncircumscribed and objective (enhypostata) and homoousia and co-eternal and absolute. The followers of Marcellus appeared to be guilty of insincere jugglery with words, and their acceptance of the homoousion must have seemed, in the light of their theory, to involve a repudiation of the objective character of the Persons of the Trinity, for all their protestations to the contrary.

The position of the moderate Conservatives, or semi-Arians, came to be (ap. Epiph. *haer*. 73.1) that they professed, not homoousios, but homœousios, the term which they thought better expressed the meaning assigned to homoousios at Nicæa. In their explanation of homoousios, if we confine our consideration to the single point which formed the main issue at Nicæa, they were substantially correct, although it goes without saying that homœousios was open to serious objection, as Athanasius was quick to perceive. Just as homoousios involved associations which led beyond the immediate object of the Council's definition, so homœousios, if pressed, might lead to Arianism and polytheism. Homoousios was, however, still suspect of Sabellian tendencies, and the Synod of Ancyra (ap. Epiph. *haer*. 73.11) declared that, if anyone should call the Son homoousios or tautoousios with the Father, he should be anathema— making an identification between the two terms homoousios and tautoousios similar to that between homoousios and monoousios which pseudo-Athanasius's *expositio fidei* had expressly disclaimed.

After this the more extreme Conservatives, led by Macedonius, drifted into denial of deity to the Holy Spirit; they are the people aimed at by Athanasius in the passage from his letter to Serapion, quoted above, in which he

R

suggests that they believed in a dyad instead of a triad. The moderates, on the other hand, under the able guidance of Basil the Great, were converted, by arguments such as those of Athanasius in the *de synodis*, into champions of the Nicene creed, though even yet their emphasis fell, as we shall see, on a somewhat different aspect of the truth than that which has been uppermost in the explanations of Athanasius himself. The downright Arians denied both homoousios and homœousios, as, for instance, Eunomius, who writes (*lib. apol.* 26) that neither homoousios nor homœousios is to be accepted, since the former implies materiality (genesis) and division of the ousia, and the latter implies equality of the ousiai. The extreme Arians were by this time perfectly clear about their disbelief in the real divinity of the Son.

The extreme champion of orthodox formularies, Epiphanius, held firmly to the middle path, renewing the claim that homoousios neither denoted a bare unit nor divided the substance. The Son, he wrote (*haer.* 65.8), can neither be heteroousios from Him that begat Him, nor tautoousios, but homoousios. We do not admit tautoousios, he wrote again (*haer.* 76.7), for fear that the term may be regarded by some as an approximation to Sabellius, but we say homoousios, signifying by "the homo-" that the Persons are perfect, that the Son is out of the Father, perfect out of perfect, and the Holy Spirit also perfect. In the earlier work, entitled *ancoratus*, he claims (6.4) that the homoousion is the bond of the faith, for if you admit the homoousion, you have broken the power of Sabellius. Homoousios (*ib.* 6.5) indicates a single hypostasis (i.e. individual substance, in the old untechnical sense), and yet it signifies that the Father is objective (enhypostatos) and the Son objective and the

Holy Spirit objective. Without confessing the homoousion, he repeats (*haer.* 69.72), there is absolutely no disproof of heresies; for as the serpent detests the smell of bitumen, so Arius and Sabellius detest the formula of the true confession, homoousion. Epiphanius, then, is adamant in claiming that the homoousion was incompatible with either of the current forms of heresy; it was a bulwark both against Arian subordinationism and against Sabellian uni-personalism.

It has already been pointed out that, in order to oppose the rising school of Macedonius (which inherited an exclusive title to the name semi-Arian after the Cappadocian reconciliation with the Nicene party), Athanasius applied the term homoousios to the Holy Spirit. Apparently Basil avoided taking similar action, on precautionary grounds. In the same way, in order to preclude misunderstanding and prejudice, he always refrained from calling the Holy Spirit by the title Theos, though he fully believed in the truth which the ascription of that title would convey (Greg. Naz. *or.* 43.68). Yet he writes (*de fid.* 4) that we baptise into a homoousios Trinity. The application of the adjective to the Trinity itself, as distinct from the Persons, soon gave rise to a regular formula, "consubstantial Trinity," of which instances occur in Cyril of Jerusalem *ep. ad Constant.* 8 (A.D. 351, but there is a slight doubt of the authenticity of these concluding words of the letter); Epiphanius *haer.* 36.6.4; the Council of Constantinople (A.D. 382) *ep. syn.* ap. Thdt. *h.e.* 5.9.11; Didymus of Alexandria *de Trin.* 2.6.9; and (in the form of a doxology) pseudo-Macarius *hom.* 17.15.

The stages by which orthodox semi-Arianism was led to the full acceptance of the Nicene formula may be illustrated

in the person of Basil. At first he was cautiously suspicious
of the homoousion, and wrote (for the correspondence, though
it has been strongly contested, seems not improbably to
be genuine) to Apollinarius, later heresiarch, for a resolution
of his doubts. He asks (*ep.* 361) how the homoousion can
soundly be applied to objects in reference to which there is
no common antecedent genus nor antecedent matter, nor
separation of one object so as to form a second; it seems to
him that the phrase "similar without variation" (a notable
semi-Arian formula) would better fit the situation than the
homoousion. Apollinarius replied, in the letter numbered
362 in the collection of Basil's correspondence, with a fully
Athanasian explanation, and follows it up, in the letter
numbered 364, with the statement that the homoousion
indicated the Son to be not similar to God, but God, as
being a true offspring and of the same ousia as Him that
begat Him.

In the genuine books against Eunomius (dating about
363–5), Basil uses the word homoousios more than once of
secular objects in its original and proper sense, and once
theologically, in the same sense, that is to say the sense
accepted by Eusebius at the Council of Nicæa: the Son, he
says (*c. Eun.* 1.20), has been called 'radiance' that we may
perceive the fact of His being united to the Father, and
'expression of His hypostasis' in order that we may recognise
the fact of His being homoousios. So already, writing to
Maximus (*ep.* 9.2), he had complained that Dionysius of
Alexandria went so far in subordinating the hypostaseis as
to undermine the homoousion; but he proceeds at once (3)
to interpret the homoousion himself as meaning "similar in
ousia without variation," as suggested in the letter to Apol-

linarius. It is not the divine identity but the divine equality which Basil uses homoousios to secure.

Later on, in order to clear himself from the charge of belittling the Nicene formula, Basil composed a letter which shows the unmistakable influence, in thought and language, of the *de synodis* of Athanasius. In this missive (*ep.* 52.1) he professes himself an heir of the fathers who at Nicæa promulgated their great decree about the faith, but admits that the term homoousion was not only misrepresented by opponents, but was also still under suspicion in some quarters which were substantially more orthodox.

Moreover, it had been criticised a century before in the matter of Paul of Samosata. The Synod of Antioch had maintained that homoousios tended to imply a relation similar to that existing between different copper coins, each possessing a common participation in the anterior substance copper; such language, says Basil, may be all very well in connection with copper coinage, but there is no anterior underlying substance in the case of God the Father and God the Son; what can be conceived as anterior to the Unbegotten? Continuing (*ib.* 2), he says that the Council of Nicæa, after stating that the Son was Light of Light and out of the ousia of the Father, added the homoousion, in order to indicate that whatever conception of light may be ascribed to the Father will apply equally in the case of the Son; for, he says, collaterals [though what about the copper coins?] are not called homoousios with one another; that expression is appropriate when the same nature (physis) obtains between the cause and that which derives its existence from that cause. Here he is on the verge of formulating the unity of substance, though he just falls short of stating it.

Again, he writes (*ep.* 214.4, dated A.D. 375), If you ask me shortly to state my own view, I shall reply that ousia bears the same relation to hypostasis as the common (τὸ κοινόν) has to the particular; each of us at the same time partakes of existence through the common principle of ousia, and by his own personal properties is constituted So-and-so. In theology, too, the principle of the ousia is common, like goodness or deity; but the hypostasis is recognised in the individual property of Fatherhood or Sonship or Sanctifying Power. If anyone asserts that the prosopa are anhypostata (without hypostasis), the statement is absurd; but if it is agreed that the prosopa exist in genuine hypostasis, then they must be enumerated, that the principle of the homoousion may be maintained in the unity of the godhead. Basil's statement is not as clear as might be desired; his formal definitions are abstract and unsatisfactory (see below pp. 275ff.); but he does seem to realise that the homoousion bears some kind of relation to the problem of unity as well as to that of equality. He probably thought, according to the principle of the solidarity of the human race, that the whole of human nature is presented in each individual man, so that his argument from particular men afforded a not entirely inadequate illustration of the unity of God. He certainly seems to imply that the only fact which constituted the several hypostases of the godhead was that of Fatherhood, Sonship and Sanctification, and that, apart from these 'idiomata' of presentation, the ousia of the three Persons was identical.

The whole argument of a passage in his sermon *c. Sabell. et Ar. et Anom.* (4) seems to require the implication of identity of substance. Arguing strongly for the view that, while he recognised two distinct hypostaseis, he still maintained the unity of God, "as image," he writes, "the Son reproduces the exact model without variation, and as offspring He preserves the homoousion." The image-metaphor guarantees so to speak, the identity of form between the Persons, and the offspring-metaphor guarantees the identity of matter. This interpretation is confirmed by the words with which the section opens. Basil affirms that when he says 'one ousia,' he does not mean to imply two separated objects produced out of one; the Son derives His objective existence out of the Father as arche; Father and Son do not derive their being out of a single antecedent ousia; they are not collaterals (adelpha) but father and son; and the identical character (τὸ ταὐτόν) of the ousia is to be accepted, since, in the imagery of the old metaphor of divine unity, the Son rays forth in entire perfection from a Father who remains in entire perfection.

Indeed, he had disclaimed the merely generic sense of ousia, as equivalent to εἶδος (species), in the treatise c. Eunom. (1.23); as the Father is free from any kind of composite character, so the Son also is absolutely simple and un-compounded, and the expression 'similarity,' as applied to the relation between them, is not conceived as depending on identity of species, but on their actual ousia; the godhead has neither form nor figure, and therefore it follows that similarity, in this connection, must be due, not to any qualities or attributes held in common, but to the ousia itself, just as equality in the same connection resides, not in measurements of bulk, but in 'identity' of power. The identity of the divine ousia in the several Persons is there-fore not, in Basil's view, a matter of their belonging to a single species, but of their several expression unimpaired of an identical single ousia, which is concrete, incapable of any limiting or qualifying relation, and exhaustive of the content of the being of its several presentations: the prosopa are constituted by the permanent and objective presentation of this ousia, respectively, as Paternal, Filial, and Sanctifical.

Already in the *de Spiritu sancto* (45) Basil had argued that the unity of the Persons was not a collective unity, and that the real meaning of the monarchy was seen in a unity of ousia, though he does not actually employ the term 'identity' (ταυτότης). We do not number the Persons, he said, by addition, making an increase from one to plurality, nor do we speak of first, second, and third; indeed he denies that he had ever heard the expression 'second God.' While we worship God out of God and confess the particularity of the hypostaseis, "we rest in the monarchy" and do not scatter the divine principle into a separated multitude; it is the one form which is seen in God the Father and in God the Only-begotten, imaged through the undeviating character of the godhead; the Son is in the Father and the Father in the Son. In the homily against the Sabellians and Arius and the Anomoeans (4) the word 'identical' does occur, as has been quoted already.

This key doctrine, like so much else that was crucial in Basil's thought, comes from Athanasius (*de decret.* 23). The principle, says Athanasius, has to be preserved that the Son is truly immutable and unchangeable; and how otherwise could He be such unless He is the own offspring of the Father's ousia? for this title, like that of 'radiance,' must be taken as maintaining His 'identity' with His own Father. With him identity is linked up with the fact of being homoousios, not only in the sphere of God, but in the world of men. As we have seen before, he argues (*de syn.* 53) that similarity does not belong to ousiai; it only applies to appearances (σχήματα) and attributes; with reference to ousiai the right term to use is not resemblance but 'identity.' He illustrates his point by observing that what makes one man resemble another is not his ousia but appearance and 'character'; that is to say, external or internal relations. He makes a similar remark, again in the course of an argument from 'likeness' to the homoousion, in the correspondence with Serapion (*ad Serap.* 2.3): we are homoousios with those whom we resemble and with whom we share 'identity'; men, he repeats, being like and possessing 'identity' with one another are homoousios with one another, for all possess the 'identical' qualities of mortality, corruptibility, mutability, and creation out of non-existence. We need not stop to discuss here the validity of the argument from the solidarity of the human race, which was adopted by the Cappadocian Fathers. But his insistence on associating 'identity' with homoousios gives a sufficiently clear indication of the lines on which the mind of Athanasius worked about the Trinity.

Basil took up the term 'identity,' though with some diffidence. Note, he says (*hom.* 23.4), the similarity of the Son to the Father; by that, as he explains, he means 'identity,' safe-guarding, however, the particularity of the Son and the Father; he bids his hearers recognise the paternal 'form' (morphe) in the hypostasis of the Son, quoting "I am in the Father and the Father in me," which, he claims, does not imply "fusion of substances but identity of 'character.'" Identity of ousia is combined with the possession by the several Persons of distinguishing particularities ($\gamma\nu\omega\rho\iota\sigma\tau\iota\kappa\alpha\grave{\iota}$ $\grave{\iota}\delta\iota\acute{o}\tau\eta\tau\epsilon\varsigma$), as he explains carefully in the work against Eunomius (2.28); the fact of being begotten or unbegotten is simply such a distinguishing particularity, which supervenes upon the divine ousia with a view to providing a clear and unconfused conception of the Father and the Son; Father and Son are both alike light, the one unbegotten light and the other begotten light; as between light and light, no opposition arises, but in so far as the one is begotten and the other unbegotten, a contrast supervenes; for this, he adds, is the nature of the idiomata, that within the identity of the ousia they manifest distinction. Basil can fairly claim to be at bottom Athanasian.

The term identity passed into the ordinary currency of theological language, and it is indeed astonishing that so little attention is called to its emphatic significance by modern text-books. Thus the Semi-Arians (ap. Epiph. *haer*. 73.9.7) argue that the phrase 'similar in ousia' is inadequate as a description of the Son's relation to the Father, because it fails to express the truth that his ousia is identical with that of the Father. Theodore of Mopsuestia (*frag.* in Swete 2. 328 line 21) states that there are not three different ousiai, but one ousia recognised in the identity of the godhead. The identity of the divine ousia in the three Persons is a very frequent theme in Cyril of Alexandria. To take only two instances: he declares (*dial. de Trin*. 1, 408C) that although the Son veritably exists in His own hypostasis, yet He is not to be distinguished from the Father as a human being is distinguished from his fellows or according to the law of bodily objects; they have a union of nature which is of an ineffable character, although there is no fusion between the hypostaseis in such a manner as that the Father and the Son are one and the same; each possesses a real subsistence, but their unity is guaranteed by the identity of the ousia. Again (on *St. John* 525D) he compares the divine Wisdom to the human understanding up to this point, that the Wisdom of the God and Father, that is to say the Son, is not a thing different from the Father so far as relates to the identity of their ousia and the undeviating similarity of their nature (physis). Anastasius of Sinai (*Hodegus*, Migne 89.56A) sums up all in an epigram: the Son is a secundity of hypostasis in an identity of physis.

The result of this insistence on the identity of the ousia is seen in the changing emphasis with which the doctrine of the monarchy now comes to be regarded. There is no longer any suggestion that God is one simply by reason of the fact that the second and third Persons may in the last resort be resolved back into the first Person, since they derive their origin from Him. The fact that now comes to be emphasised is that the Father is manifested in the Son and in the Holy Spirit wholly and without any detraction. The three Persons no longer lead back to a unity that is primarily found in one Person; they are in a real sense one in themselves. This new sense of 'monarchy' appears, for instance, in Epiphanius (*haer.* 62.3); we are not introducing polytheism, he asserts, but proclaiming monarchy, and in proclaiming monarchy we confess the triad, a monad in a triad and a triad in a monad, one godhead of Father, Son, and Holy Spirit. So he, too, like Basil, "rests in the monarchy."

The Cappadocian Settlement finally fixed the statement of Trinitarian orthodoxy in the formula of one ousia and three hypostaseis. It was worked out largely by Basil, supported by the strenuous efforts of the uncompromising Epiphanius, preached by the inspired populariser, Gregory of Nazianzus, and elaborated by the acute and speculative mind of Gregory of Nyssa. Most of the vitally significant terms employed in determining this theological settlement have already been described. Something, however, should be said about the term physis (φύσις). This word is an empirical rather than a philosophical term. Its most important controversial use arose in connection with later disputes over the Incarnation. It refers to much the same thing as ousia, but it is more descriptive, and bears rather on function, while ousia is metaphysical and bears on reality. The Persons of the Trinity have one physis because they have one energeia: their activity is in each case divine and that divine activity admits of no variation. Physis therefore, more readily than ousia, supports a generic meaning. At the same time it must be remembered that this meaning is by no means necessary. A number of instances could be quoted in which 'one physis' signifies 'one object possessing a certain character or displaying a certain function.' It is unnecessary to elaborate this fact here, as it is chiefly important in connection with the Cyrilline doctrine of the unity of Christ. In relation to the Trinity, however, 'of one physis' can just as well imply 'of identical function or nature' as 'of similar function or nature'; and as long as the definition 'one ousia' clearly implied identity of substance, so long would 'of one physis' support an interpretation which implied that the Trinity was in a real sense a single object.

A simple illustration may help to make the whole position clear. The pulpit of St. Mary's Church at Oxford is a pragma, thing, or object. It is a hypostasis, as being a concrete, objective entity, existent in fact and not merely in thought. It is a prosopon, as an object empirically distinct from other and possibly similar objects, such as the pulpit in the Church of All Saints, further along the street. It is a physis, as employed for preaching. And it is an ousia, as analysed in substance and content into an actual instance of all that is connoted by the conception of pulpitry in general. Some of these words are capable of bearing a generic sense. But it should be observed that all of them can denote a single concrete entity, and in the illustration just presented all of them do so denote a single entity. Similarly, as applied to the being and the Persons of the deity, in the classic exposition of Trinitarian doctrine constructed by the Fathers of the fourth century, prosopon, hypostasis, and ousia all equally denote single concrete entities, and physis denotes the characteristics of such a single entity. To the Greeks, God is one objective Being, though He is also three Objects.

This view of the matter differs in conception, though not in effect, from the Latin view, according to which God is one Object and three Subjects (una substantia, tres personæ). Neither the Latin language, nor the ordinary Latin intellect, was capable of the subtlety of the conception which approved itself to the Greek theologians. Latin theology took its own path, and Augustine attempted, perhaps not very convincingly, to correlate the three Subjects by the analogy of subject, object, and relation (de Trin. book ix.), presenting it in the very fully elaborated example of mind, knowledge of self by the mind, and love with which the mind loves both itself and its own knowledge. He tried a surer method of

approach (*ib.* book x.) with his psychological illustration of
the co-ordination in a unified human consciousness of
memory, understanding, and will, and the consequent
argument from the mental constitution of man, the highest
of God's creatures, to a more objective multiplicity in the
creative Mind. By such means attention was firmly riveted
on the essential unity involved in the divine triplicity, and a
road was paved to the conception of the mutual interpenetration of the three Persons.

Among the Greeks, the same goal was ultimately reached
by a different route, not psychological but metaphysical, as
befitted the Greek intellect. For the Greeks were not only
concerned to defend the language of tradition and the
descriptive teaching of the Bible; they were always anxious,
with genuine speculative interest, to infer from the Biblical
data what God really is. The theological problem was to
them an exercise in Christian philosophy, no less absorbing
for its own sake than necessary to be undertaken in order to
preserve the gospel against practical polytheism or dissolvent
unitarianism.

The wisest of the Latins were fully conscious that the
Greek doctrine of the Trinity was essentially different from
their own. They owned that there was something paradoxical in the attempt, necessary as it was, by finite human
intellects to give expression to the nature of the infinite
mystery of God. This recognition enabled them to grasp
that any doctrine of God is only a human allegory, true
enough in so far as it presents a faithful picture of the
revelation disclosed by God for man's practical apprehension,
but quite inadequate to convey a complete account of what
God is in His own perfect nature. On this understanding,

they were ready to allow that two different definitions of the being of God might well be equally true to fundamental divine fact. Both were based upon analogy, and analogies must not be pressed in detail beyond the points which they are intended to cover. Putting the matter from a different standpoint, the creeds might be compared to accurate signposts rather than to exhaustive charts.

Jerome indeed had violently denounced the formula of three hypostaseis (*ep.* 15) and branded it as Arian. It is clear from his language that he identified hypostasis with substantia exclusively in its generic sense. Through thinking in Latin rather than in Greek terms he failed to detect the subtlety and true meaning of the Greek conception. He therefore regarded the Greek upholders of the formula as heretics. But Augustine was neither alarmed nor even surprised to find that the Greeks interpreted the Trinity differently from the Latins. "For the sake of describing things ineffable," he wrote (*de Trin.* vii.4 (7)), "that we may be able in some way to express what we are in no way able to express fully, our Greek friends have spoken of one essence and three substances, but the Latins of one essence or substance and three persons." Either practice is legitimate, provided that such expressions are "understood only in a mystery," for God can be more truly conceived than expressed, and exists more truly than He can be conceived; the transcendence of the godhead surpasses the powers of ordinary discourse.

Four centuries later, the fact of Greek and Latin divergence was noted in the West with deep suspicion. The Greek doctrine had been revived by Irish teachers, whose habit of rational speculation matched that of the Greeks, but with far less general profundity of theological insight. At the beginning of the ninth century the Celts, who in a Greekless Western world were once more in possession of at least some measure of Greek culture, knew that hypostasis, though equivalent in theology to the Latin persona, really meant not subject but object. The consequence may be traced in the horrified protest of Benedict of Aniane, who died in 822 (*opuscula* iii., Migne *P.L.* 103.1413B). The 'Scoti' were employing an argumentation that was superstitious, apocryphal, and ignorant of the true faith. They based it on the Greek statement of the faith, which required the profession of one ousia, that is, one natura or essentia, and three hypostaseis, which could be translated into Latin either as 'three personæ' or as 'three substantiæ.' In the Latin language, says Benedict, only the term essentia should be applied to God's being; substantia was indeed used also, but improperly, because to Greeks 'substantia' strictly implied the same thing as persona, not the same thing as natura. But the "moderni scholastici," especially among the Irish, had taken advantage of these facts to pose their "syllogismus delusionis." (Benedict's orthodox Latin mind was as greatly scared of the irresponsibility of logic as St. Bernard's was when confronted by Abelard.) By means of this they deduced that a Trinity exists, as of Persons, so of Objects (substantiarum), playing on the double interpretation of hypostasis. Benedict clearly did not realise that hypostasis does not really mean at all the same thing as persona, nor that in the authentic Greek doctrine of the Trinity God, regarded as object, is indeed three. But in that age it is to his credit that he even recognised the meaning of hypostasis in any connection.

A generation later than Benedict of Aniane, the doctrine of the Trinity is expounded by John Scotus in its Greek form without any sign of conscious repudiation of Western orthodoxy. This enigmatic Irish Christian philosopher, who translated pseudo-Dionysius and Maximus Confessor into Latin, is obviously thinking in terms of Greek theory. "In order," he claims (*de divis. naturæ* 1.13, Migne *P.L.* 122.456B), "that the devout activity of pious minds may have something to conceive and express about the ineffable and incomprehensible. . . holy theologians have devised and transmitted the following devout 'symbolic' [credal, or allegorical?] statement of the faith, that we should believe with our heart and profess with our lips that the divine goodness consists in the three objects (substantiæ) of a single essence (essentia)." Contemplating, he continues, the one ineffable universal cause they proclaimed the unity; but regarding that unity not in solitude and sterility but in a marvellous and fertile multiplicity, they recognised three objects (substantiæ) presented by the unity, namely the ingenerate, the begotten, and the processive.

Anselm (*epp.* 1.74, Migne *P.L.* 158.1144C), as a devout student of St. Augustine, was again aware that Greek and Latin doctrines differed, but equally unconcerned; "owing to lack of a term which will properly signify that plurality which is discerned in the most high Trinity, the Latins claim that three persons are to be believed in one substance, but the Greeks, with no less loyalty, confess three substances in one person." He states the antithesis with less accuracy but with enhanced paradox by substituting 'one person' for 'one essence' in his account of Greek theology. But by this time the difference, though still recognised, begins to be slurred over. Roscelin, the aggressive nominalist who had been compelled in 1092 to recant the tritheism alleged against himself, regards the divergence as a mere matter of verbal form. In his abusive letter to Abelard (inter Abelard *epp.* 15, Migne *P.L.* 178.365B), he asserts that "by persona we mean nothing else than we mean by substantia, though by terminological custom we triplicate persona and not substantia, while the Greeks triplicate substantia."

St. Thomas Aquinas (*summa theol.* 1.29.3) saw through Jerome's error in identifying hypostasis with the abstract sense of substantia, and (*ib.* 1.29.2) admitted that the two words really had the same meaning. Nevertheless, since substantia was equally capable of expressing the abstract or the concrete, he deprecated its use as the translation of hypostasis, and preferred subsistentia, defined as that which "per se existit, et non in alio." This was indeed precisely what hypostasis meant. But Aquinas himself failed to express entire recognition of the fact. Instead, he thought that hypostasis simply meant 'individual,' like the Latin persona and (as he might have added, but did not) the Greek prosopon: "secundum vero quod supponitur accidentibus, dicitur hypostasis vel substantia." The only distinction which he could make between persona and hypostasis was that he took hypostasis to signify an individual in any class of objects, "communiter in toto genere substantiarum," but confined persona "in genere rationalium substantiarum," that is, to individuals of the human species. It is unnecessary to carry the investigation further. Enough has been said to show that over a long period of centuries the most observant and profound of Western theologians recognised the characteristic meaning of the Greek doctrine to be that of 'three Objects,' and not 'three Subjects'; and were nevertheless content to think the Greeks as likely to be right as they themselves.

CHAPTER XII

UNITY IN TRINITY

THE doctrine of the Cappadocians was substantially the same as that of Athanasius, from whom they had learned it. But their emphasis was different. They have been accused—quite unjustly and inaccurately—of being practically tritheists. That was not the case. By ousia they meant a single identical object, regarded from the standpoint of metaphysical reality; not merely similarity of being. But for two reasons they insisted much more strongly than Athanasius on the objective triplicity of God. They themselves came out of the semi-Arian tradition, in which only with difficulty was the entire separation of the three hypostaseis overcome. And their battle was against extreme Arians, who insisted on the triplicity of hypostaseis in order to prove their contention that the hypostaseis were unequal. With these antecedents, and against that enemy, they accepted the objective triplicity as the basis of their thought, and from that position advanced to the assertion that because the three hypostaseis were equal, they must further constitute a single identical ousia. They were too firm in their belief in the unity of God to be able to rest in the conception of the similarity of the hypostaseis; that doctrine was bound to lead on to the dogma of substantial identity. But the groundwork of the Cappadocian Fathers' thought lay in the triplicity of equal hypostaseis, and the identity of the divine ousia came second in order of prominence to their minds. That is the reason why Basil, for instance, in arguing for the equality of the three Persons, so often uses language about the ousia of God that fails to go beyond the ascription of a common generic stuff to the several hypostaseis. "Substance and hypostasis bear the same relation of common and particular as do animal and John Doe: we maintain one ousia in the godhead in order to avoid giving a different rationale of the Persons" (*ep.* 236.6). But, after all, that is the main thing which Basil had to prove, and moreover is all that the Nicene Council originally set out to state.

If the community of ousia is taken as implying an antecedent matter, divided up into the three Persons, says Basil (*c. Eunom.* 1.19), that is as great a blasphemy as saying that the Persons are unequal, as the Eunomians frankly did: the right way of understanding the community of ousia is by the recognition that the same account must be given of one Person as of another; if the Father, for instance, is regarded as possessing the content (ὑποκείμενον) of light, then the ousia of the Son is also light; and on this reasoning the godhead is one. Again (*ib.* 2.4), the mere fact that names differ does not imply any necessary variation in the ousia: Peter and Paul have different names, but there is one ousia of all mankind.

Here it needs to be remembered that though the analogy holds good up to a point, yet in fact the cases are very different. In the case of different men, the unity of ousia is generic and does not lead on by a necessity of thought to identity of ousia. And besides, the differences that distinguish different human beings are manifold; but the differences that distinguish the divine Persons consist simply in the 'idiotetes' expressed in the names of Fatherhood, Sonship, and Sanctification, which signify, as will be seen shortly, the manner in which the substance is imparted and expressed. So it is true that an element has to be recognised in the godhead which is common, and other elements must be distinguished which are individual: faith confesses the distinction in hypostasis and the community in ousia; hypostasis is the badge of the individuality of each, while the principle of community is referred to the ousia (*ep.* 38.5). Yet the whole unvaried common substance, being incomposite, is identical with the whole unvaried being of each Person; there is no question of accidents attaching to it; the entire substance of the Son is the same as the entire substance of the Father: the individuality is only the manner in which the identical substance is objectively presented in each several Person. (On *ep.* 38 see Index of References.)

Idiotes, or 'particularity,' is the term chosen to express this individual characteristic. The difference between the Persons, says Basil (*c. Eun.* 1.19), consists in their plurality and in the 'particularities' which characterise each: and again (*ep.* 38.8), everything that belongs to the Father is seen in the Son, and everything that belongs to the Son belongs also to the Father, since the Son abides whole in the Father and again possesses the Father whole in Himself; the hypostasis of the Son is, so to speak, the 'form' and presentation (prosopon) of the recognition of the Father, and the Father's hypostasis is recognised in the form of the Son; there remains the supplementary particularity with a view to the clear distinction of the hypostaseis. These particularities are called by Basil γνωριστικαὶ ἰδιότητες ('identifying particularities') (*ep.* 38.5, *c. Eun.* 2.29), and they consist in being gennetos and being agennetos (*c. Eun. ib.*): or as in Greg. Naz. (*or.* 25.16), agennesia, gennesis, and ekpempsis (promission). They are modes of being, not elements in being. Later theology called them for obvious reasons ἰδιότητες ὑποστατικαί (pseudo-Cyr. *de ss. Trin.* 9: "agennesia and gennesis and ekporeusis (procession): in these hypostatic particularities alone do the three holy hypostaseis differ from one another.") In the form 'idioma' this term goes back to Alexander of Alexandria (ap. Thdt. *h.e.* 1.4.52), who states that being agennetos is the only idioma of the Father.

The fact that these three particularities merely represent modes in which, as has been said, the divine substance is transmitted and presented, was expressed by the phrase τρόπος ὑπάρξεως, 'mode of existence.' The word hyparxis means, in the simplest sense, existence. Hypostasis and ousia, says Athanasius (*ad Afr.* 4), mean 'existence'; for they are, and they 'exist.' But the word carries a certain association with the sense of beginning. The hyparxis of life, remarks Irenæus (*haer.* 4.20.5), comes about by sharing in God: and Eusebius (*eccl. theol.* 1.9.2) states that when the Bible speaks of the hyparxis of created things, it testifies that they all were created through the Logos. It is therefore possible to argue that when the phrase 'mode of hyparxis' is applied to the divine Persons, it may, at least in the case of the second and third Persons, originally have contained a covert reference not merely to their existence, but to the derivation of their existence from the paternal arche.

The term seems to have been rescued by Basil from the schools of logic, and subsequently adopted generally into the theological tradition. The word knowledge, he observes (*ep.* 235.2), covers many senses; an object may be known by reference to number, size, effect, mode of hyparxis, time of generation, or ousia; the Eunomians demanded that Basil should profess knowledge of the ousia of God; but he hesitated to say more than that he knew what was knowable of God, and that other knowledge of Him passed human comprehension. Again (*de Sp. sanct.* 46) he says that the Spirit is a living ousia, lord of sanctification, whose relationship to God is disclosed by His procession, but the mode of whose hyparxis is preserved ineffable. His friend Amphilochius of Iconium (*frag.* 15) insists that the names Father, Son, and Holy Spirit do not represent ousia as such, but "a mode of hyparxis or relation."

In the fourth (pseudonymous) book of Basil against Eunomius, which may possibly have as its author Didymus, the blind theologian of Alexandria (inter Bas. ed. Ben. vol. i. 283B), this point, that the term agennetos expresses not the ousia of God, but His mode of hyparxis, is elaborately proved: for if objects that have a different hyparxis of their being must be held to possess also a different ousia, .then various members of the human race are not homoousioi, for Adam had one hyparxis, being formed out of the earth, and Eve had another, since she issued from Adam's rib, and Abel another, as he was born of human intercourse, and the Son of Mary another, for He was born of the Virgin alone: hence agennetos and gennetos do not refer to the ousia of the Father and the Son, but to their mode of hyparxis. In this passage, the origin of existence is clearly taken as determining the mode of existence in each given instance of temporal being. It may be inferred that by implication the point stressed in the divine instances is also the process by which each Person comes to have His being imparted, as much as the manner in which that being, once imparted, is expressed. The Father affords a negative instance, as He does not come to be from any source, but exists underivatively; the Son comes to be derivatively, by generation, from the Father. The matter is, however, only one of academic interest, since, whether the term really means 'mode of existence' or 'mode of obtaining existence,' in practice it is exclusively employed to cover the facts involved in the latter conception; while, on the other hand, since the relations between the divine Persons have no temporal reference but express eternal processes continually operative within the divine being, it might well be said that there is no difference for thought between those processes themselves and their initiation.

The phrase also occurs in Gregory of Nyssa (*c. Eun.* 3.6.63, vulgo 8, Migne 45.793A), at about the same date as in the example last quoted, but not in the technical Trinitarian sense. The instance does, however, further illustrate the association of the phrase with origins. Arguing against the view that the Son had a temporal beginning, Gregory points out that the Son, as creator, had no affinity with the creation; if He had such affinity with His works in any other respect, it would have been necessary to admit that He did not diverge from the creation in respect of the mode of His hyparxis either: but this is not the case. Pseudo-Justin several times employs the phrase of the Trinity, as, for instance, when he states (*exp. rect. fid.* 3) that the terms agennetos and gennetos and ekporeutos do not express ousia but modes of hyparxis; or when he says (*ad orth. resp.* 139) that the divine Persons differ not in ousia but in their modes of hyparxis, and that this difference in modes of hyparxis does not destroy their unity in ousia. Pseudo-Cyril (*de ss. Trin.* 8) repeats that the Holy Spirit proceeds from the Father, not by way of generation but by way of procession—it is, he adds, another mode of hyparxis, just as is the generation of the Son; and he compares Adam, who was in the literal sense agennetos, Seth, who was gennetos, and Eve, who "proceeded" from Adam's side. The whole passage, with much else, is transcribed by John of Damascus into the first book of his *Orthodox Faith* (*fid. orth.* 1.8, 135B, C). Maximus Confessor again (*myst.* 517B) remarks that the Holy Monad is a triad in its hypostaseis and mode of hyparxis.

So far the connection with origins appears to be maintained. Nevertheless, Leontius of Byzantium employs both tropos (mode) of hyparxis and logos (principle) of hyparxis in relation to the two natures of Christ (*c. Nest. & Eut. prol.*, Migne 86.1269C; *ib.* 1, 1304B). In this connection the phrases have no reference to origins, but mean simply 'mode of existence,' or 'constitutive principle.' The same remark applies to the passage (*ib.* 1285A) in which the phrase is applied to the human soul, which is said to be circumscribed both in its own principle of hyparxis and through being associated with a circumscribed body. In like manner John of Damascus (*c. Jacob.* 52) remarks that the incarnation was not an act of the divine nature, but the mode of a second hyparxis. The possibility therefore remains that the association with origins is mainly an accident, arising from the inherent nature of the case when the phrase was applied to the divine Persons. But in any event, as has been said, it makes no practical difference to the sense. The term

mode of hyparxis was applied, from the end of the fourth
century, to the particularities that distinguish the divine
Persons, in order to express the belief that in those Persons
or hypostaseis one and the same divine being is presented in
distinct objective and permanent expressions, though with
no variation in divine content.

One salutary consequence followed from the fact that the
basis of thought was now laid in the triplicity of objective
presentation rather than the unity of essential being. It
meant the end of subordinationism. There was no longer
any question but that the Son and Holy Spirit are indeed
equal to the Father as touching divinity, since each is a
presentation of an identical divine being. The history of
Arius had indicated that subordinationism leads either to
unitarianism or to polytheism, or to a mixture of the two.
The only sense in which the doctrine could survive in
Catholic theology was in strict and sole relation to the
doctrine of arche. According to this doctrine, the Father's
mode of hyparxis involves a logical, though of course not a
temporal, priority, in that the two derivative modes of
hyparxis, those of the Son and of the Holy Spirit, depend on
it for their source. But such priority involves no superiority.
The doctrine of the Trinity, as formulated by the Cappadocians, may be summed up in the phrase that God is one
object *in* Himself and three objects *to* Himself. Further
than that illuminating paradox it is difficult to see that human
thought can go. It secures both the unity and the trinity.

Still in strict relation to the arche, the subordinationist
tradition derived from Origen left yet another legacy to
theology in the doctrine of the double procession of the Holy
Spirit. Origen expressly subordinated the Spirit to the Son.

He decided that piety and truth required acceptance of the theory that all things came to be through the Logos, as St. John had said; nor was it possible to exclude from the range of the expression 'all things' the being of the Holy Spirit; the Spirit, however, must be recognised as more honourable than them all, and first in rank of all that derive their being from the Father through the Son; he further suggests a reason why the Spirit is not called Son, as Christ is—because He does not derive from the Father direct, but appears to require the ministry of the Son for His hypostatisation (on *St. John* 2.10, 75, 76). The Catholic Origenists reproduced the kernel of this teaching in their assertion that the Holy Spirit proceeds from the Father through the Son. It is most significant that the Antiochene school, represented by the 'creed of Theodore' and by Theodoret, denied the double procession and asserted that the Spirit proceeds directly from the Father. "We neither regard the Spirit as a Son," says the 'creed of Theodore' (Hahn *Symbole*[3] p. 302), "nor as having received His existence through the Son." "If Cyril means that the Spirit has His existence from the Son or through the Son," says Theodoret in answer to Cyril's ninth anathema (Thdt. 5.47B), "we reject this teaching as blasphemous and impious." The Alexandrians and Cappadocians were Origenists; the Antiochenes were not.

The double procession was explicitly taught, on the lines laid down by Origen, in the *Ecclesiastical Theology* of Eusebius (3.6.1–3). Not only is the Spirit conveyed through the Son to those whom the Father wills, but He comes into being through the Son; the Son is creative of all derivative beings (geneta), even of the existence of the Paraclete-Spirit; the Spirit is not to be identified either with God or with God's Son, since He does not derive His origin from the Father similarly to the Son, but through the Son. The Holy Spirit, in [Athanasius] *exp. fid.* 4, is a procession (ekporeuma) of the Father, ever in the hands of the Father who sends Him and of the Son who sustains Him. In Athanasius, the Spirit has the same rank and function (physis) relative to the Son, as the Son bears to the Father (*ad Serap.* 1.21): the Spirit is called, and is in fact, the image of the Son, as the Son is the image of the Father (*ib.* 1.24, cf. 1.20): the Spirit is not external to the Logos, but by reason of being in the Logos is therefore through Him in God (*ib.* 3.5).

Basil is, characteristically, more hesitant. It is stated (*ep.* 38.4) that the Spirit depends on the Son, as being the channel of His ministration, though the existence of the Spirit is linked with the Father as cause. Basil himself certainly contemplates with sympathy the view that as the Father is seen in the Son, so is the Son seen in the Spirit (*de Sp. sanct.* 64), which is pure Athanasian doctrine; and maintains (*ib.* 45) that the one Spirit is through one Son linked to one Father. Epiphanius, the antipathetic critic of all theological aberration, was indeed no spiritual child of Origen, yet he was capable of acute thought. To his view the Spirit proceeds from the Father and receives from the Son (*ancor.* 7), and is out of the same substance of the Father and the Son (*ib.*). He is Spirit of the Father and Spirit of the Son, not through a process of combination like that which associates human soul and body, but centrally to both alike (ἐν μέσῳ πατρὸς καὶ υἱοῦ), out of the Father and the Son (*ib.* 8); the Holy Spirit is "from both," a Spirit out of the Father, for God is spirit (*ib.* 70).

Gregory of Nyssa begins by reproducing current views. Father, Son, and Holy Spirit are so inter-related, that in no conception or statement properly attaching to the divine nature does the Spirit manifest the slightest variation, except for the single fact that He is recognised individually in respect of objective being, inasmuch as He is out of God and is of Christ (*adv. Maced.* 2). He proceeds out of the Father and receives out of the Son (*ib.* 10). The Father cannot be conceived apart from the Son, nor can the Son be apprehended apart from the Spirit; the Son is ever in the Father, and the Holy Spirit ever with the Son (*ib.* 12). When is the Spirit divided from the Son, so that, if worship is offered to the Father, worship of the Spirit be not included with the Son? (*ib.* 24). The Spirit accompanies the Word as the breath of man accompanies man's word (*or. cat.* 2).

But he goes further. The Eunomians alleged that the Spirit was created by the sole God through the Only-begotten. Gregory accepts the divine monarchy and the theory of causal dependence, while maintaining the Trinity. As the Son is linked to the Father, he writes (*c. Eun.* 1.42.691, Migne 45.464B, C), and, though He derives His being from the Father, yet is not posterior in time with respect to His existence; so the Holy Spirit is attached to the Only-begotten, and the Son is only conceived as anterior to the objective being (hypostasis) of the Spirit in logical thought, in respect of the principle of causation; periods of time have no place with reference to the pre-eternal life of God. These words appear to imply the double procession. Elsewhere (*non tres dei*, Migne 45.133B, C) he is more explicit. While we confess, he observes, the invariability of the divine nature, we do not deny the difference between the Persons in respect of cause and being caused, by which alone we conceive it possible to distinguish one from another; we believe that one is the cause, and the other out of the cause; and again we recognise a further distinction in that which is out of the cause, for one is directly out of the first, but the other proceeds out of the first through that which comes directly; the title Only-begotten therefore rests indisputably with the Son, and the fact of the Spirit's procession out of the Father is equally certain, because the mediating position of the Son both preserves to Him the title of Only-begotten, and also does not exclude the Spirit from His 'natural relation' to the Father. It is here transparent that Gregory conceived the being of the Holy Spirit to be so grounded in the being of the Son, as that in turn is grounded in the being of the Father.

In Cyril and later writers the expression "out of the Father through the Son" becomes a regular formula for the procession of the Holy Spirit. The Spirit, says Cyril (*ador.* 9E), is poured forth substantially out of both, that is out of the Father through the Son. He is the unvaried image of the Son (*thes.* 33, 336D). He derives intrinsically and substantially from the Father in the Son (*thes.* 34, 340A). So, too, Maximus Confessor, to carry the matter no further, defends the double procession by reference both to Cyril and to Latin Fathers (*opusc.* 70C, D), arguing that the doctrine does not imply that the Son is the cause of the Holy Spirit, since the Father is the one cause of Son and Spirit, but that the Spirit proceeds through the Son; and again, he maintains (*qu. ad Thal.* 63, 238D) that as the Holy Spirit is by nature in substance the Spirit of the God and Father, so He is by nature in substance the Spirit of the

Son, since He ineffably proceeds out of the Father substantially through the begotten Son.

Such was the last legacy of subordinationism to theology. It is strange to reflect that while this theory in its first beginnings tended to rend the Trinity into three disjunct entities, in this its last phase it contributed to the strengthening of the sense of the divine unity by binding into a coherent and organic relation the conceptions entertained of the three divine Persons. The three have one physis, God, observes Gregory of Nazianzus (*or.* 42.15); their ground of unity (ἕνωσις) is the Father, out of whom and towards whom are reckoned the subsequent Persons, not so as to confuse them but so as to attach them. The doctrine of monarchy had begun by basing the unity of God on the single Person of God the Father, and was thereby crippled in its effort to account for the existence of three divine Persons. So long as three equally divine Persons were recognised, it was no real explanation of the claim of Christianity to be a monotheistic faith simply to affirm that only one of them was ultimate. The question was bound to arise, in that case, whether the other two Persons were truly God at all. Arius concluded that they were not. The Athanasians, on the other hand, developed a real doctrine of divine unity, which faced and, so far as might be, solved the paradox of a monotheistic trinity.

The doctrine of divine monarchy then came to afford a welcome theory of the relations in which that unity was grounded, a service which it was infinitely better capable of performing than that of safeguarding the unity itself. Granted, now, that the three Persons represent objective presentations of the one divine Being, the generation of the Son and the procession of the Spirit indicate relationships between the Three that assist towards a conception of the reality of the One. And when the being of the Spirit became further linked in thought to that of the Father by the intermediary being of the Son, the result was not only to conform to suggestions revealed in Scripture—and Scripture was always the basis and material of patristic theology—but also to strengthen the association of the several Persons and diminish the risk of their being conceived as disjunct individuals of a species. The unity appears the more real, when the triplicity is seen to be throughout a strongly organic triplicity, and when it is recognised that the act of procession is not so much a new act as the completion of the act of generation, which is in turn no less fundamental a characteristic of God than the fact of His being agenetos or uncreate.

The sense of this contribution of the doctrines of monarchy and of the double procession to the realisation of the divine unity is apparent in Gregory of Nyssa, and affords a striking testimony to the singular acuteness of his mind. The Son "is linked to" (συνάπτεται) the Father—the word is characteristic of him: the Spirit "is attached to" (ἔχεται) the Only-begotten (c. Eun. 1.42, p. 252 above). The Father, the Son, and the Holy Spirit are recognised as ever with one another in a perfect trinity "consequentially and conjunctively" (ἀκολούθως καὶ συνημμένως) (adv. Maced. 12, in a context also quoted p. 252). It is significant that the Antiochene school, which declined to accept the unifying conception of the double procession, was also the school which failed to arrive at a satisfactory statement of unity in relation to the Person of Christ. Theodore and his followers were better at analysis than at synthesis.

It has been stated that the particularities of being unbegotten, begotten, and processive are not merely the distinguishing features of the several objective presentations of the godhead, but are the sole distinguishing features. The implication of this fact is that the unity of God, though sometimes in the background, continued to be held with great tenacity. Accordingly, there was discerned in God only one will and one 'energy' (principle of action). This doctrine indeed has its roots far back. Origen (on *St. John* 13.36, 228) observes that the will of God is present in the will of the Son, and the will of the Son is undeviating from the will of the Father, so that there are no longer two wills but one will, which single will provides the reason for our Lord's assertion that "I and the Father are one." He repeats (*c. Cels.* 8.12) that the Father and the Son are two 'things' (pragmata) in objectivity, but one in consent and harmony and identity of purpose. Athanasius (*c. Ar.* 3.66) follows Origen in maintaining the the position that there is one will which proceeds from the Father and is in the Son, so that from this fact the Son may be seen in the Father and the Father in the Son. The tradition is maintained in Basil, who claims (*de Spir. sanct.* 21) that the divine will follows the divine ousia, and is consequently seen similar and equal, or rather identical, in the Father and the Son; which is the ground of the statement, "he that hath seen me hath seen the Father" (*St. John* xiv. 9).

It is true that the word here translated 'will' is, in all the cases above quoted, thelema, and not thelesis. It refers rather to the result of an act of will than to the act itself or to the faculty by which the act is made. At the same time, in the Greek of the patristic period the distinction between the two forms is not invariably maintained. And the community of will points to a much closer unity between the Persons when it is expounded, as it is by Gregory of Nyssa (*c. Eun.* 2.216, Migne 984A), as implying that the Son not only possesses but is the Will of the Father, just as He is the Word and Wisdom of the Father. (Compare Clement *strom.* 5.1, 6.3, "the Word of the Father of all is the Wisdom and most manifest Goodness of God and His almighty Power . . . and almighty Will.") But indeed no community of will could be closer than that which was in the mind of Athanasius in the passage just cited; for the words immediately preceding those quoted are to the effect that the Son, with that will (thelesis) with which He is willed from the Father, Himself loves and wills and honours the Father. It is therefore clear that the conception of a community of will between the Persons extends to the act of will, and not only to the resolutions formed by it.

As God is one in will, so is He one in operation or 'energy.' This doctrine goes back to Athanasius, where it forms part of his proof of the deity of the Holy Spirit. Thus he argues at some length (*ad Serap.* 1.19) that, since the Father is light and the Son is the radiance from that light, the Holy Spirit, being the agent by the reception of whom mankind receives its enlightenment, must be discernible in the Son; when, therefore, we are enlightened by the Spirit, it is Christ who in Him enlightens us, since St. John has said that it is Christ who is the true light that enlightens every man. Similarly, the Father is the source and the Son is called the river that flows from that source, yet the Scripture says that we drink of the Spirit, because in drinking of the Spirit we drink Christ: and again Christ is the true Son, but it is through receiving the Spirit that we are made sons and have received the Spirit of adopted sonship. So he concludes (*ib.* 28) that there is a holy and perfect triad expressed in Father and Son and Holy Spirit, which contains nothing foreign or derived from an external source; its nature is self-consistent (literally, "similar to itself") and indivisible, and its 'energy' is one; for the Father acts invariably through the Word in the Holy Spirit. Thus the unity of the holy triad is preserved, and so one God is preached in the Church, who is over all and through all and in all; over all, as Father, the arche and fount; through all, through the Word; and in all, in the Holy Spirit. It will be observed here again that the unity of God, or divine monarchy, is no longer based primarily on the fact that the first person of the Trinity is arche. On the contrary, it is asserted that the one God is expressed as Father over all and as Son through all and as Spirit in all. The full significance is attached to the divine function in each of the three several Persons. Yet this function is not exercised by them in individual isolation, and it is expressly stated that the Trinity as a whole has in operation only a single energy.

Similarly, it is maintained (*ib.* 30) that if God is a triad, as indeed He is, and this triad has been shown to be indivisible and undissimilar, then it must possess but a single holiness and a single eternity and immutability. The same is true of the divine grace, which is the bounty bestowed by God in triad; it is granted from the Father through the Son, and we could possess no community in the gift save in the Holy Spirit; when we partake of Him we possess the love of the Father and the grace of the Son and the community of the Spirit Himself. From these facts, Athanasius proceeds, it is shown that the energy of the triad is single (*ib.* 31 *init.*). The argument is repeated substantially (*ib.* 3.5) with reference to the phenomena of prophecy. When St. Paul stated (*Acts* xx.23) that the Holy Spirit testified to him in every city that bonds and afflictions awaited him, it must be remembered that the Spirit is not outside the Word but is in the Word, and through Him is in God; graces are given in virtue of the triad, and in their distribution, as St. Paul writes to the Corinthians (1 *Cor.* xii.4–6), there is the same Spirit and the same Lord and the same God who works all in all, for the Father works through the Word in the Spirit. It is clear that to Athanasius a single divine operation is manifested in the particular acts of the several Persons, an operation as truly and definitely single as is the ousia which is manifested in their several objective presentations.

Basil (*c. Eun.* 3.4) maintains that the deity of the Holy Spirit is indicated by the fact, on which he enlarges, that the energy of the Holy Spirit is co-ordinate with that of the Father and the Son. His brother argues ([Bas.] *ep.* 189.6) that if we observed the operations issuing from the Father and the Son and the Holy Spirit to be different from one another, we should conjecture from the contrast of the operations that the natures performing them were different also; but if we perceive that the operation of Father, Son, and Holy Spirit is single, the conclusion necessarily follows from the identity of the operation that the nature is united; and he asserts (*ib.* 7) that the identity of the operation in Father, Son, and Holy Spirit clearly indicates the undeviating character of the physis. As is remarked by the author of Basil's fourth book against Eunomius (280C), those whose operations are identical have a single ousia; there is a single operation of

Father and Son; therefore there is also a single ousia of Father and Son.

Since the argument so often proceeds from identity of operation to identity of being, and not in the opposite direction, it would seem clear that the former doctrine occasioned less difficulty than the latter and was even more widely held: none but the one absolute God can produce divine results. Hence Gregory of Nyssa is in a position to state (*non tres dei*, Migne 45.133A) that the Father is God and the Son is God; but this assertion does not preclude the truth that God is one, because in the godhead there can be discerned no difference either of nature or of operation. And again (*comm. not.*, Migne 45.180C) he observes that the Persons of the godhead are not separated from one another either in time or in place or in purpose or in pursuit or in operation. He has a careful discussion of the whole matter in *non tres dei* (Migne 125C, D). In men, he says, in spite of the solidarity of the whole race, each individual acts separately, so that it is proper to regard them as many; each is separated into an individual unit by the fact of the independence of his 'energy.' This is not so, he proceeds, with God. The Father never acts independently of the Son, nor the Son of the Spirit. Divine action, however differentiated in human conception, always begins from the Father, proceeds through the Son, and is completed in the Holy Spirit; there is no such thing as a separate, individual operation of any Person; the energy invariably passes through the three, though the effect is not three actions but one.

Subsequent writers show no diminution of strength in their sense of the divine unity. Gregory of Nazianzus (*or.* 31.16) maintains in a memorable sentence that each of the divine Persons possesses a unity with the associate Persons no less actual than with Himself, by reason of the identity of ousia and of power; and this is the ground of the divine unity. Amphilochius of Iconium is the author of a strong statement, preserved in a fragment which is quoted in the *Concilia* (Hardouin 3.864C: several other fragments are quoted by Theodoret from the same sermon in which this extract is said to occur). It takes the form of a rhetorical question. How can the works of Me and of my Father be distinguished, seeing that there is a single will (thelesis) and word and knowledge and wisdom and nature and godhead? In Didymus of Alexandria (*de Trin.* 2.1) it is the Trinity and not any one Person or combination of Persons, that sits upon an eternal throne regarding the abysses, and is heard though it is silent, and hears those who are silent, and knows what shall come to pass before it comes to pass, and brings about all things by a word and swifter than a word and by the sole act of willing: by an incomprehensible mystery this Trinity possesses a single will, and its utterance and graces proceed from a common act: though each several Person had the capacity to do all things independently in perfection, yet, in order to indicate their co-operation and the undeviating character of their ousia, the creation was fulfilled by the holy triad jointly. Cyril of Alexandria (*dial.* 6 *de Trin.*, 618E) allows that the creative will of each one of the divine Persons is indeed an activity of that Person, but maintains nevertheless that it extends throughout the whole godhead and is a product of the supernatural ousia; thus the Father works, but through the Son in the Spirit; and the Son works, but as the power of the Father, since His individual being is from the Father and in the Father;

and the Spirit works, because he is the Spirit of the Father and the Son, universally active.

This thought is worked out by Cyril at considerable length in a passage of his commentary on *St. John* (858B to 859E). He is discussing the parable of the Vine and the Husbandman, and explains that this latter title is ascribed to the Father, in order that He might not be left idle and inactive in our conception of the work of spiritual sustenance which is carried out by the Son in the Holy Spirit. The rectification of our condition, he says, is a work of the whole holy and consubstantial triad, and the will and power to do all the actions done by that triad extend throughout the whole divine nature. For that reason praise is rendered from men to the Trinity, both in its entirety, and Person by Person; for it is God whom we call Saviour, and when graces are bestowed upon us we do not acknowledge them separately to the Father and separately to the Son or to the Holy Spirit, but ascribe our salvation truly to the single godhead; and even if we determine to apportion certain of the blessings bestowed on us, or of the activities displayed in nature, to each several Person, none the less we believe that all proceeds from the Father through the Son in the Spirit.

Accordingly Cyril denies either that the Son is alone in quickening the branches of the Vine with life and productive power, or that the providential care indicated by the use of the title Husbandman is confined to the Person of the Father alone. Each process, properly speaking, is a distinct operation or energy of the divine ousia, which belongs, says Cyril, to "God conceived in a holy and consubstantial triad." Both operations therefore, that of quickening and that of providential oversight, are operations of the Trinity. This must be so, he adds, because the Son is intrinsically and truly in His own Father, and possesses in His own physis Him that begat Him, and everything is brought to fulfilment through both, in the Spirit, as out of one godhead; for where undeviating identity of nature is perceived, there the act of operation is not divided, even though it may appear to an observer that the conduct of the operation is manifold and diverse. Since, then, he concludes, we recognise one ousia, that is to say true and intrinsic (φυσικός) godhead, in three objective presentations, namely the Father, the Son, and the Holy Spirit, it is incontrovertible that what we describe as an operative act of one, is an accomplishment of the whole and single godhead, in accordance with its intrinsic power. (Cf. *c. Nest.* 4.2, 103A.)

Somewhere about the beginning of the eighth century an anonymous but extremely important theological treatise was composed by a writer otherwise unknown. He is the real author of a large part of the most striking sections of the *Orthodox Faith* of John of Damascus, who simply incorporated the work of the unknown into his own book. The work itself passed under the name of Cyril, and is published at the end of the standard editions of his writings. In this work the author, to whom it is convenient to refer as pseudo-Cyril, contrasts (*de ss. Trin.* 10) the separation of the hypostaseis of individual men with the unity of the godhead; it is proper to speak of two or three or any number of men, as it is of any creatures, but not proper to speak of a plurality of Gods. In the incomprehensible Trinity community and unity are concretely expressed through the coeternity, through the identity of the ousia and the energy and the will, through the concordance of purpose, through the identity of authority and power and goodness—I do not say similarity, he interjects, but identity—and through the single dynamic initiative (ἔξαλμα κινήσεως).

There is, he continues, one ousia, one goodness, one power, one will, one energy, one authority; one and identical; not three similar to each another, but a single identical motion of the three hypostaseis; for each of them enjoys unity in relation to the others no less than towards Himself—the Father, the Son, and the Holy Spirit are in every respect one entity, save for ingeneracy and generation and procession. Again he says, later in the same chapter, that when we look to the godhead and the first cause and the monarchy, to the one and identical motion and purpose of the godhead, and to the identity of the ousia and the power and the energy and the lordship, then what is presented to us is single. But when we regard the objects in which the godhead is expressed, or, to speak more accurately, the objects which the godhead is, and what comes out of the first cause time-lessly, uni-gloriously, and indivisibly, then there are three objects of worship. The passage is a brilliant and convincing summary of the conclusions at which the whole process of Greek speculation about the nature of God arrived at last, through centuries of intellectual effort and rational discrimination.

CHAPTER XIII

THE TRIUMPH OF FORMALISM

IT is abundantly clear that the ousia of God is not to be understood as an abstract species, but as a single undifferentiated substance, identically expressed in each of the three Persons. It is true that on occasion, in order to meet the arguments of some particular opponent, a theologian might employ a line of reasoning which failed to imply the full truth. Instances of such reasoning, when ousia may be quoted as bearing a generic sense, are not in themselves evidence that the ousia of God was ever conceived generically by the theologians concerned, or that they would have employed such a usage in conducting an argument on ground of their own choice. When pressed, and except for inadvertence, the writers on whose works contribution has hitherto been laid all taught that God is a single being, as is guaranteed by the doctrine of identity of ousia. They insist that by identity they mean identity and not similarity, and their contention is borne out by their several expositions of the unity and singularity of all divine motion, operation, and energy. But it is now necessary to point out that, side by side with this long-sustained consistency of teaching a parallel tendency arose, at least in certain circles, to treat ousia in a much more abstract sense, and therefore in a sense far more nearly approaching the generic. A movement took place away from constructive reasoning towards formal definition; from pure thought towards the logic of thought; in a sense, though only in a rather misleading sense, from Platonism to Aristotelianism.

In Gregory of Nyssa this tendency is not yet apparent. For instance he writes (*ep.* 24) that the ousia of the several Persons, whatever it really is—for it is ineffable in speech and incomprehensible in conception—is not parted into any contrariety of nature; there is no difference of ousia in respect of the holy Trinity apart from the order of the Persons and recognition of the hypostaseis. Each Person is a concrete individual entity, yet in the three there is discoverable only a single content. The Father is an ousia, he writes (*comm. not.*, Migne 45.177A), the Son is an ousia, the Holy Spirit is an ousia, yet there are not three ousiai because the one ousia is identical. Gregory illustrates this unity (*c. Ar. et Sab.* 12; but the authenticity of this work is disputable) by the co-existence in a single mind of diverse sciences, each of which, so to speak, covers the whole extension of the consciousness that contains them. In a man's soul two or more sciences congregate; they are not over-crowded by one another in the mind and location of the soul; though many in number they have free space and are mutually pervasive [the last two words at any rate appear to give the sense of a singularly obscure Greek phrase]; they fill the soul and one does not withdraw from another, so that they present a single appearance of ousia [i.e. content], since they are settled in one identical mind; yet they differ from one another inasmuch as one is the science of medicine and another the science of philosophy; it is exactly the same with the Father and the Son. This profound and pregnant passage appears to lead in a direction similar to that indicated by the later doctrine of 'perichoresis' or co-inherence of Persons.

In Cyril again a single divine ousia is presented identically in the three Persons, as has been shown in passages already quoted, and could be illustrated by innumerable further instances. Thus (on *St. John* 16E) the Father and the Son, though distinct individuals, are seen in one another by reason of the identity of ousia. Elsewhere (*ib.* 850E) the Son is immanent in the ousia of the God and Father; and (*ib.* 925C) the Holy Spirit is not conceived as foreign to the ousia of the Only-begotten, but proceeds intrinsically out of it, and is nothing other than He, so far as relates to identity of nature, even though He is conceived individually. Statements of a similar kind are reiterated in the *Thesaurus*. Thus he writes (*ass.* 12, 111E) that since the Son is the peculiar property of the Father's ousia, He carries within Himself the Father entire, and is Himself entire in the Father according to the identity of ousia: (112C) the Persons are in identity of ousia and none possesses anything which excludes another from the intrinsic property thereof: (*ib.* 109E) by the statement, "I and the Father are one," our Lord indicated His identity of nature with Him that begat Him, but also indicates by the further statement, "I am in the Father and the Father in me," that, in spite of this identity of godhead and unity of ousia, they are not to be conceived as an object numerically one in the sense that it is sometimes called Father and sometimes called Son, but that both Father and Son are individually objective.

The word homoousios remains to be considered. It will be recalled that, although Athanasius employed this term in a sense which included the ascription of identity of substance to the Persons to whom homoousios was applied, nevertheless this sense was not traditionally included in the term. What it originally and commonly meant was simply 'of the same stuff.' Basil again seems to have followed Athanasian doctrine, but in a fumbling and almost half-hearted manner, so that the student of his writings needs to assure himself, from other indications than the mere use of the word homoousios, as to the fact of Basil's adherence to the doctrine of identity of ousia. It has also been stated that the semi-Arians were substantially correct in their view that homoousios, as employed in the creed of Nicæa, really meant what they preferred to express by the word homœ-ousios. As this was the word's original sense—and it must be remembered that homoousios was commonly applied to all sorts of objects which had no connection whatever with theology—it is not surprising that to this sense it once more reverted. Its real work for theology had been completed so soon as the doctrine of Athanasius had been otherwise safeguarded by the general adoption of the phrase 'identity of ousia.'

Instances may subsequently occur in which homoousios bears an Athanasian implication, but by the time of Cyril it has normally become equivalent to ὁμογενής. Thus Cyril observes (on *St. John* 849C) that the Son is 'homogeneous' with the Father, that is to say homoousios; and again (*dial.* I *de Trin.*, 391C) that the Son, having sprung from the very ousia of the God and Father, will not be an alien or foreigner to Him that begat Him, but homoousios with Him and conformable and ὁμοφυής. Of course, the identity of substance follows from this fact, because there cannot possibly be two Gods, and the doctrine of identity provides the one way out of an admission of polytheism; but this truth depends on inference, and is no longer expressed immediately in the term homoousios, as it had been by Athanasius a couple of generations before.

Another reason, based in theology, existed to support and justify the reversion in the sense of homoousios. As early as in Eustathius of Antioch it had been stated that our Lord's soul was rational and homoousios with the souls of men, just as His flesh was homoousios with the flesh of men, since it proceeded from Mary (fragment quoted by Theodoret *Eran.* 1, 56B). In such a connection as this, homoousios could only mean "made of stuff from the same lump." The phrase was taken up and quickly became a commonplace. Theodoret (*ib.* 2, 139D) purports to quote Ambrose for the formula "homoousios with the Father in respect of the godhead and homoousios with us in respect of the manhood." In the East the expression 'homoousios with us' is found principally in Antiochene writers and, as a fellow Syrian, in Apollinarius and his school. But it was adopted by Cyril and popularised by him (e.g. *c. Nest.* 3.3, 80B). Cyril has no hesitation in employing homoousios in the same context to express both identity of substance with God and similarity of substance with men. Henceforward, therefore, the sense of homoousios is definitely generic, and the reason clearly is in some measure the assimilation of 'Theology' (or the doctrine of God) with Christology.

This fact has an important bearing on the sense of ousia adopted by the two authors named Leontius in the sixth century. Through exaggerated assimilation of the theory of the Trinity to the theory of the incarnation, assisted by a strong tendency towards schematic formalism, a marked change has overtaken the sense of ousia as normally employed. It is true that Leontius of Jerusalem rejects the possibility of an ousia which is a mere abstraction; such a thing is separable in thought but does not exist in practice. Thus he writes (*c. Monoph.* 51, Migne 1797C) that an hypostasis without ousia and an ousia without objectivity (anhypostatos) are alike inconceivable. The Byzantine says (*c. Nest. et Eut.* 1, 1277D) that the word hypostasis denotes an individual, but the word objective (enhypostatos) denotes the ousia, indicating that it is not an accident which exists in some other object, as do attributes, whether primary or secondary. An attribute, he says, is not an ousia, that is to say a pragma or 'thing' with objective existence, it is something that is observed relative to an ousia; but an ousia without objectivity is an impossibility. He means that an ousia, being the universal of concrete objects, must exist in each of those objects. He is fully aware of Aristotle's distinction between particular ousiai and the one common ousia which is involved in particular objects, and it is not impossible to quote him for instances of ousia in the sense of 'object.' But there is no doubt whatever that the sense in which he consistently and almost exclusively employs ousia is the logical sense of 'essence,' which is practically equivalent to 'universal.'

He is soaked in abstract logic and has a tedious passion for formal classification. For instance, he is careful to recall (fragment 2009C) that genus and differentia and species contribute jointly to the ousia of each particular object, and for that reason they are given the name of 'essential'; but property and accident are non-essential (ἐπουσιώδης). To take another example, he observes (*c. arg. Sev.* 1945B) that the factors which determine the nature (physis) of an object contribute to the ousia, but the factors which determine its hypostasis are of the nature of accidents; in the case of a man, his ousia is determined by the terms animal, rational, mortal, but his hypostasis is determined by shape, colour, size, parentage, education, occupation. In the definitions with which the *de sectis* opens (although it now appears that this work is not earlier than the seventh century and has no connection with either Leontius, it displays similar abstract tendencies), the author even makes the astonishing statement that, in the Fathers, ousia means the same as physis, that both represent the same conception as is expressed by secular philosophers in the word 'species' ($\epsilon\hat{\iota}\delta o\varsigma$), and that species is the term applied to a plurality of different objects; hypostasis on the other hand, which he says (with a nearer approximation to the truth) is employed by the Fathers in the same sense as Person (prosopon), means the same thing as the philosophers express by 'individual' ($\check{a}\tau o\mu o\varsigma$ $o\grave{v}\sigma\acute{\iota}a$). These extracts are sufficient to show not only the interest in precise definition, but also the fatal tendency to obliterate vital distinctions between the meanings of various philosophical terms. It is not strictly accurate to say that hypostasis and prosopon bear the same sense, though in theology they are rightly applicable to the same objects, and may be held to be practically equivalent. It is grossly untrue to affirm that theologians had employed ousia in the sense of species. The writer would have been nearer the mark if he had said that ousia and hypostasis were synonymous. He was simply reading his own definitions into the work of his predecessors, in order to present a formally balanced equation between the group of terms expressing divine trinity and the group of words expressing divine unity. Such efforts, by a formal arrangement of the objects of thought, contributed a good deal to the cause of abstract simplicity. They did so at the cost of reducing to a monotonous unreality all the finer shades of meaning which are indigenous in the Greek language and had hitherto been so effectively employed by Christian theologians.

It is true that both the Leontii were almost wholly occupied with Christology, and their ideas were developed with that subject mainly in view. Ousia was always capable, in a suitable context, of meaning 'secondary substance,' and in this sense was applied at least as early as Chrysostom to the human nature in which Christ assumed a share. At that period secondary substances were often not treated as abstract, but accepted more or less vaguely as actually existent universals. This was a legacy from Plato. It introduces, however, quite a different conception to speak of the two ousiai of Christ, in such a way as to make the human ousia no longer mean the total physical substance of the whole race, but the metaphysical analysis of Christ's individual humanity; and to make the divine ousia similarly mean not the content of God but the metaphysical analysis of Christ in His divine aspect. Yet this is the step which the Leontii took. In Christology, as in reference to the Trinity, ousia stands no longer for an object but for an analysis. Furthermore they consciously and increasingly assimilated the terminology proper to the analysis involved in the one doctrine to that involved in the other doctrine. Thus Leontius of Byzantium says (c. arg. Sev. 1917D) that in the case of the Persons of the Trinity identity of ousia unites while contrariety of hypostasis divides; but in the case of the incarnation contrariety of ousia separates while identity of hypostasis unites.

This unfortunate habit could not but result in detracting from the peculiar value of the orthodox definition of the Trinity, as being one object regarded as real, in itself, and three objects regarded as objective, to itself. The sense of ousia on which this definition depends, was inapplicable to the two natures of Christ. It would make nonsense of orthodox Christology to apply the phrase 'two ousiai' to Christ in the sense of two primary ousiai. In effect, that was the fundamental error of Nestorianism. True, the Leontii speak much more frequently of two physeis than of two ousiai. But in a number of instances they do say 'two ousiai,' and this could only mean 'two universals,' or 'two abstract analyses.' Consequently, when Trinity and incarnation are compared, and reduced to the formulæ 'three hypostaseis and one ousia' and 'one hypostasis and two ousiai' respectively, the former definition necessarily comes to mean merely 'one analysis of reality in the three Persons,' instead of 'one identical concrete substance in the three Persons.' The doctrine of identity of substance is not, of course, lost to theology, but it is lost to this particular definition, and unless other steps are taken to secure its expression, the way is paved to tritheism. This danger was not academic; it actually ensued. It was in the sixth century that an outbreak of tritheism occurred, and had to be seriously refuted.

It is therefore worth while quoting further instances of this mode of teaching. "The mystery of the Trinity," says Leontius of Jerusalem (c. Monoph. 18), referring to an unnamed 'Father' for the statement, "is just the reverse of the mystery of the incarnation." Leontius himself (*ib.*) lays down the formula, which sounds like a popular rhyme or a children's catechism, "in the case of the holy and super-essential Trinity, unity of hypostaseis in a single physis; in the case of the holy and ineffable incarnation of the Word, unity of physeis in a single hypostasis." The statement is theologically correct of the incarnation. It is also correct, so far as it goes, of the Trinity, but in this case it does not represent the whole truth; it omits the crucial identity of concrete ousia. Nevertheless, people trained to think in the manner of this catechetical jingle would quickly be induced to suppose that it did contain the whole truth, and to infer that three Persons in one substance meant no more than three Persons in one nature. The mind which can bear to talk about two ousiai in Christ is in danger of losing its grip on the true doctrine of God. Yet this fallacious mode of thought is characteristic of the man. In *c. Nest.* 2.13, for instance, he argues that, if it is right to maintain that three hypostaseis are enousios (find their analytical reality) in a single ousia, it is also proper to maintain that two natures are enhypostatos (find their objective expression) in a single hypostasis. He is again equating the two different doctrines to the necessities of an assimilated formula. He does not here, indeed, speak of two ousiai, but of two natures (physeis). But he could so speak; an instance occurs in *c. Nest.* 2.4 to illustrate the possibility.

There is one redeeming feature in a bad business. His view of physis, and by implication, of ousia, was not wholly abstract. He is quite clear that a physis can only in thought be separable from a concrete object; it cannot exist in the abstract air. He maintains, in the context quoted (*c. Nest.*

2.13), that the two physeis of Christ are objectified in an
identical common hypostasis; not in the sense that either
resides anhypostatos therein, but that both are enhypostatos
in relation to it. This fact enables Leontius to present a
clear and satisfactory scholastic definition of the incarnation.
It is not in his conception of the relation of physis and
hypostasis that he is at fault. But when he turns to the
Trinity, and applies a form of definition which attaches the
whole concrete element in the conception to the hypostasis,
treating the physis as concrete solely in its dependence on
the hypostasis, his theory fails to exclude tritheism. The
only concrete residua are the hypostaseis, and they are three.
His abstract view of physis would not have mattered if he
had, as emphatically he ought to have, retained the traditional
conception of ousia as itself expressing a concrete entity, a
primary ousia. The whole mischief lay in his deplorable
assimilation of ousia to physis, which made of it, not perhaps
a secondary ousia (which would have involved a definite
form of tritheism, with three Gods all made of a common
stuff), but an abstract analysis, which might or might not
imply identity, as opposed to similarity, of substance.

There had nearly been a similar disaster a couple of
centuries earlier, over the term hypostasis. On this occasion
the offender was none other than Basil. In the working out,
by the Cappadocians, of the exact senses to be attached to
terms of theological definition, Basil, who like the Leontii
was learned in all the logic of the heathen, had dallied
dangerously with a tendency to identify hypostasis with
idioma. If this suggestion had been adopted, the concrete
character of the Persons would have been jeopardised, as in
the sixth century the concrete character of the divine

Being was jeopardised. Fortunately, the hints thus thrown out, which implied a different sense in hypostasis from that which it normally bore, were disregarded; there seems to be no trace of a subsequent usage in which hypostasis conveys any other sense than that of the whole concrete object.

Basil distinguishes hypostasis (*ep.* 38.3) from the indeterminate principle of ousia, which fails to arrive at stability (stasis) owing to the universality of the matter signified; and identifies it with the principle which expresses what is universal and uncircumscribed in a particular pragma by means of non-essential idiomata: again (*ib.* 6), hypostasis is defined as the group of idiomata about each particular object, the individualising sign of the existence of each object. He repeats the same notion, *ep.* 214.4, arguing that the ousia bears the same relation to the hypostasis as does the common element to the particular element; so that in the godhead hypostasis is recognised in the idioma of Fatherhood, Sonship, and Power of Sanctification, while ousia is illustrated by abstract conceptions such as goodness and deity.

As Basil was inclined to define the term, it covered only such abstract elements in an object as were left over when the physis or abstract ousia had been subtracted. But as his successors, and indeed his contemporary theologians, employed it, it meant the concrete whole, objectively presented—ousia plus individuality, not individuality as distinguished from ousia. Hypostasis signifies genus, species, differentia, property, and accident combined in an actual thing, not merely the last two of the five elements in the analysis. Thus Epiphanius (*ancor.* 81.7) asserts that the Holy Spirit in the form of a dove was by Himself a hypostasis, and Gregory of Nyssa (*c. Eun.* 2 (vulgo). 13, Migne 472D) states that the titles of the Persons denote merely the distinguishing particularities of the hypostaseis; he does not say, as Basil might have said, that they are the actual hypostaseis. According to the Fathers, remarks Eulogius (*frag.* in Migne 86.2948A), hypostasis simply means ousia plus idiomata. John of Damascus, at the close of the great patristic period of constructive thought, expressly defines hypostasis (*dialectica* 30) as "ousia with accidents," existing of itself. Basil, though he really held the doctrine of identity of ousia, as has previously been shown at length, seems nevertheless to have been tempted to jettison the concrete character of both ousia ("indeterminate principle of ousia") and hypostasis, in the interests of an abstract logic incapable of expressing the real truth which he was trying to define.

But this was only a passing episode, and even its author handled the matter fumblingly, without pressing home his formal theory. It was promptly forgotten, and left no ill effect on the theological tradition The case was far otherwise with the later aberrations of Leontius, which had serious and lasting consequences. For instance, Eulogius of Alexandria, who died in 607, accepts (*frag.* from the *synegoriai*, Migne 2953D) the fatal view that ousia means that which is observed in common in many instances, and in equal proportions—"not more of it in one instance and less of it in another." This means that he holds ousia to cover just the same facts, and no more, as are covered by genus, species, and differentia.

He proceeds to illustrate by defining the ousia of man as "flesh ensouled in a rational soul," and refers to a further refinement, made in the interests of Christology, (which he has already explained in an earlier fragment, 2952Aff), to the effect that man himself is composed of two ousiai, the ousia of soul being different from the ousia of body, though there is only one ousia of manhood regarded as a whole. Eulogius does not seem to realise the full force of the inference that if these two ousiai, by being united in a single hypostasis in each man, become a single ousia, the two ousiai of Christ might also become united into a single ousia—a consequence which he stoutly denies, giving as his reason the argument that in this case there must have been a whole class of Redeemers instead of only one. This deduction is based on the assumption that ousia is a generic term, and that the formation of a single Christ-ousia would imply a whole new class of hybrid God-men. Christ's uniqueness depends on His not belonging to any one class, but to two at once—a position which is claimed for no one else. The whole argument affords an interesting lesson in the perils of abstraction. Perhaps Eulogius' last word on the subject may be represented in the statement (2952C) that in Christ a union of two ousiai produced a single hypostasis and Person, and that although the analogy with human body and soul only illustrates the point with some obscurity, consolation is to be derived from the reflection that the incarnation transcends all other unions and indeed exceeds human comprehension. Yet Eulogius has a clear head and is no fool.

More serious yet than Eulogius, on account of the vast influence which he exercised, is the adherence of Maximus, a truly great man, to the abstract view of ousia. Again and again Maximus equates ousia with species (eidos), distinguishing it from hypostasis by saying that the latter term denotes a particular instance embodying the ousia or eidos; and he ascribes (e.g. *opusc.* 77B) two ousiai to Christ. He even makes an egregious error of fact, presumably having acquired the habit of reading his revered Gregory of Nazianzus through the spectacles of Leontius or his school; for (*opusc.* 151C, Migne 91.276A) he accepts a definition of ousia as, according to the philosophers, a self-subsistent pragma independent of other objects for its existence, but, according to the Fathers, the physis-entity that is predicated of many objects different in hypostasis from one another. He is well aware of the definition, derived from the classical school of Plato and Aristotle, which makes of ousia a concrete object, but believes that the theological tradition interpreted ousia in the other Aristotelian sense of abstract universal.

The reason why theologians so completely reversed the genuine tradition in the sixth and seventh centuries can hardly be entirely disconnected with the triumph of the Council of Chalcedon. This is not the place to enlarge on a theme which properly belongs to Christology. But it should not be out of place to observe that Chalcedon did in effect encourage abstract negations at the expense of rational analysis. The clumsy Occident intervened as teacher in a matter which it had not properly learned and did not really understand. Under its influence, the Council of Chalcedon made no contribution to thought beyond the demarcation of the ground between true and false lines of enquiry.

The doctrine of the Trinity had already been admirably defined, because it had been defined concretely in both its crucial terms, ousia as well as hypostasis. In Christology, hypostasis was concrete enough, but physis was abstract.

Nestorian efforts to make physis concrete only led towards Nestorianism. Cyril made a great effort to produce a concrete psychological conception of the natures of the God-man which should both preserve their distinction and yet present them in a union concretely intelligible. He was probably never very fully understood, and, though his orthodox intentions were vindicated at Chalcedon, his actual line of approach was abandoned, and never renewed except by Monophysites. Chalcedon negatived Nestorianism, and negatived the Monophysite conclusions wrongly drawn from Cyril's premisses. Negatively, it was a crowning mercy: it suppressed psychology, to the avoidance of untold heresy, though also to the complete postponement of positive Christological advance. Official Christology remained negative and abstract, and for that reason abstraction became a necessity of theological thought. The next stage necessarily came to consist in a refinement of the accepted abstractions in the cause of clearer and ever clearer statement. But this process did not and could not lead to clearer comprehension and insight into substantial truth and fact.

As we have seen, assimilation of Christology and 'Theology' led immediately to the invasion of Trinitarian doctrine by like abstractions. The theological situation appears to have been saved by an accomplished and truly profound thinker, pseudo-Cyril, whose very name is unknown, author of the treatise *de sacrosancta Trinitate* which is printed at the close of the collections of Cyril's writings. This great and admirable work marks two distinct developments. As will shortly be shown, it introduces the term 'perichoresis' (co-inherence) to the discussion of Trinitarian problems; and it restores the true meaning of ousia. It speaks of God (cap. 7) as a single ousia, godhead, power, will (thelesis), energy, arche, etc., descried and worshipped in three perfect hypostaseis, which are inconfusedly united and inseparably distinguished into Father, Son, and Holy Spirit. Once more the unity of God is made the basis of definition, and once more the hypostaseis are defined as perfect presentations of the one, identical, supreme Being. God is "descried and worshipped" in three objective hypostaseis, but He is definitely one.

The true doctrine thus restored was permanently secured when John of Damascus incorporated into his influential treatise on the *Orthodox Faith* about two-thirds of pseudo-Cyril, with scarcely the alteration of a word. The teaching of pseudo-Cyril thus became part of the acknowledged standard of orthodox Oriental theology. In the *dialectica* (cap. 4), which forms the prelude to the larger work, John himself propounds the definition of ousia as $\pi\rho\hat{a}\gamma\mu a$ $a\vartheta\vartheta\acute{u}\pi a\rho\kappa\tau o\nu$, a thing of which the existence is independent of that of other things: God is one such ousia, and every creature is another; and this is true, even though God is an ousia surpassing all ousia ($o\vartheta\sigma\acute{i}a$ $\vartheta\pi\epsilon\rho o\acute{u}\sigma\iota os$). The doctrine of the Trinity was again explicit, in the form of one God in three 'Persons' and not three Persons in one godhead.

CHAPTER XIV

CO-INHERENCE

THE Cappadocians had had to defend themselves against the charge of tritheism, and Gregory of Nyssa wrote a treatise to explain exactly why that charge against his teaching failed. But in the sixth century, when theological thought was in its abstract phase and the three hypostaseis were the only elements in the conception of the Trinity that were anchored safely in concrete objects, a real outbreak of tritheism occurred. It was Christology which was the immediate occasion of the Trinitarian error. The account given of John Philoponus, the ablest leader of the Tritheists, in 'Leontius' *de sect.* 5.6, is borne out by the fragments of two chapters from his work entitled *Diaitetes*, which are preserved in the *de haeresibus* of John of Damascus (cap. 83). Philoponus was a Monophysite of a moderate type, who propounded a doctrine based on the teaching of Cyril. Like Nestorianism, his heresy represented an attempt to reach the concrete. He distinguished very clearly, and in full accordance with the history of the word in orthodox Fathers, between the generic sense of physis and the particular sense. In the former, as he stated quite correctly, physis is an abstraction. But as such it has no real existence; it only exists as embodied in a particular physis, that is to say, in an actual instance. Hence, he concluded, physis amounts to much the same thing as hypostasis, and the existence of a physis implies the presence of a corresponding hypostasis. If therefore, he argued, Christ be admitted to possess two physeis, He must have had two hypostaseis; since this is absurd, it follows that He had only one physis. Accordingly Philoponus contended for the formula, 'one nature incarnated of God the Word.'

The extracts preserved do not give any full account of his Trinitarian views. But they do state enough to show that in regard to the ascription of a single physis to the Trinity he adopts the generic and abstract sense of physis. We confess, he remarks in illustration of his general view of physis and hypostasis (ap. Joh. Dam. *haer.* 104A), one physis of Father, Son, and Holy Spirit, but maintain three hypostaseis or Persons, of which each is distinguished from the others by a particularity; for what would be a single physis of godhead, that is, the common principle of the divine physis, if regarded in and by itself, and not separated by the complementary conception of the particularity of each hypostasis? The inference appears to be that in any real or concrete sense of the word physis Philoponus maintained the existence of three physeis in the godhead. This inference is confirmed by what follows, in which he asserts, in further support of his general argument, that at the union of two .physeis in the incarnation, the 'divine nature' in the Incarnate does not refer to the common divine nature of the godhead but to the particular embodiment thereof which is to be discerned in the Second Person of the Trinity; "we understand the term physis in an individual sense." Unfortunately, no reference appears to be preserved relating to ousia. But it is easy to see that if he had grasped the truth of the single identical concrete ousia of God, instead of understanding the common essence of the godhead in an abstract sense, he might have found that the concrete physis which he desiderated was embodied in that ousia, without triplicating a distinct physis in each of the three hypostaseis.

The prevalence of such difficulties and of such theories required to be counteracted. And countered it was by pseudo-Cyril. Not only did he recall theology to the true and concrete doctrine of identical ousia, but he gave it a term to express the co-inherence of the three Persons in one another. This term was perichoresis or in Latin circum-incessio.

The doctrine itself of the co-inherence of the three Persons in one another goes far back. It is really involved in the doctrine of the identity of the divine ousia as expressed in each Person. It is further implied in the development of the view that what may be called, for lack of a better term, the psychological centre of God is to be sought in the ousia rather than in the Persons, with its formulation in the statement of a single identical will and energy. Thus Athanasius remarks (*ad Serap.* 3.4) that the Son is omnipresent, because He is in the Father, and the Father is in Him; the case is different with creatures, which are only to be found in separately determinate localities; but the Spirit who fills all things clearly is exempt from such limitation, and must therefore be God, and is in the Son as the Son is in the Father. Again he says (*ad Serap.* 4.4) that the Spirit belongs to the ousia of the Word and belongs to God and is said to be in Him; He is not called Son, yet is not outside the Son; if we partake of the Spirit we possess the Son, and if we possess the Son we possess the Spirit. Again (*ib.* 12), since the Son is in the Father, He is also present in everything in which the Father is present; nor is the Spirit

absent; for the holy, blessed, and perfect Trinity is indivisible. Such thoughts were inherited by the Cappadocians
whose dependence on Athanasius it is temerarious to
minimise, and reappear in closely similar form in the super-
Athanasian Cyril.

Before passing on, it is worth glancing at Hilary, since he
learned his theology in the East. What Hilary has to say
deserves consideration, both for the way in which he himself
puts his views, and for their obvious dependence on his
Greek teachers. It seems impossible, he says (*de Trin.* 3.1),
that one object should be both within and without another,
or that the divine Persons can reciprocally contain one
another so that one should permanently envelop, and also be
permanently enveloped by, the other; human wit will
never succeed in giving a complete explanation of this
paradox, though it can, if it likes, come to recognise its
significance and intelligibility; "what man cannot understand, God can be." The clue is to be found in the special
nature of God. The Father, first (*ib.* 2), is without and
within all things, He contains all and can be contained by
none, and so forth. This is all quite good Greek patristic
traditionalism. The Son (*ib.* 4) is perfect offspring of perfect
Father; hence those properties which are in the Father are
the source of those with which the Son is also endowed;
the Son is wholly Son of Him who is wholly Father; the
fullness of the godhead is in the Son; and each is in the
other mutually, for as all is perfect in the unbegotten
Father, so all is perfect in the only-begotten Son.

Elsewhere (*de Trin.* 9.69) he argues from the Athanasian
conception of the Son as image, emphasising the idea that
this conception works both ways; as the Father is reflected

in the Son, so is the Son reflected in the Father; further, if this statement corresponds with realities and the delineation is mutual, the likeness that reflects must in either case be of the same nature as the object which it reflects, though at the same time they are not separate, since both are one. Perceive, he says, their unity in the indivisibility of their nature, and apprehend the mystery of that indivisible nature by regarding the one as the mirror of the other; but remember that the Son is the mirror, not as a likeness reflected by the splendour of a nature outside Himself, but as being a living nature indistinguishable from the Father's living nature, derived wholly from the whole of His Father's nature, having the Father's nature in Himself because He is the only-begotten, and abiding in the Father, because He is God. All this is finely put, and in language free from unnecessary technicalities. And it marks a new advance in that it presents the conception of the several Persons of the godhead 'containing' one another. The exact significance of this essentially Greek phrase will appear in a moment.

As has been said, particular emphasis was laid by the fourth-century Fathers on the fact that the Father is in the Son and the Son in the Father and the Spirit in both. But at first the language in which the fact was expressed did not progress far beyond the actual phrases of Scripture; which means, in effect, that the fact was accepted, and arguments were based on it, but as yet little attempt was being made to present a reasoned interpretation of it. Basil shows his independence by arguing strongly (*de Spir. sanct.* 63) for the use of the phrase "be with" (συνεῖναι), in preference to "be in" (ἐνεῖναι), in describing the relations of the divine Persons. But this is not, as might appear at first sight, an argument for pluralism. He proceeds to give examples to indicate that the former expression is more properly applied to such things as are associated inseparably, and that the latter expression is only proper to the relations of God with creatures. Heat, for instance, is said to reside 'in' a hot iron (from which it is separable), but 'with' the actual fire; health (another separable feature) resides 'in' the body, but life 'with' the soul. The word 'with' is thus to be preferred where the relation to be expressed is intimate and inherent and inseparable. However, the word 'in' was too Scriptural and too firmly fixed in the tradition to be extruded.

Cyril, in the next century, was specially insistent on the unity of the divine Persons, and made some independent efforts towards an explanation of it, basing his examples mainly on the fact of identical ousia; that is, advancing once more from unity to plurality rather than in the reverse direction. He stated (*thesaurus ass.* 32, 284E) that the Son possesses a single ousia with the Father and, so to speak, indwells ($\dot{\epsilon}\nu\upsilon\pi\dot{\alpha}\rho\chi\epsilon\iota$) in the identity of the nature with ($\pi\rho\acute{o}s$) Him that begat Him; and again (*ib. ass.* 12, 111E), that since the Son is the property of the paternal ousia, He wears or bears ($\phi o\rho\epsilon\hat{\iota}$) the Father entire in Himself and is Himself entire in the Father; this relationship, as Cyril expressly states, is the consequence of the identity of ousia. The holy triad, he remarks again (*ib. ass.* 32, 311A), is interwreathed ($\dot{\alpha}\nu\alpha\pi\lambda\acute{\epsilon}\kappa\epsilon\sigma\theta\alpha\iota$ $\delta\iota'$ $\dot{\epsilon}\alpha\upsilon\tau\hat{\eta}s$) into a single godhead by means of the identity of ousia, so that the divine ousia alone is the absolute good. This metaphor is not dissimilar from that adopted by Novatian (above, p. 221). The earlier Latin Fathers were fruitful in anticipating the results of later Greek theology, throwing out suggestions of great fertility, but lacking the depth of conscious deliberation, produced in the Greeks by the necessity of facing acute and well-trained opposition. Hence Latin theology seems by comparison unaware of its own brilliance, and after Augustine certainly never developed its conceptions with a philosophical power in the least comparable with that of the Greeks.

In the commentary on *St. John* (28Dff.) Cyril gives several illustrations of his meaning; the Father is not 'in' the Son in the sense in which one physical object is inside another, nor like a basin in a basin; but as the subject of an extremely exact portrait might exclaim, "I am in this picture and this picture is in me"; or the quality of sweetness in the honey on a man's lips might claim a similar unity with the honey; or the warmth declare its union with the fire. The first of these three illustrations is borrowed from Athanasius (*c. Ar.* 3.5). It is not very happy, except in so far as it emphasises the exactitude with which the representation of one ideal content is reproduced in the several Persons; but it may be taken in connection with Hilary's more profound exposition of their mutual imagery. The last two examples recall those advanced by Basil in arguing for 'with' as against 'in.' Their point is that although the sweetness and the warmth are conceptually distinguishable from the honey and the fire, yet practically and necessarily they are inseparable and co-extensive. The same point is made in a rather different way, still as a consequence from the identity of ousia, by Procopius of Gaza (*ep.* 104), who observes that the products from the arche are not expelled from it, but are retained entirely undeparted from it, owing to the identity of ousia, even though as individual Persons they do issue forth.

But a much more important advance was made along a different line. Attention has already been called to the use by Hilary of the conception that the several Persons mutually 'contain' one another. This is strikingly developed by 'Gregory of Nyssa' (*adv. Ar. et Sab.* 12). The word χωρεῖν (contain) had for centuries been accepted as a technical expression for the pervasion of all created things by God. Originally it could mean either to be extended and fill space, or, transitively, to 'hold' a certain measure, in the sense that a pewter pot may hold an imperial pint. God, as all-pervasive Spirit, is omnipresent in all space and 'holds' all extended matter; He 'contains' the universe. It was by a most valuable extension of this conception that it now came to be applied to the mutual relations of the divine Persons.

If the Father is perfect and fills all things, the writer asks, what is left for the Son, who is also perfect, to contain? His answer is that the Father and the Son are receptive and permeative (χωρητικός) of one another, and, as thus 'containing' one another, would be equal in extension; the one is enveloped in the other (περιέχεσθαι), but not in like manner with human instances of envelopment, in which the enveloping substance has an empty space in which to hold the substance enveloped; with God the relation is mutual. Here follows the simile of the sciences jointly and commonly pervading a single mind, to which reference has been made above in a different connection (p. 266). So far as extension can be conceived in relation to deity, the Father and the Son are mutually interpenetrative like the sciences, and extend over identical space and are receptive of one another, and are one, differing only in hypostasis and title, and reside

in one another, like perfume in the atmosphere. The special
interest of this illustration is due to its abandonment of the
ancient type of analogy, drawn from material objects such
as light or fire or water, in which the several Persons are
represented by disparate elements, in part substances and
in part attributes. It substitutes a metaphor in which the
entities that typify the Persons are strictly equivalent.
None of the three sciences that occupy the mind is either
more or less objective than the other two. No room here
remains for further subordinationist misunderstanding.

The idea was taken up. Nilus writes (*epp.* 2.39) that the
Son is like in all respects to His own Father, so that the
Father is extended in Him and He is contained by the
Father. And Cyril, in a passage already summarised (on *St.
John* 28D ff.) says that the Father is not contained in the
Son after the manner of a basin in a basin, but that He is
extended in the Son and manifested in Him; since He is
wholly in the Son, therefore the Son wholly is perfect, as
permeative of (χωρητικός, literally, 'capable of containing')
the perfect one (29B). Again, he remarks (*dial.* 3 *de Trin.*,
467C), following the argument of *adv. Ar. et Sab.*, that
since the Father fills all things he cannot see the possibility
of any scope for the process of filling ascribed to the
Son by St. Paul (*Ephes.* i.23), apart from the fact that each
Person is in the other substantially (οὐσιωδῶς). The Son,
in other words, can only "fill all things" because He is
contained in the Father who fills all things.

The fact, then, of the co-inherence of the divine Persons
was well established, though no convenient term had as yet
been invented to describe it, beyond the use of phrases
indicative of mutual content, based on a rather crude, though

expressive and not really misleading, metaphor from the mensuration of physical capacity. The conception was closely allied to the conception of identity of concrete ousia, and as the latter fell into the background, between Cyril and Leontius, so did the former. But both together were revived by pseudo-Cyril, who may thus claim to acquire, by his restoration and development of Cyril's teaching, some sort of title to Cyril's name which has been attached to his writing. But the idea of 'perichoresis,' the term which he now applied to the conception of co-inherence, already had an interesting history. Contrary to what is frequently stated, it did not historically belong to the Trinitarian cycle of ideas at all. Its only theological use, until pseudo-Cyril, was Christological, and it meant, until pseudo-Cyril, something quite different from co-inherence.

The noun 'perichoresis' itself does not seem to occur at all until Maximus Confessor, the seventh-century opponent of the Monothelites. The earlier history of the term must be studied in its verb, περιχωρέω. This word is employed by 'Macarius of Egypt' (de pat. et discr. 5) in the sense of 'encircle' or 'encompass.' It next occurs three times in Gregory of Nazianzus. Life and death, he observes (or.18.42), though they appear to differ as far as possible from one another, yet 'reciprocate' and resolve themselves into one another; life comes from corruption and leads through corruption to corruption; death releases us from earthly ills and often transfers us to the higher life. The word clearly implies an interchange produced by the revolution of successive cycles. It means the same when he says (or. 22.4), in speaking of the phenomena of satiety, that all things 'reciprocate' into one another and are the subject of revolution. And the same meaning is retained when he maintains (*ep.* 101, 87C) that our Lord in His human nature is often referred to by titles properly and strictly indicative of His divine nature; like the natures, he points out, so also the titles are mingled, and 'reciprocate' into one another—in brief, are alternative. (Cf. Gr. Nyss. *c. Eun.* 1.95, M. 280B).

In addition, there is the compound, ἀντιπεριχωρέω, to be considered. This word occurs in what looks like a gloss in the text of Leontius of Byzantium (*c. Nest. & Eut.* 2, Migne 1320B), which states expressly that in speech the two natures of Christ "are interchangeable" (for that really is what the word amounts to); one may be predicated, instead of the other, of the one Christ who is in both. The corresponding sense of 'interchangeability' (referring not to Christology but to the alternative prepositions in the formula of the double procession of the Holy Ghost, 'out of' the Son or 'through' the Son) survives in the noun antiperichoresis in the writings of John Veccus and George Pachymeres at the end of the thirteenth century.

We come now to Maximus. In the course of his scholia on Dionysius (on Dion. *ep.* 4.8) this author quotes perichoreo, of the two natures of Christ, from Gregory of Nazianzus (*ep.* 101). He also employs it himself in the same connection (*ambig.* 112b D), saying that the human nature (it is important to observe that it is this which forms the subject of the sentence, not the divine nature), by virtue of being inconfusedly united with the divine nature, has entirely περικεχώρηκε, 'interchanged,' 'become reciprocal,' with the divine nature, possessing thenceforward absolutely nothing that is detached or separated from the deity which is hypostatically united to it. The meaning here cannot be 'interpenetrate,' because no one ever had the hardihood to suggest that the human nature is capable of interpenetrating the divine; the process, where it is alleged, is always in the opposite direction, and that for reasons sufficiently obvious.

Maximus also employs the noun 'perichoresis,' and this seems to be its first appearance on the stage of patristic philology. (It is quoted by Liddell and Scott from Anaxagoras as meaning 'rotation'.) To take first a neutral instance, having no bearing on theology, he writes (*quaest. ad Thalass.* 59, 202B) that as man cannot see physical objects in the dark, so he cannot perceive spiritual objects without spiritual illumination. Then he continues that salvation of souls is the proper end of faith; the end of faith is the true revelation of the object of faith; true revelation of the object of faith is the ineffable 'completion of the cycle' (perichoresis), according to each man's measure of faith, of what has been believed; and 'completion of the cycle' of what has been believed means the recurrence (ἐπάνοδος) of the believers at the end to their own beginning. The language of the last sentence, relating to recurrence to an end which coincides with a beginning, is decisive for the meaning of perichoresis. Maximus also uses antiperichoresis (*schol. in* Dion. *div. nom.* 5.8.7) in the sense of revolution or alternation, giving as instances night and day, harvest and seed-time.

When therefore he comes to apply perichoresis to the problems of Christology, we find that it means reciprocity of action. He takes as illustrations the interchange in the moment of giving utterance between the spoken word and the conception which it expresses, both called logos in Greek (*disp. Pyrrh.* 187A), and, commonly, the reciprocal actions of cutting and burning which are performed by a red-hot knife (e.g. *opusc.* 102B). His object in employing the term was not to explain the unity of the one Christ, but the singleness of action and effect which proceeded from the two natures united in His Person. And it should be added that he always calls the process a perichoresis of the two natures 'to' ($\epsilon i s$ or $\pi \rho \acute{o} s$) one another, never a perichoresis 'in' ($\epsilon \nu$) one another or 'through' ($\delta \iota \acute{a}$) one another. The idea in the background is simply the metaphor of rotation from a fixed point back to that point again.

This brings our investigation down to pseudo-Cyril; and since perichoresis is a Christological term, hitherto apparently unused with reference to Trinitarian problems, it is better to turn first to his use of it in Christology. He remarks, in a passage (*de ss. Trin.* 22) not appropriated by John of Damascus, that the divinity was the anointing element in the Christ ['the anointed one'] and the humanity the element anointed. By anointing, he continues, is meant the perichoresis of the entire chrism into the entire anointed; a merely superficial anointing, such as that bestowed on kings and high priests, does not make them Christs; and even though the grace bestowed by the chrism penetrates the receiver, yet this permeative unction is only one of grace, not strictly of the chrism; hence only the Lord is a true Christ. The implication clearly is that in His case the chrism of divinity permeated His humanity. The perichoresis has become, in the author's eyes, a process of unification between the two natures in our Lord.

A little later (*cap.* 24) he enumerates some of the results of the junction and perichoresis of the two natures; they include the deification of the flesh and the making man and creature of God the Word—not, however, in such a sense as that the two natures are changed into a single compound nature, but because the two natures are united hypostatically and receive an inconfused and unaltering perichoresis into one another. This perichoresis, he adds, proceeds not from the flesh but from the divinity, since it is impossible for the flesh to perichorein through the divinity; but the divine nature, having once permeated (περιχωρήσασα) through the flesh, bestows on the flesh an ineffable perichoresis with itself. Here it is to be observed that the process is one-sided and is one of penetration; the preposition 'through' appears. Again, in discussing the interchange of properties (ἀντίδοσις ἰδιωμάτων) between the two natures (which however in the last resort only amounts to a verbal formality), he observes (*cap.* 27) that each nature interchanges with the other what belongs to itself, through the identity of hypostasis and the perichoresis of the natures into one another; so that it is possible to say that 'God appeared on earth' and that 'this Man is uncreated and impassible.'

What pseudo-Cyril appears to have in mind is a permeation or co-inherence between the two natures similar to that which Gregory of Nyssa conceived between the Persons of the Trinity in his simile of the different sciences extended in a single consciousness. The two natures are not confused, but as each occupies the whole extension of the same hypostasis they must, on the physical metaphor, be regarded as interpenetrative. And just as it might be said of the scientist, 'This is a mathematician' or 'This is a physician,' so it can be said of Christ in the concrete, 'This is God' or 'This is Man.' In reality, since the process of permeation is one-sided, and especially since neither of the co-inherent entities in the case of Christ is conceived of as genuinely concrete, the metaphor is forced and not profoundly illuminative of the Christological problem. It is little more than word-play to maintain that two abstractions are co-inherent.

Whether or not this change in the meaning attached to perichoresis was deliberate it is impossible to decide. But it may be conjectured that it was accidental; partly because the word is of very rare occurrence, and in consequence bore no very clearly defined theological connotation; and partly because philologically it is a compound derivative of $\chi\omega\rho\acute{\epsilon}\omega$, which means either 'to go' or 'to contain,' and had been used from time out of mind to express the permeation of matter by God. For the purpose of eliciting this particular sense of 'permeation,' the philological link formed a most felicitous accident. To one who held a strong view of the co-inherence of the two natures, and was acquainted with the fact that the idea of perichoresis had been employed by Gregory of Nazianzus and Maximus to describe the relations of the two natures, and was moreover familiar with the stock illustration of the red-hot knife, so common in Maximus, the accidental connection of $\pi\epsilon\rho\iota\chi\omega\rho\acute{\epsilon}\omega$ and $\chi\omega\rho\acute{\epsilon}\omega$ may well have been decisive in determining him in all innocence to find in perichoresis a sense which as yet it had never possessed.

However, once found, it is immensely to our unknown author's credit that he perceived the fruitfulness of its application to the Persons of the Trinity. This was indeed his greatest and wisest innovation. If the conception of interpenetration is forced in relation to the natures of Christ, it is an admirable description of the union of the three

Persons of God. And it was necessary to find some such simple and expressive term for the purpose. As has been emphasised already, both ousia and hypostasis, the crucial terms in the doctrine of the Trinity, are concrete. It follows that the doctrine, for the sake of completeness, ought to be capable of being defined from the aspect of either term. From the aspect of a single concrete ousia, expressed objectively in three presentations, the being of God is clearly stated, and monotheism is safeguarded in the doctrine of identity of ousia. But owing at first to the accidents of controversy, and later to the abstract tendencies of the sixth century, the aspect in which God came to be more commonly regarded was that of three objects in a single ousia. The uppermost term is now hypostasis, and it becomes an eminent practical necessity to formulate a definition which, beginning from the uppermost term, will equally well express the truth of the monotheistic being of God. Without such a definition, the recurrence of tritheism was almost inevitable—not because the truth was unknown or unappreciated, but because in the absence of a convenient and illuminative formula the minds of the unwary are apt to be drawn away from central truths to invent heresies on the perimeter. Nor does 'the unwary' necessarily mean the most obtuse. The ablest minds may be the narrowest.

This definition was provided in the formula of the perichoresis or circumincessio of three co-inherent Persons in a single substance. Pseudo-Cyril enunciates the single ousia boldly. We assert that each of the three possesses a perfect hypostasis, he says (cap. 9), but maintain one ousia, simple, final (the subsequent passage shows that this is equivalent to 'concrete'), perfect, in three perfect hypostaseis; so again (cap. 10), we call the holy Trinity one God. He continues by explaining the consistency of this doctrine with the fact of the three hypostaseis; they are united, he says, not so as to be confounded, but so as to adhere to (ἔχεσθαι) one another, and they possess co-inherence in one another without any coalescence or commixture. Again, he quotes (cap. 23) the text "I am in the Father and the Father in me," as evidence of the co-inherence in one another of the hypostaseis, and the undeparting session (ἵδρυσις) of the Son in the Father, as Word, as Wisdom, as Power, and as Radiance.

It is interesting to note how the old sun-and-radiance metaphor is gathered up and preserved in the new formulation of the co-inherence: our author, like a good theologian, brings forth out of his treasures things both new and old. But it is even more important to observe how subtly and silently the phraseology of perichoresis has been changed. It is no longer perichoresis 'to' one another, but perichoresis 'in' one another. The former was the traditional form, when the term was used for Christology and in its original sense. It is sometimes retained by pseudo-Cyril for Christology, from sheer habit; and sometimes altered. But in relation to the Trinity it is never used, either by him or by John of Damascus, who took the term over from him and employed it frequently. Perichoresis 'to' one another might imply that the Persons were equivalent or alternative; perichoresis 'in' one another implies that they are coterminous and co-extensive. It forms the exact reverse of the identity of ousia. How different the implications of these two different prepositions are, is indicated by the protest of Nicephorus of Constantinople (*ad Leonem III*, Migne

100.184D) that to say the divine hypostaseis are transformed and 'alternate' ($\pi\epsilon\rho\iota\chi\omega\rho\acute{\epsilon}\omega$) 'into' one another is the heresy of Sabellius.

Nothing of importance remained to be added to the Greek patristic definition of the Trinity. It stands as a monument of inspired Christian rationalism. John of Damascus, as has been said, took up and popularised the doctrine of perichoresis, but there was nothing for him to add to it. He emphasised its point by laying stress (*fid. orth.* 1.14) on the "mansion and session" ($\mu o\nu\grave{\eta}$ $\kappa\alpha\grave{\iota}$ $\ddot{\iota}\delta\rho\upsilon\sigma\iota\varsigma$) of the hypostaseis in one another. He also revived the assimilation of the definitions of the Trinity and the incarnation (*de nat. comp.* 4): in the holy Trinity we speak of three hypostaseis united by their perichoresis; why then refuse to admit in the incarnation two natures united by their perichoresis? But the assimilation is only partial, directed against the Monophysite position; and the true and full doctrine of the Trinity was by now too securely established for confusion to be caused. There is no revival of the false analogies of Leontius. The only criticism that might seem substantial is that the whole doctrine of unity rested on physical metaphors. But, as pseudo-Cyril had pointed out in an entirely different connection (cap. 12), since we find many terms used metaphorically in Scripture concerning God, which are more directly applicable to physical objects, it needs to be recognised that it is impossible for mortal men to comprehend or to discuss God except by using symbols derived from mortal experience. Both he and all other competent theologians were completely on their guard against mistaking anthropomorphic or physical metaphors for more than what they purported to be. The Arians had fallen into this pitfall; the children of Athanasius went free.

* * * *

In retrospect, it appears that the long history of the evolution of Trinitarian doctrine is the record, on the one hand, of orthodox insistence on the true and full deity of the three Persons historically revealed, as against the attempts of heresy to maintain the doctrine of divine unity by mis-conceived and mischievous short-circuits. This orthodox insistence was based primarily on scriptural fact, but also, as comes out more and more clearly, on the philosophic sense that the being of God needs to be justified to reason alike as transcendent, as creative, and as immanent. On the whole these three adjectives fairly express the special characteristics of the three Persons, at any rate in relation to the universe, which is as far as human knowledge can very well expect to reach. The conception of the Father as anarchos arche, Source without other source than itself, safeguards the supremacy of God over created objects and His absolute distinction from them all. Whatever there was of religious value in the Gnostic assertion of a divine transcendence so complete that it could not bear direct contact with the world, is preserved when the divine agency in creation is assigned to God the Son; at the same time, because the Son is fully God, the truth is maintained that both creation and redemption (or re-creation) are acts of God. The immanence of the Spirit, in the special work of sanctification but also in the general guidance of the universe to the end designed for it, asserts the principle that God is not only transcendent in the fullest degree, not only active in controlling the world *ab extra,* but also operative in it from within. It was assumed that the divine relationships disclosed in the course of revelation, made through religious history and assisted by reflection on the constitution of the universe, correspond to real and permanent facts in the life of God. God is self-consistent. In revealing Himself to men He cannot be untrue to Himself, or misrepresent His own nature.

On the other hand, the history is the record of a long struggle, in the face of heresy, to express and explain, consonantly with the retention of the facts of experience, the true unity of God. By a full use of the subtlety of Greek thought and language, it was laid down that God is a single objective Being in three objects of presentation. This may be paraphrased in the expression, already employed, that He is one object in Himself and three objects to Himself. Alternatively, the result of the extended theological process may be summed up, in language more modern than any used by a Greek Father, but in loyalty to the spirit and meaning of Greek theology, in the formula that in God there are three divine organs of God-consciousness, but one centre of divine self-consciousness. As seen and thought, He is three; as seeing and thinking, He is one. He is one eternal principle of life and light and love. Yet the life implies reproduction within the Trinitarian cycle of the divine being; the light is reflected in a social order of morality; and the love is embodied in a genuinely mutual activity. To claim more is perilous to Christian monotheism. To claim less is treacherous to Christian history.

GENERAL INDEX

x

GENERAL INDEX

GENERAL INDEX

INDEX OF PATRISTIC REFERENCES

[The editions named in this Index are those which have been used in the text. 'Ben.' = Benedictine ed.; *G.C.S.* = *Die Griechischen Christlichen Schriftsteller der ersten drei Jahrhunderte* (the "Berlin Corpus," 1897 ff.); *C.S.E.L.* = *Corpus Scriptorum Ecclesiasticorum Latinorum* (the "Vienna Corpus," 1866 ff.). Under most headings, the references to Migne (*P.G.* and *P.L.*) have been added for convenience, whether this edition has been used or not. When it has been used, it is cited without brackets. Where the reference is not just '*P.G.*' (or '*P.L.*'), but '=*P.G.*' (or '=*P.L.*'), it is to be understood that Migne is a reprint of the text named.

As regards the individual Patristic writings, their commonly received dates as well as notes on their authenticity have been inserted where desirable and possible. The Patristic References are given in heavy type; those to the pages of this book in Roman type. The use of square brackets indicates that a passage is not by the Patristic writer under whose name it occurs, but has found its way into the edition cited, either through his own quotation of it or through modern editors. In a few instances somewhat fuller references are given in this Index than in the text.]

ADAMANTIUS, DIALOGUE OF (before 400 A.D.). Ed. *G.C.S.* [*P.G.* 11.1713–1884]. **1.2, 804** C., 200.

ALEXANDER, Bp. of ALEXANDRIA (d. 328 A.D.). Apud Theodoret, *H.E.;* ed. *G.C.S.* [*P.G.* 82.881–1280]. *Theod. H. E.* [**1.4.29**], 26; [**1.4.38**], 174; [**1.4.46**], 12 f.; [**1.4.52**], 245.

AMBROSE (Bishop of Milan; c. 339–397 A.D.). Apud Theodoret, *Eranistes;* ed. J. L. Schulze–J. A. Noesselt [=*P. G.* 83.27–336]. *Eran.* [**2.139** D], 269

AMPHILOCHIUS (Abp. of Iconium; c. 340–400 A.D.). Ed. *P.G.* 39.13–129. *Frag.* **15 (112** C.D.), 246. *Frag.* [in Hardouin, **3.864** C], 261.

ANASTASIUS, SINAITICUS (Abb.; d. later than 700 A.D.). Ed. *P.G.* 89. *Hodegus*, **56** A., 233.

ANCYRA, SYNOD OF (358 A.D.). Synodal Letter apud Epiph. *Haer.* 73.2–11. [**73.9.7**], 232; [**73.11.10**], 207 f.

ANSELM, ABP. of CANTERBURY (1033–1109 A.D.). Ed. *P.L.* 158, 159. *Epp.* **1.74,** 239.

ANTIOCH, SYNOD OF (268 A.D.). Apud M. J. Routh, *Reliq. Sac.*, iii, 289–316. **290** f., 201; **291,** 203; **293,** 201; **310** f., 201; **312,** 201.

APOCRYPHAL LITERATURE. Ed. C. Tischendorf for *Evv.* and *Apocc.;* C. Tischendorf–R. A. Lipsius–M. Bonnet for *Acta Apost.* *Protevang. Jac.* **6.3,** 22.

INDEX OF PATRISTIC REFERENCES

INDEX OF PATRISTIC REFERENCES

INDEX OF PATRISTIC REFERENCES

INDEX OF PATRISTIC REFERENCES

INDEX OF PATRISTIC REFERENCES

INDEX OF PATRISTIC REFERENCES

MACARIUS MAGNES (perhaps
the Bp. of Magnesia of the
same name who accused
Heracleides at the Synod of
the Oak, 403 A.D.; but see
T. W. Crafer's *Apocrit.*, p.
xx]. Ed. C. Blondel [Paris,
1876).
Apocrit. **2.9**, 173 f.; **3.11**, 190;
3.43, 163; **4.26**, 199.

MAXIMUS THE CONFESSOR (monk
c. 580–662 A.D.). Ed. F.
Combefis (Paris, 1675)[=*P.G.*
90, 91; also 4.15–43², 527–
576].
Quest. ad Thalass. **57**, **192** A,
171; **59**, **202** B, 293; **63**,
238 D, 253 f.
Quest. et Dub. **20**, 63.
Scholia in Dion. Areop. In *Ep.*
4.8, 292; in *Div. Nom.*
5.8.7, 293.
Opuscula. **70** C, D, 253; **77** B,
279; **102** B, 294; **151** C, 279.
Disp. cum Pyrrho. **187** A, 293.
Mystagog. **517** B, 248.
Ambig. **105** b, 169; **112** b D,
292.

MELITO (Bp. of Sardis; 2nd cent.).
Ed. E. J. Goodspeed (*P.G.*
5.1207.1224).
Fgmt. **7**, 77.

METHODIUS (Bp. of Olympus;
martyred c. 311 A.D.). Ed.
G.C.S. (*P.G.* 18.9–408).
Symposium. **8.8**, 16.
De autex. (='On Freewill'). **2.**8,
63; **5** f., 28–31; **8.1**, 191.
De res. **2.30.8**, 199; **3.6.4**, 173.
De creatis. **4.1**, 7.

NEMESIUS (Bp. of Emesa; 4th–
5th cent.). Ed. *P.G.* 40.503–
818.
De nat. hominis. **608** A, 32.

NICEPHORUS, PATRIARCH OF
CONSTANTINOPLE (c. 750–829
A.D.). Ed. *P.G.* 100.170–
1066.

Ad Leonem III (811 A.D.).
184 D, 298 f.

NILUS THE ASCETIC (of Ancyra
[not of Sinai]; d. c. 426 A.D.).
Ed. *P.G.* 79.
Epp. **2.39**, 34, 290.
Ad Eulog. **11**, 170.
De Oratione. **66**, 14.

NOVATIAN (Roman, mid 3rd
cent.). Ed. W. Yorke Fausset
(Camb., 1909) [=*P.L.* 3.861–
970].
De Trinit. **31**, 221.

ORIGEN (Alexandrine; c. 185–
255 A.D.). Ed. *G.C.S.* where
available; for the *Philocalia*,
J. A. Robinson (Cambr.,
1893); elsewhere ed. Ben.
[=C. V. Delarue], with sup-
plements in *P.G.* (11–17).
Comm. in Gen. Comm. **3**
[=*Philocal.* **23**.**14**], 53.
Fgmt. in Gen. [=Euseb. *Prep.
Ev.*, **7.20**], 171.
Hom. in Exod. **9.3**, 94.
Hom. in Levit. **13.4**, 192.
Hom. in Num. **12.1**, 192.
Adnot. in Deut. On **16**, **19–20**,
175.
Hom. in Jesu Nav. [=*Jos.*]
20.1, 68.
Selecta in Pss. fgmt. **1** [=*Dela-
rue* **2.513** B C], 73.
Exposit. in Prov. On **8.22**, 191.
Comm. in Cant. **84** A, 94, 161.
Schol. in Cant. On **7.1**, 52.
Hom. in Jer. **9.4**, 154; **16.5**,
66; **18.5**, 22; **18.6**, 67.
Comm. in Ioan. (Books 1–5
before 232 A.D. [at Alex.];
rest later [at Caes.]).**1.19**,
111, 118; **1.20**, **119**, 9;
1.24, **151**, 127, 189; **2.2**, 16,
114 f.; **2.2**, 17 f., 144 f.;
2.3, 19, 73; **2.3**, **20**, 120 f.;
2.10, 73, 51; **2.10**, 75, 51;
179; **2.10**, 75 f., 250; **2.11**,
79, 51; **2.17**, **123**, 26; **2.24**,
156, 171; **2.25**, **162**, 23;
2.28, **172**, 135; **2.31**, **189**,
69; **2.35**, **215**, 164; **2.37**,